This book is to be returned on or before 523-4
the last date stamped below.

OBSERVING THE CONSTELLATIONS

OBSERVING THE
CONSTELLATIONS

THE MITCHELL BEAZLEY GUIDE TO THE STARS

JOHN SANFORD

ACKNOWLEDGEMENTS

I want to thank my co-authors Michael Marten of Science Photo Library, who was responsible for the choosing and finding the additional photographs used in the book; and Wil Tirion, whose expertise in astronomical chart making is combined with his artistic talent in our maps. One's first book is always (I suppose) daunting, and an understanding, helpful, and firm editor is a necessity. Robin Rees of Mitchell Beazley proved to be all the above and then some. I appreciate being kept on-track and on schedule by Robin. My traveling companions to Chile, where many of the southern hemisphere photographs were made, were extraordinarily understanding and helpful during our short but fruitful trip: Charlie Oostdyk, Joel Harris, and Verryl Fosnight. An active amateur astrophotographer we met on a Halley's Comet trip in 1986, Noel Munford, helped by shooting several constellations missed on my trips, and Director Ed Krupp and Bob Webb helped out at Griffith Planetarium when we needed absolutely that last constellation photo. Lastly, heartfelt thanks to Liz Johansson, who always encouraged and gave me time to write during the 10 month gestation of this book.
J.S.

Observing the Constellations

Edited and designed by Mitchell Beazley International Limited, Artists House, 14-15 Manette Street, London W1V 5LB

Executive Editor	Robin Rees
Art Editor	Mike Brown
Advisory Editor	Nick Booth
Proofreader	Mark Hendy
Production	Ted Timberlake

Astrocartography	Wil Tirion
Photography Editor	Michael Marten

© Mitchell Beazley Publishers 1989

British Library CIP Data for this book are available from the British Library

ISBN 0 85533 748 6

Typeset in Gill Light by Litho Link, Welshpool
Printed and bound in Hong Kong by Mandarin Offset International Limited

PHOTO CREDITS

Constellations

All the photographs of the constellations are by John Sanford except for Antlia/Pyxis, Carina/Volans, Centaurus, Dorado/Mensa, Eridanus, Hydrus/Tucana, Pictor, Reticulum/Horologium, Vela, which are by Noel T. Munford, and Camelopardalis and Fornax/Sculptor/Phoenix, which are by Griffith Planetarium.

Other photographs

©Anglo-Australian Telescope Board: 46, 95, 173; © Chuck Edmonds/OCA/SPL: 96; European Southern Observatory: 166; European Space Agency/SPL: 145; Gordon Garradd/SPL: 51; © Kim Gordon/OCA/SPL: 10, 18, 103, 135; Hale Observatories/SPL: 58; © David A. Hardy/SPL: 26; Dr R.F. Haynes et al, Molonglo Telescope, University of Sydney/SPL: 66; © Rick Hull/SPL: 52, 130, 142; Dr William C. Keel/SPL: 1, 14, 30, 74; Francis Leroy/Biocosmos/SPL: 59; Dr Jean Lorre/SPL: 106, 160, 165; © Jack Marling/SPL: 56; Robert H. McNaught/SPL: 48, 87; D.K. Milne, CSIRO/SPL: 168; NASA/SPL: 78, 138; National Optical Astronomy Observatories/SPL: 86; NRAO/AUI/SPL: 55; John Bedke, Observatories of the Carnegie Institution of Washington: 45; Royal Greenwich Observatory/SPL: 110; Rev. Ronald Royer/SPL: 2-3, 38, 81, 99, 117, 133; John Sanford/SPL: 22, 34, 41, 148, 155; Dr Rudolph Schild/Smithsonian Astrophysical Observatory/SPL: 13, 42, 122; UK Schmidt Telescope Unit, © Royal Observatory, Edinburgh: 64, 70, 92 (with David Malin), 104, 118, 126, 151, 169 (with David Malin); US Naval Observatory/SPL: 36; Dennis di Cicco/SPL: 109

The photographs credited to SPL can be obtained from SCIENCE PHOTO LIBRARY, 112 Westbourne Grove, London W2 5RU

Suggested further reading

Allan, R. H., *Star Names, Their Lore and Meaning*, Dover Press, New York, 1963.

Burnham, R., Jr., *Burnham's Celestial Handbook*, 3 vols, Dover Press, New York, 1966, 1978.

Eicher, D. J., *The Universe From Your Backyard*, Astromedia, Milwaukee and Cambridge University Press, Cambridge, 1988.

Hartung, E. J., *Astronomical Objects for Southern Telescopes*, Cambridge University Press, Cambridge, 1968.

Hirschfield, A. and Sinnott, R. W., *Sky Catalog 2000.0*, 2 vols, Cambridge University Press, Cambridge and Sky Publishing Corporation, Cambridge, Mass., 1985.

Laustsen, S., Madsen, C., and West, R. M., *Exploring the Southern Sky*, Springer Verlag, Berlin, New York, 1987.

Norton, A. P., *Norton's Star Atlas*, 16th ed., Sky Publishing Corporation, Cambridge, Mass., 1973.

Sulentic, J. W. and Tifft, W. G., *The Revised Catalog of Nonstellar Objects*, University of Arizona Press, Tucson, 1973.

Tirion, W., *Sky Atlas 2000.0*, Cambridge University Press, Cambridge and Sky Publishing Corporation, Cambridge, Mass., 1981.

Tirion, W., Rappaport, B., and Lovi, G., *Uranometria 2000.0*, 2 vols, Willmann-Bell Inc., Richmond, VA, 1987, 1988.

Vehrenberg, H., *Atlas of Deep Sky Splendors*, 4th ed., Cambridge University Press, Cambridge, Sky Publishing Corporation, Cambridge, Mass., and Treugesell-Verlag, Dusseldorf, 1988.

CONTENTS

INTRODUCTION

Welcome to **Observing the Constellations!** This book was conceived to fill a gap for a guide to how to observe all 88 constellations. Discussion in some detail of the major telescopic objects in each group has been relegated to "observing manuals" in the past, and it is hoped that readers will find this colorful new approach easy to use.

Observing the Constellations will give the beginning astronomer, and perhaps the more experienced binocular or telescope observer, enough information about stars, galaxies, clusters and nebulae to stay busy for some time. The mythology boxes for each group highlight often hard to find information, while the maps build to form a complete star atlas. I have tried to combine these elements in a readable and entertaining volume which can form a reliable reference base for further involvement in astronomy.

One of the most wonderful things about astronomy is that you can go into it as far as you wish, from being just informed enough to point out a few constellations to a child or friends, to becoming an avid astrophotographer willing to guide a telescopic camera for hours at a time. There is room for all tastes and levels of enthusiasm. Many people fit into the category of "armchair astronomer", and in urban society that is completely normal, but never to have the joy of seeing a tiny moon poised on the limb of Jupiter, or the thrill of finding a supernova or comet invisible to the naked eye, is to miss half the experience. I hope that with this book in hand (and a red flashlight), you will be motivated to go out and see firsthand the heavenly wonders described herein.

John Sanford   February 1989

HOW TO USE THE BOOK

Turn to the hemispheres on pages 8 and 9 if you are starting your quest from scratch. Page 8 shows a whole sky map for the northern hemisphere, and page 9 for the southern. The months of the year are shown around the circumference of each hemisphere. Look at the relevant hemisphere, and rotate it until the current month is at the bottom. In the northern hemisphere, the chart then shows the sky that is visible when facing south at around 11 pm GMT. In the southern hemisphere, the chart shows the sky that is visible when facing north at around 11 pm GMT. Turn the charts clockwise by 15° for each hour before 11 pm, and anti-clockwise for each hour after 11 pm. (The sky rotates by 15° per hour from east to west because of the Earth's daily rotation.) The hemisphere maps divide the sky into the patterns of stars that form the constellations, and having discovered which are on view, individual constellations can be looked up in alphabetical order in the main body of the book.

The basic reference for each constellation is a detailed color map showing its stars and other astronomical objects. The maps contain all but the very faintest stars visible to the naked eye, and include virtually all the telescopic objects mentioned in the text and listed in the tables. The maps can also be used to plot the locations of comets and novae, the two most common ephemeral astronomical bodies. If used in the dark, maps should be viewed in red light which does not affect the dark-adapted eye.

The star maps are accompanied by photographs of the constellations they represent to show how they actually appear in the sky (an arrow indicates north), and tables provide the detail that keen amateurs will require to locate and study multiple stars, galaxies, nebulae, clusters and other "deep-sky" objects.

NAMING STARS

The bright stars in a constellation are named with letters of the Greek alphabet, from α (alpha) to ω (omega). Prominent stars often have popular names too, and some stars are assigned numbers, or Roman letters. Galaxies, clusters and nebulae are often given Messier (M) numbers, after Charles Messier, an 18th century French astronomer who cataloged non-stellar objects so they would not be confused with comets, the objects he was really interested in. The New General Catalog (NGC) of non-stellar objects is a more extensive list, originally published by J. L. E. Dreyer in 1888, based largely on the work of 19th century (prephotography) observers. It has subsequently been extended, and the Index Catalog (IC) was an addendum to it.

LOCATING STARS

The astronomical coordinate system most commonly used is called Right Ascension (RA) and Declination (Dec.). These are direct projections of longitude and latitude on Earth. Imagine yourself at the center of a globe looking outwards. The globe is clear plastic, and is only marked by lines of latitude and longitude.

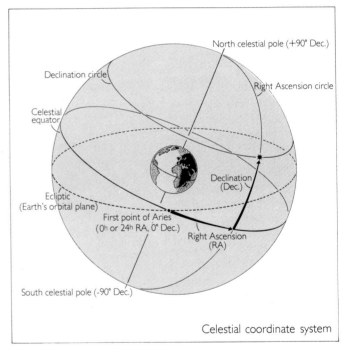

Celestial coordinate system

The 0 and 24 hours point for Right Ascension (the equivalent of longitude) is called the First Point of Aries, or the Vernal Equinox (the Earthly equivalent is the 0 and 24 hours point at Greenwich, London, from which all longitudinal measurements are made). RA is read from this point eastwards around the sky until at 24 hours you are back to the start. Because of precession (the Earth's wobbly axis of rotation) the First Point of Aries has actually moved from its original home in Aries into Pisces.

Declination is read from the celestial equator either north or south, from 0° to 90° (north pole) or −90° (south pole).

For example, the star Vega is at 18 hours 36.9 minutes in Right Ascension (18h 36.9m RA), and +36 degrees 47 minutes in Declination (+36 47 Dec.). This is only exact for one particular instant in time, on January 1, 2000 AD. The plot of the Earth's wobble only repeats itself every 26,700 years, so a mapmaker like Wil Tirion must specify a date when the axis is pointing in exactly in a certain direction for the maps and its coordinates to be exactly accurate. These epochs are usually only changed every 25 or 50 years, and we are now using 2000.0 coordinates almost universally. Since the sky only shifts about 50 arcseconds ($\frac{1}{70}°$) per year at the equator relative to this coordinate grid, this is not very significant for most uses.

STAR BRIGHTNESSES

The magnitude of stars and objects shown in the maps and tables is the brightness of the stars and objects as they actually appear in the sky – the apparent magnitude. Based on the work of Hipparchos in about 120 BC who designated the brightest stars he could see as 1st magnitude and the dimmest as 6th, it was later given a scientific basis by defining 1st magnitude stars as 100 times brighter than 6th magnitude. This means that for each step down in magnitude stars are 2.512 times brighter, so a star of magnitude 3 is 2.512 times as bright as a star of magnitude 4. For example, the star Spica is +1 and Polaris about +2 (slightly variable). This leads to negative magnitudes for the brightest objects in the sky: Venus is magnitude −4, the full moon about −12, and the Sun −26!

The further away a body is, the dimmer it appears, but there is another magnitude measure that is used to give an indication of how bright objects really are if we looked at them all from the same distance. Absolute magnitude is the estimated brightness of a body at a standard distance of 10 parsecs (parallax-seconds) (32.6 light years). The use of "pg" following the tabulated magnitude indicates that the magnitude has been recorded on a traditional photographic emulsion rather than using a modern photometer.

OBSERVING WITH BINOCULARS AND TELESCOPES

The naked eye can show us many of the sky's wonders. Planets, the stars, meteors, the Milky Way, eclipses, clusters like the Pleiades, and even the fuzzy ellipse marking the Great Galaxy in Andromeda some 2.3 million light years away, can all be appreciated in this way.

The invention of the telescope about 1607 and its use by Galileo transformed the view of the heavens. Telescopes gather light to make faint objects more visible – it is no use just having high magnification. A 20-inch (50-cm) telescope and a 200-inch (5-m) telescope may have the same magnification, but whereas the former will typically permit viewing of objects at distances of up to xx light years, the latter will see 15 billion (thousand million) light years, almost to the edge of the Universe! So aperture is important if you want to look at faint objects. The eye when dark adapted has a pupil aperture of about 6-7 mm. A 50-mm binocular objective lens gathers over 50 times the light of the human eye (when talking about areas the squares of the apertures must be compared). An 8-inch (20-cm) telescope has about 1,600 times the light gathering power of the eye.

Binocular observing is a good way to learn the sky, because first you have to have a good idea where you are pointing them in order to match up an object to the map. There are few constellations that fit exactly entirely into a binocular field, however. Lyra, Crux, and Sagitta come close if you have low power, wide field, binoculars. Usually a section, such as the Big Dipper's bowl, or Orion's Belt, are more the size a binocular

field will encompass – 3 to 5 degrees. The first figure in describing binoculars is the magnification, and the second is the diameter of the objective (large) lens in millimetres. Common combinations are 6 × 30, 7 × 35, 8 × 56, 10 × 70, and 15 or 20 × 80. One other measure gives the brightness that is possible, and this is called the exit pupil. This is given by dividing the objective size by the power. A maximum of 7 is possible since that is the diameter of the dilated human eye when dark adapted. Any higher and the light is wasted. Lower, and the field is not as illuminated as possible. It is easy to see that 7 × 50, 8 × 56 and 10 × 70 all satisfy the criterion of the 7 mm exit pupil, and are best for looking at faint objects. 20 × 80 binoculars are good for astronomy despite the 4 mm exit pupil because their 80 mm lenses gather much more light, and the 20 power helps resolve objects like clusters and close stars. Steadily held, and a tripod is essential, this last instrument will show you virtually every object described in this book. With prices of over $400 for adequate beginning telescopes, I frequently recommend that beginners invest in a good pair of binoculars and perhaps a photo tripod to hold them steady, rather than buying a flimsy "toy" telescope.

The telescope is a wonderful invention. It not only makes things closer, but it makes them brighter. However, let us recall that a cheaply made, poorly mounted small telescope, such as are frequently supplied through department stores, often prove such a disappointment that the user is "turned off" astronomy. One adage in our hobby goes, "You can see a lot with a steadily mounted small telescope, even of mediocre optical quality, but you can't see anything with a poorly mounted one, no matter how good the optics." Suspicion should be directed to any adverts stressing the magnifying power of a telescope. It is how well it shows what you are looking at and how still the image stays, rather than raw magnification which is important.

A beginning telescope should have at least an 80-mm objective lens (3.1 inches), and a sturdy tripod and mount which allows accurate following of astronomical objects as they cross the sky. A few improvements can be made to most small telescopes, such as using a weight hanging under the tripod to add mass, and the use of better eyepieces (get a .965 to 1¼ inch adaptor, then use good quality eyepieces), tightening up the tripod legs-to-head connection, etc. All go to improving the steadiness and sharpness of the view of the small telescope.

The use of an astronomical telescope could fill a book itself, but I will try to give a few hints for general usage here rather than trying to describe all the kinds and equipment available to the amateur astronomer. First, once your finder telescope is aligned, use it to acquire the object you want to see. If it is too small or faint, use a nearby star and "offset" the telescope to where you think it should be (from the map). Tighten the movement clamps slightly, and start looking with the lowest power available in the main scope. You may have to scan a bit in RA or Dec., but take note of where you started so you can return to that spot to start another "search pattern". Assuming you have followed your telescope manual's directions for setting up and polar aligning, you can also try using the setting circles supplied with most equatorially mounted telescopes. Try this with an easily seen first magnitude star a few times before tackling a galaxy or other fainter objects. Above all when observing, be comfortable! Strive for a relaxed but alert receptive state of mind. Some beginners race from object to object without appreciating anything. Those galaxies are not going anywhere, so contemplate and study rather than see and run. A higher power eyepiece will make the sky darker, and frequently helps see fainter objects better. Often cupping your hand around the eyepiece will help screen out any extraneous light and allow you to see better. I believe that sitting down is a far better position for the astronomer than standing, and you will be able to see through the eyepiece better if you can hold your head steady. Keep in mind that looking with one eye is an acquired art, and it will be learnt through practice. An experienced observer can always see more than a beginner, so look on and become experienced! As you gain experience and expertise, you may want to report your observations to some organization which can use them to further science. A good

recent example was the Halley Watch, which organized hundreds of amateur observers and gather their descriptions, drawings, and photographs of Comet Halley. There are groups for variable stars, meteors, solar system observations, as well as several nova and supernova search groups both in Europe, America and Australia.

ASTRONOMY WITH A CAMERA
Astrophotography is a hobby many thousands of amateur astronomers enjoy. Much has been written, and several recent books have treated the subject fully. An outline of the major points of technique is given briefly:

Turn the map for your hemisphere until the current month is at the bottom. The map then shows the constellations on view that month at approximately 11 pm GMT (facing south in the northern

Northern Hemisphere

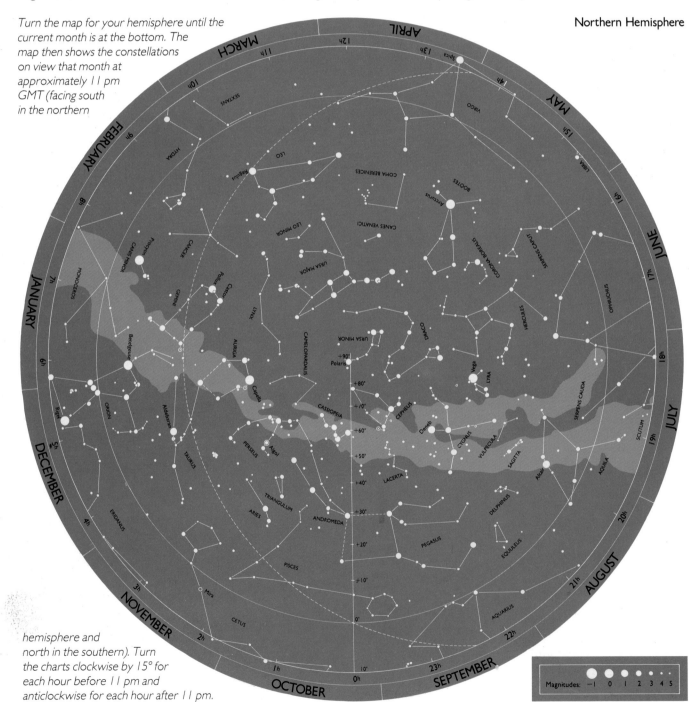

hemisphere and north in the southern). Turn the charts clockwise by 15° for each hour before 11 pm and anticlockwise for each hour after 11 pm.

1. A tripod mounted camera and ultra fast film (1600 ISO and faster) can capture stars to fainter than naked eye limit in a 15 second exposure at f/2.

2. A camera mounted "piggyback" on a driven telescope with lenses from 24-mm to 300-mm can do wonderful work on the quality of many of our photographs (note the captions for specific techniques).

3. Through the telescope ("prime focus") work requires guiding during the exposure because there are few commercial mounts for small telescopes which drive accurately enough for this type of demanding work.

4. Lunar and planetary and bright double star photography can be done at prime or even higher scales providing the telescope drives smoothly and the mount is sturdy enough to prevent shutter jiggle. Slower fine grain films are recommended for bright subjects.

At the time of writing, the best amateur work in black and white is being done on hypersensitized Kodak 2415 Technical Pan film, which has become fairly standard for long exposure deep sky work. In color, hypered Konica (Sakura) 400 and 3200 are preferred along with Fujichrome 1600D and Fujichrome 100 pushed a stop or two for color transparencies. New films and electronics will no doubt change the future of astrophotography in ways we can hardly imagine.

The constellation labels are orientated north up and south down. To make the connection between the maps a 20° overlap is shown. The solid line is the celestial equator, and the dotted line is the ecliptic.

Southern Hemisphere

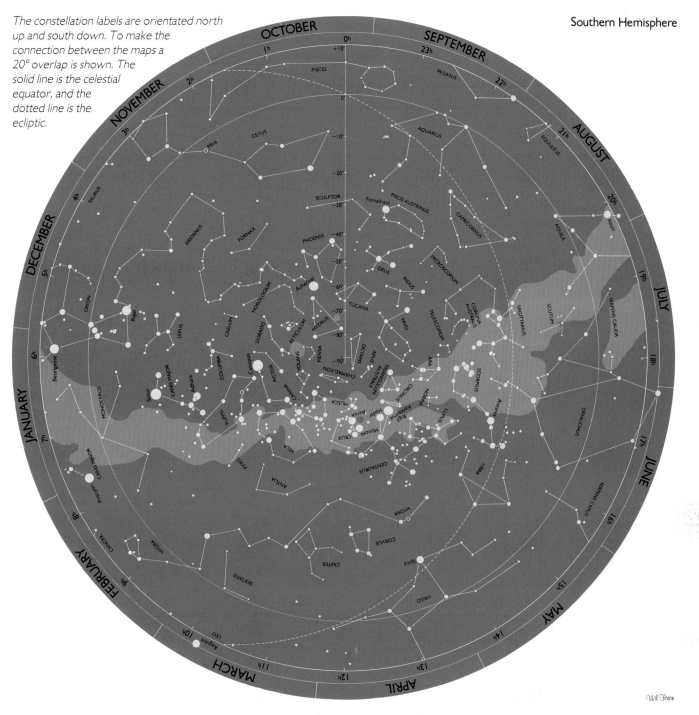

ANDROMEDA

Andromeda Galaxy, M31.
Located 2.3 million light years away, M31 (NGC 224) is a giant spiral galaxy that dominates our "Local Group" of galaxies. It has two small companions: the elliptical galaxy NGC 205, which is seen on the right; and the elliptical galaxy M32 (NGC 221), which is the bright, star-like object below and left of M31's center. The photograph was taken by California amateur Kim Gordon using a 5.5-inch (140-mm) Wright–Newtonian telescope on hypered Konica 400 color negative film with a 25-minute exposure.

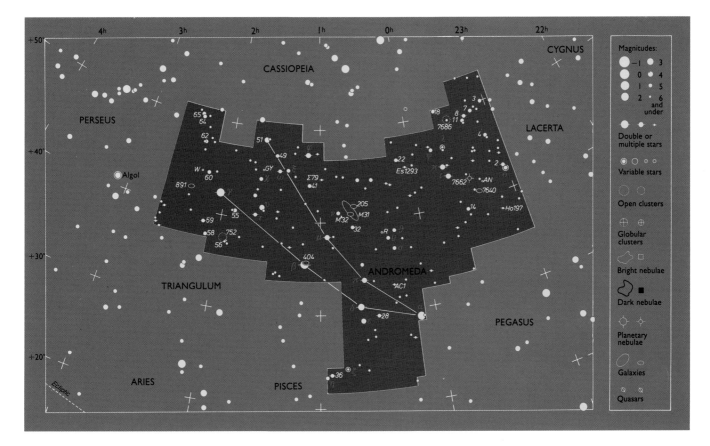

Andromeda, the chained or girdled lady, is a large and important fall constellation. It is located between Cassiopeia and Pisces. Andromeda is seen in the sky with her arms stretched out in supplication, lying on her side with her head at the upper left corner of the Great Square of Pegasus, and her feet near Perseus. At northern latitudes she rises late in the evening in the summer, and is almost overhead at 9 pm by mid-November. The most striking feature of Andromeda is that the largest and nearest spiral galaxy is located in the northern part of the figure, Messier 31 (M31), or the Great Galaxy in Andromeda. It appears as a fuzzy elongated patch of light at about 4th magnitude. This is probably the most distant object visible to the naked eye, modern estimates making it 2.3 million light years away. In binoculars or a telescope M31 is a fascinating object, with two smaller and fainter companion galaxies also conspicuous in the field at low powers.

Multiple Stars

Double stars found in Andromeda (except for Gamma (γ)) tend to be faint, but those listed below are worth hunting for at the positions given. The best star of the group must be Gamma (γ) or Almach (sometimes misspelt Almaak), which is one of most beautiful double stars in the sky. The primary is of spectral class K0, a bright orange, and the secondary star (a very close double or triple itself) is A0, which appears bluish or blue–green in contrast. The separation of the AB pair is presently 10 arcseconds. The secondary star is seen as a very close double or as a single star at times, because the elongated orbit of its companion closes to less than 0.1 arcseconds, unresolvable in any earth-based telescope. This happened last in 1952, and the

widest separation was in 1982 at nearly 0.6 arcseconds. This duplicity was discovered by F. W. Struve in 1842 at Pulkova. At the distance published for Gamma, 260 light years, the actual separation of BC averages 30 Astronomical Units (AU), while the distance from A to BC is something like 800 AU (1 AU is equivalent to the distance from the Earth to the Sun). In a good 8-inch (20-cm) aperture telescope with good steadiness and high power, the BC pair appears as two tiny blue disks just touching. This smaller pair is a good test for the larger telescope and "seeing" (steadiness) conditions.

Another close double star which is also a binary system is 36 Andromedae. Here we are looking more or less "down" or "up" at the orbit, i.e. we see it at a high inclination. The period of the second star is 165 years and it was closest to the primary (i.e. at periastron) in 1957 at 0.6 arcseconds. Having passed that, it is now opening to the maximum separation of 1.4 arcseconds, which will be reached about 2040. These yellow suns of 6.0 and 6.4 magnitude are another test pair for good optics and good seeing. 36 is found between Eta (η) and Zeta (ζ).

The Great Galaxy

The nearby spiral galaxy called M31, or NGC (New General Catalog) 224, is the closest known spiral-type galaxy. Only the irregular neighbors of the Milky Way, the Magellanic Clouds, are closer to us. We look through a screen of stars of our galaxy the Milky Way (all closer than 5,000 light years) across the intergalactic expanse of over 2 million light years to see the Andromeda Galaxy and its smaller elliptical companions NGC 205 and NGC 221 (M32). M31 is thought to be similar to our galaxy in structure but about half as large again in diameter, or about 180,000 light years. It has two major spiral arms, but they are difficult to trace owing to much dust in the plane of the galaxy and the fact that the disk is inclined to us at over 70 degrees. M31 is an excellent binocular object which may best be seen in a large pair of astronomical binoculars. The binocular view shows an elongated haze for about 1.5 degrees in either direction.

In the telescope, individual parts of the M31 system can be seen; the larger the aperture the better. The nucleus of M31, for example, is an almost starlike point with the haze of the millions of Population II (redder) stars surrounding it and suffusing the field with their soft glow. The small elliptical galaxy M32 is just at the visual edge of the galaxy to the south, with the fainter NGC 205 opposite and about a degree away. In 8-inch (20-cm) and larger telescopes a star cloud in one of the arms named NGC 206 can be glimpsed as a fuzzy elongated ball about the size of M32 but quite a bit fainter. In 16-inch (40-cm) instruments, with good seeing conditions, the brightest blue supergiants in this cloud and elsewhere in the arms begin to resolve visually into tiny 17th-magnitude points. Also at this faintness, many of the globular clusters surrounding M31 can be seen, not quite sharp starlike points at high powers. Many novae and one supernova (which in 1885 reached 5th magnitude) are seen in M31. The Hubble Space Telescope and its descendents will allow closer observation of planetary nebulae and gaseous nebulae in M31, as well as stars similar to our Sun in this enormous system. At such vast distances from us, the Sun would be very faint, appearing to have a brightness of only 29th magnitude! Two other galaxies should be mentioned here. NGC 404 is an easily found round spot in the same field with 2nd-magnitude Beta (Mirach). It is a 12th-magnitude elliptical which was not charted on some star atlases, resulting in a good number of spurious "comet discoveries" in the 1960s and 1970s. If you spot such an object (faint and fuzzy) be sure to give it an hour or so to be certain it is moving relative to nearby stars before calling or telegraphing a "discovery" to the Center for Astrophysics in Cambridge, Massachusetts. NGC 891 is a relatively nearby large spiral galaxy seen edge-on. In an 8-inch (20-cm) or larger aperture instrument it is seen as a large (12 arcminute) long streak with a dark lane particularly prominent with greater telescopic apertures. It is not a bright object (12th magnitude), and therefore requires a Moonless night and pure sky to be seen well.

Planetary Nebula

The single bright planetary nebula known in Andromeda is NGC 7662. It looks bluish green through a telescope, caused by strong, doubly ionized oxygen atoms. With a larger telescope (greater than 16-inch (40-cm) aperture) this object also shows a pinkish central region. The central star is quite faint, although a central spot can be seen at times. The object is about 30 arcseconds in diameter and about 9th magnitude, so can be seen with anything from a 3-inch (75mm) refractor on up.

The Variable R Andromedae

R Andromedae is a red long-period variable star which has an unusually great range of brightness – from 5.1 to 14.8. So from naked eye brightness, R goes down to the limit of a 10-inch (25 cm) telescope. The period is 409 days for this Mira-type star, and its spectrum is overlain with a rich set of titanium and zirconium lines. These are most evident when the star is faint, meaning large and cool, but fade as the star heats up and contracts during each cycle. R is found eadily, since it is a member of the little Sigma (σ), Theta (θ), and Rho (ρ) asterism.

TELESCOPIC OBJECTS IN ANDROMEDA
Double and Multiple Stars

Name	RA	Dec.	Separation (arcseconds)		Mags.		Year
Ho 197	23h 11.5m	+38° 13'	AB	0.4	8.3	8.6	1958
			AC	42.6	8.3	8.7	
			AD	47.2	8.3	8.7	
Σ 3050	23h 59.5m	+33° 43'		1.3	6.0	6.0	1967
Es 1293	00h 05.2m	+45° 14'	AB	12.9	6.5	13.5	1925
			AC	21.6	6.5	9.5	1934
AC 1	00h 20.9m	+32° 59'		1.6	7.5	8.0	1959
36	00h 55.0m	+23° 38'		~1	6.0	6.4	1959
Σ 79	01h 00.1m	+44° 43'		7.8	6.0	6.8	1967
φ (Phi)	01h 09.5m	+47° 15'		0.5	4.6	5.5	1960
τ (Tau)	01h 40.6m	+40° 35'		52.3	4.9	10.1	1925
γ (Gamma)	02h 03.9m	+42° 20'	AB	10.3	2.3	5.3	1967
			BC	0.5	5.5	6.3	1959
59	02h 10.9m	+39° 02'		16.6	6.1	6.8	1949

Deep Sky Objects

Name	RA	Dec.	Type	Size	Mag.
NGC 7640	23h 22.1m	+40° 51'	Gal. Sb	10.7' × 2.5'	10.9
NGC 7662	23h 25.9m	+42° 33'	Plan. Neb.	30" × 20"	9.2
NGC 205	00h 40.4m	+41° 41'	Gal. E6	17' × 10'	8
M32 (NGC 221)	00h 42.7m	+40° 52'	Gal. E2	7.6' × 5.8'	8
M31 (NGC 224)	00h 42.7m	+41° 16'	Gal. Sb	178' × 63'	3.4
NGC 404	01h 09.4m	+35° 43'	Gal. E0	4.4' × 3.3'	10.4
NGC 752	01h 57.8m	+37° 41'	Open Cl.	50'	5
NGC 891	02h 22.6m	+42° 21'	Gal. Sb	13.5' × 2.8'	12.0

Spiral galaxy NGC 891. Located 40 million light years away and seen edge-on, NGC 891 has a distinctive, dark lane of dust that bisects its central bulge. This dark lane can be seen in larger amateur telescopes. A supernova was seen in NGC 891 in 1986–87. The picture was recorded at optical wavelengths by a CCD camera mounted on a telescope at the Whipple Observatory, Arizona. A CCD, or charge-coupled device, is a type of light-sensitive silicon chip.

ANTLIA/PYXIS

NGC 2997 is an impressive spiral galaxy, type Sc, located some 30 million light years away. In this optical CCD picture, the pink concentrations in the spiral arms are HII (ionized Hydrogen) regions, where populations of massive stars have recently formed; their color is due to their strong emission of Hα light as electrons and protons recombine to form electrically neutral hydrogen (HI). The picture is a composite of two frames recorded by a CCD camera at the 60-inch (1.5-m) telescope at the Cerro Tololo Inter-American Observatory in Chile.

Antlia and Pyxis are among the most inconspicuous of constellations, and are discussed together for convenience. Antlia contains no stars brighter than the 4th magnitude, and although Pyxis has two stars above 4th, they are undistinguished. Both are predominantly southern constellations, centred near to −30° of celestial latitude. For northern observers, they are at their best vantage in the early spring. Antlia reaches culmination (i.e. at its highest point in the sky) at around 10pm on April 1, with Pyxis culminating a month previously (10pm on March 1). Pyxis precedes Antlia by about one hour of Right Ascension, equivalent to 15° of celestial longitude. It is slightly easier to find: after all, it was once part of the great Argo Navis (see mythology box). For observers south of −40° declination, Pyxis can be located just above the 2nd-magnitude stars Zeta Puppis and Lambda Velorum. Its brightest stars make an almost-isosceles triangle above them (see map).

Antlia

Antlia has no bright stars (Alpha (α) is only magnitude 4.25) and occupies a relatively empty area. There are a few double stars within its boundaries, the most prominent being Delta (δ), a slow binary: it consists of two stars of 5th and 9th magnitude, separated by 11 arcseconds. There is also the semi-regular variable U Antliae, which has a range from about 5.7 to 6.8, and a period of about a year. There is one easily-observed galaxy (NGC 2997), and there are two other faint galaxies, NGC 3271 and NGC 3347.

Pyxis

The main object of interest for binocular and telescope obser-

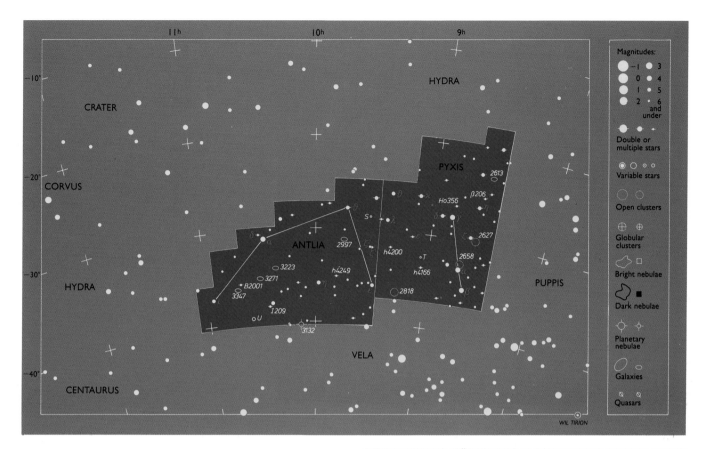

vers in Pyxis is the Milky Way, which runs through its western portions, providing observers with some small open clusters. The eastern area is unobscured and contains the worthwhile galaxy NGC 2613. There are several double stars worth hunting, including 206, Ho 356, h4166 and h4200.

Some of the most unusual novae are recurrent ones, and T Pyxidis is an interesting example. Recurrent novae are binary systems in which the primary is an older giant star and the secondary is a white dwarf. Material is continually transferred from the giant to the dwarf, but every few decades the accreted material on the dwarf explodes in a thermonuclear reaction. The apparent brightness of the star increases dramatically: the greater the time between the outbursts, the brighter the outbursts are. T Pyxidis last brightened from its normal 14th magnitude to 6.3 in January 1967. Previous maxima had occurred in 1944, 1920, 1902 and 1890. Given the roughly 20-year period between outbursts, another is due shortly.

Finally, there is a star cluster combined with a planetary nebula which is not connected to the cluster as it has a greater distance, NGC 2818. The nebula is about 40 arcseconds in diameter, faint and located at the western edge of the cluster of about 30 faint stars. At least an 8-inch (20-cm) 'scope is necessary to see this combination well.

TELESCOPIC OBJECTS IN ANTLIA
Double and Multiple Stars

Name	RA	Dec.	Separation (arcseconds)	Mags.		Year
ζ₁ (Zeta 1)	09h 30.8m	−31° 53′	8.0	6.2	7.1	1952
h4249	09h 48.8m	−35° 01′	4.3	8.0	8.1	1952
I209	10h 24.4m	−38° 35′	1.2	8.4	8.6	1954

TELESCOPIC OBJECTS IN ANTLIA continued
Double and Multiple Stars

Name	RA	Dec.	Separation (arcseconds)	Mags.		Year
δ (Delta)	10h 29.6m	−30° 36′	11.0	5.6	9.6	1932
B2001	10h 40.9m	−35° 44′	0.7	6.4	8.9	1960

Deep Sky Objects

Name	RA	Dec.	Type	Size	Mag.
NGC 2997	09h 45.6m	−31° 11′	Gal. Sc	8.1′ × 6.5′	10.6
NGC 3271	10h 30.5m	−35° 22′	Gal. Sb	2.3′ × 1.1′	11.7
NGC 3347	10h 42.8m	−36° 22′	Gal. SBb	4.4′ × 2.6′	12.5

TELESCOPIC OBJECTS IN PYXIS
Double and Multiple Stars

Name	RA	Dec.	Separation (arcseconds)	Mags.		Year
ζ (Zeta)	08h 39.7m	−29° 34′	52.4	4.9	9.1	1905
206	08h 35.4m	−25° 07′	1.8	8.2	8.4	1954
Ho356	08h 49.3m	−26° 26′	1.6	8.0	8.5	1954
h4166	09h 03.3m	−33° 36′	A × BC 13.7	6.7		1952
			BC 0.8	8.6	11.8	1947
κ (Kappa)	09h 08.0m	−25° 52′	2.1	4.6	9.8	1911
h4200	09h 20.7m	−31° 46′	3.1	7.3	7.9	1954

Recurring Nova

Name	RA	Dec.	Type	Mags.		Period
				max	min	
T	09h 04.7m	−32° 23′	Nr	6.3	14.0	7000 days

Deep Sky Objects

Name	RA	Dec.	Type	Size	Mag.
NGC 2613	08h 33.4m	−22° 58′	Gal. S	7.2′ × 2.1′	10.4
NGC 2627	08h 37.3m	−29° 57′	Open Cl.	11′	8.4
NGC 2658	08h 43.4m	−32° 39′	Open Cl.	12′	9.2
NGC 2818	09h 16.0m	−36° 37′	Open Cl.	9′	8.2

APUS/TRIANGULUM AUSTRALE

Apus is a small southern constellation which lies toward the south celestial pole and is therefore visible only to southern-hemisphere observers. Apus can be recognized by a small elongated triangle formed by its Beta (β), Gamma (γ) and Delta (δ) stars. The triangle is on a line almost halfway from Alpha Trianguli to the pole, which is unmarked by any significant stars.

Triangulum Australe, the Southern Triangle, is included with Apus for convenience.

Apus
The wide optical double Delta (δ_1 and δ_2), 103 arcseconds apart and both 5th-magnitude orange stars, leads the list of doubles in Apus. A faint but rich globular cluster, NGC 6101, is worth a look with larger amateur instruments (10-inch (25-cm) aperture and up). It is about 3 arcminutes in diameter and begins to resolve well in an 8-inch (20-cm) telescope.

A fairly large but faint globular is Index Catalog (IC) 4499, which is an 11th-magnitude ball of faint stars about 5 arcminutes in diameter. It can be located just north of Pi 2 (π_2) Octantis, on the Apus side of the constellation border.

Triangulum Australe
This is a southern constellation marked by three fairly bright stars forming an almost equilateral triangle southeastwards from Alpha (α) and Beta (β) Centauri. The constellation is circumpolar for most southern-hemisphere dwellers, and is between −60° and −70° in declination. Triangulum Australe culminates at 10 pm on June 20. The Milky Way is not particularly rich in this area, but there are a number of good doubles and multiples.

Multiple stars
Herschel 4809 is a multiple system, with the major components of magnitudes 6.5 and 8.5, separated by 1.2 arcseconds, with two further stars of 9th and 8th magnitude some 45 and 48 arcseconds away, respectively.

Iota (ι) has a 5.5-magnitude primary with a 10th-magnitude secondary star. This is an optical double, meaning the stars are at different distances to us and not connected by gravitational attraction. In 1918 they were separated by 19.6 arcseconds, but the distance is slowly decreasing, owing to the proper motion of the stars.

Deep Sky Objects
NGC 6025 is a small, open cluster (10 arcminutes in diameter) with about 30 stars of 7th magnitude and fainter. NGC 5979 is a small, round planetary nebula, almost stellar in appearance (8 arcseconds in diameter), and at magnitude 13 rather faint in an 8-inch (20-cm) telescope.

Cepheid variables
The two brightest variables in Triangulum Australe are Cepheid type stars which pulsate with periods of several days. These are the stars which when seen in distant galaxies are used as standard "candles", since their periods relate directly to their absolute magnitudes. R Triangulum Australis varies from 6 to 6.8 with a period of 3.389 days, and S Tri Aus varies from 6.1 to 6.7 in 6.323 days. These stars also change their spectral characteristics from F white stars when smallest (faintest) to G stars (yellow like the Sun) when expanded to to their fullest.

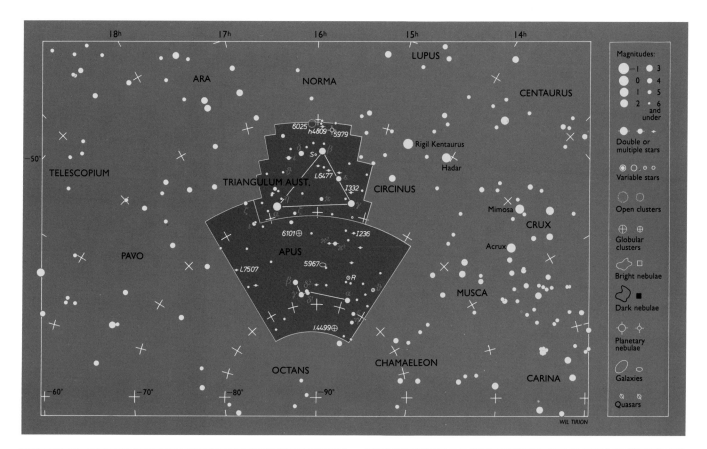

Johann Bayer

The first "modern" star atlas, and the one which served as basis for many thereafter, is Johann Bayer's **Uranometria**. Bayer was an attorney and amateur astronomer in the German city of Augsburg, in Bavaria. He was born in 1572 and died in 1625, so was approximately contemporary with Galileo. Bayer drew on the catalog of stars prepared by Tycho Brahe, the Danish astronmer, who observed from a well-equipped observatory on the island of Hven. Brahe was one of the last influential naked-eye observers, and his positions, obtained with large mural quadrants with sights, were often accurate to within 1 minute of arc. This is about half the normal eye's resolving power, so these were amazingly accurate for their time.

Bayer originated the system of using the lower-case Greek letter for the stars in descending brightness, Alpha being the brightest, Beta second, etc. After the Greek alphabet is exhausted, Roman letters are used. Later the English Astronomer Royal, Flamsteed, numbered all the stars in each constellation by order of Right Ascension with Arabic numerals, 1,2, etc. So today we see a mixture of Bayer's letters and Flamsteed's numbers when describing the stars in a constellation.

Bayer's work also defined many of the mythological figures better than previous maps had done, and he added many new groups from the "amorphae" (formless) stars which were between many of the early Greek-originated figures.

TELESCOPIC OBJECTS IN APUS
Double Stars

Name	RA	Dec.	Separation (arcseconds)	Mags.		Year
I236	14h 53.2m	−73° 11′	2.0	5.8	8.0	1947
δ (Delta)	16h 20.3m	−78° 42′	102.9	4.7	5.1	1918
L 7507	18h 12.6m	−73° 40′	2.5	6.0	9.0	1935

Deep Sky Objects

Name	RA	Dec.	Type	Size	Mag.
NGC 6101	16h 25.8m	−72° 12′	Glob. Cl.	10.7′	9.3
IC 4499	15h 00.3m	−82° 13′	Glob. Cl.	5′	11

TELESCOPIC OBJECTS IN TRIANGULUM AUSTRALE
Double and Multiple Stars

Name	RA	Dec.	Separation (arcseconds)	Mags.		Year
I332	15h 20.7m	−67° 29′	1.1	6.5	8.5	1929
L 6477	15h 47.0m	−65° 27′	1.9	6.3	6.3	1947
h4809	15h 54.9m	−60° 45′	AB 1.2	6.5	8.8	1943
			AC 45.0	6.5	9.1	1917
			AD 48.1	6.5	8.7	1917
ι (Iota)	16h 28.0m	−64° 03′	19.6	5.3	10.3	1918
Gls 230	16h 51.5m	−67° 33′	7.0	8.5	8.5	1920

Deep Sky Objects

Name	RA	Dec.	Type	Size	Mag.
NGC 5979	15h 47.7m	−61° 13′	Plan. Neb.	8″	13.0
NGC 6025	16h 03.7m	−60° 30′	Open Cl.	12′	5.1

AQUARIUS

Aquarius, the Water Bearer, is the 12th sign in the modern zodiac (the "first point of Aries" now being in Pisces) and the whole area in ancient times was associated with water or rain. The Babylonians called the area the Sea, and populated it with ocean creatures like Cetus, Pisces, Capricornus and Delphinus, all under the control of Aquarius. The Egyptian hieroglyph for water is the same as that used for Aquarius. In Roman times, the trefoil grouping and a line of stars going south into the mouths of Piscis Austrinus was a separate group, the trefoil denoting an urn or amphora.

The Helix Nebula (NGC 7293) is a cloud of gas and dust ejected from a central star, which is visible at dead center of the ring. The filamentary structure of the ring gives the impression of rapid movement, and doppler shift observations confirm this: the speed of expansion is 20–40 kilometers per second. In deep photographs the nebula looks like two overlapping rings, as in a spiral staircase, hence its name. This photograph was taken by Kim Gordon with a 20-inch (50-cm) Ritchey–Chrétien reflecting telescope. The exposure was one hour at f/8 on hypered Konica 400 film.

Aquarius is a large, important fall constellation (for northern observers). Its stars are scattered, and small groups of them form groupings or asterisms, rather than the whole resembling anything in particular. The constellation follows another zodical member, Capricornus, to the east, and occupies the area between Pegasus to the north and the 1st-magnitude star Fomalhaut in Piscis Austrinus to the south. It is on the meridian due south at 10pm on October 1.

The asterism easiest to spot is the water jar that Aquarius is holding, a "Y"-shaped trefoil which resembles the Mercedes-Benz symbol, made up of the stars Zeta (ζ) in the center, Pi (π), Eta (η), and Gamma (γ). Once you find this 2°-diameter group, just to its right (or west) you'll see Alpha (α) Aquarii, Sadalmelik. Overall, there are about 100 naked eye stars.

This large group contains many double stars of note, especially Zeta (ζ), central star of the trefoil, which is a close (1.9 arcseconds) binary, which is now opening (i.e. the separation is increasing) owing to orbital motion.

Globular Clusters

There are also two bright globular clusters, both recorded by Messier, M72 and M2, the latter being one of the better globulars in the sky. M2's total integrated magnitude is 6.0, so it may be visible to a sharp-eyed observer on a really dark night. The cluster becomes a ball of faint and very evenly bright stars of 13th magnitude and fainter in a 10-inch (25-cm) telescope. M73 is an asterism of stars which Messier mistook for a nebula.

Planetary Nebulae

There are two planetary nebulae of note, the bright Saturn

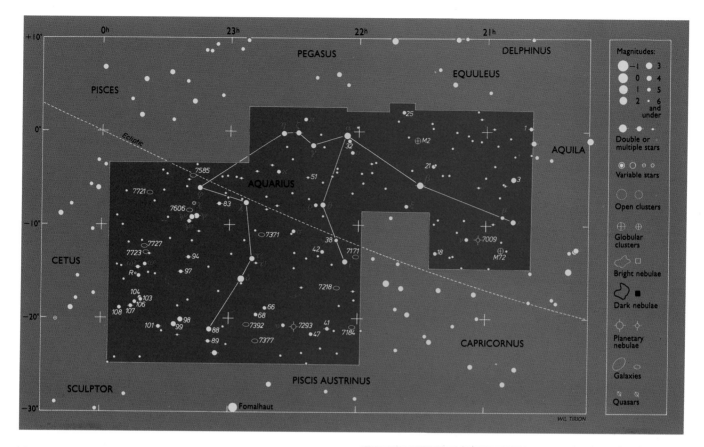

WIL TIRION

Nebula (NGC 7009) and the Helix Nebula (NGC 7293), largest – and presumably closest – of the planetary nebulae. The Saturn Nebula was so named because in a small telescope its outer shell looks like a faint ringed planet. The large (15 arcminute diameter), but faint, Helix is located in southern Aquarius. This wonderful object appears like a large, dim smoke-ring in 20 × 80 binoculars. A dark, clear night is necessary to view it well, when it can be seen in steadily held 7 × 50 binoculars. In a rich-field telescope with an Oxygen III filter, the contrast is increased, and the object becomes easy to see.

There are quite a number of galaxies in Aquarius, all being round 12th magnitude or fainter. Those brighter than 13th are listed in the table.

Planetary Nebulae

Planetary nebulae are expanding shells of gas which surround a central star in the final stages of its evolution from a giant to a dwarf. As the star evolves mass is lost as a shell of gas. They were named by Sir William Herschel in 1785 because of their telescopic similarity to planets, though something of a misnomer, because they are neither planets nor nebulae. Around a thousand are known, and though the most famous are circular in shape, the vast majority (70% of the total population) possess two lobes. The central star is usually blue and hot (30,000–400,000K), and heats up the surrounding gas shell. It has been observed that as the star fades the gas shell expands, but the exact mechanism of mass loss remains elusive.

TELESCOPIC OBJECTS IN AQUARIUS
Double and Multiple Stars

Name	RA	Dec.	Separation (arcseconds)	Mags.		Year
41	22h 14.3m	−21° 04′	5.0	5.6	7.1	1959
51	22h 24.1m	−04° 50′	AB 0.5	6.5	6.5	1960
			AB × D 113.7	10.1		1917
			AC 54.4	10.2		1917
			AE 132.4	8.6		1917
ζ (Zeta)	22h 28.8m	−0° 01′	1.9	4.3	4.5	1975
89	23h 09.9m	−22° 27′	0.4	5.1	5.9	1959
101	23h 33.3m	−20° 55′	0.9	4.8	7.1	1958
107	23h 46.0m	−18° 41′	6.6	5.7	6.7	1971

Deep Sky Objects

Name	RA	Dec.	Type	Size	Mag.
M72 (NGC 6981)	20h 53.5m	−12° 32′	Glob. Cl.	6′	9.3
NGC 7009	21h 04.2m	−11° 22′	Plan. Neb.	25″ × 100″	8.3
M2 (NGC 7089)	21h 33.5m	−0° 49′	Glob. Cl.	13′	6.5
NGC 7171	22h 01.0m	−13° 16′	Gal. Sb	3′ × 2′	12
NGC 7184	22h 02.7m	−20° 49′	Gal. Sb	6′ × 2′	12
NGC 7218	22h 10.2m	−16° 40′	Gal. Sc	2′ × 1′	12
NGC 7293	22h 29.6m	−20° 48′	Plan. Neb.	>12′	13
NGC 7371	22h 46.1m	−11° 00′	Gal. Sb	2′ × 2′	12
NGC 7377	22h 47.8m	−22° 19′	Gal. El	2′ × 2′	12
NGC 7392	22h 51.8m	−20° 36′	Gal. Sb	2′ × 1′	12
NGC 7585	23h 18.0m	−04° 39′	Gal. S	2′ × 2′	10.7
NGC 7606	23h 19.1m	−8° 29′	Gal. S	6′ × 2′	10.7
NGC 7721	23h 38.8m	−06° 31′	Gal. Sc	3′ × 1′	12
NGC 7723	23h 38.9m	−12° 58′	Gal. Sb	3′ × 2′	11
NGC 7727	23h 39.9m	−12° 18′	Gal. S	4′ × 3′	11

AQUILA

Aquila is a prominent group in the summer sky, with the Milky Way running through it. Aquila is located straight south (on the meridian) at 10 pm on August 15. Altair, Alpha Aquilae, at magnitude 0.77 is the 12th brightest star seen from Earth (including the Sun). During the summer it is about 45° above the horizon as seen from mid-northern latitudes, and can be recognized by its pure white light and the presence of two fainter stars, one above and one below, about 2° away; Gamma (γ) and Beta (β), respectively.

Aquila is a treasure-trove in binocular and telescope fields. A prominent dark dust cloud is silhouetted against the Milky Way, and is just visible to the naked eye north of Gamma. It forms a distinct "C" shape against the background of our Galaxy in 7 × 50 binoculars. This dark area is number 143 in Edward Emerson Barnard's catalog of dark nebulae published in 1919 (and subsequently expanded).

Altair, the eagle star, is at a distance is 16 light years, making it one of the closer bright stars. The spectral type is A7, indicating a fairly young Sirius-type star. Altair is known for its rapid rotational rate, discovered by the broadening of its spectral lines (from the Doppler shifting of the approaching and receding limbs). It turns in about 6½ hours. In comparison our Sun rotates in about 25 days.

Multiple Stars

There are a number of good double stars, clusters, and planetary nebulae worth observing. Some of the doubles you might try to find are: Σ 2404, a small orange double, with components of 7th and 8th magnitude, which were separated by 3.6 arcseconds in 1957. 23 Aquilae is a triple, with components of magnitude 5.3 and 9.3 separated by 3.4 arcseconds and a magnitude 13.7 star some 12 arcseconds away (only visible in larger telescopes). Chi (χ) is a good test for an 8-inch (20-cm) instrument, with components of magnitude 5.6 and 6.8 at 0.5 arcseconds separation. Pi (π) is a little easier, with stars of magnitude 6.1 and 6.9, 1.4 arcseconds apart. Σ 2587 is an easy pair for 3-inch (7.5 cm) and larger telescopes, with stars of magnitude 6.7 and 9.4 at 4.1 arcseconds distance.

Deep Sky Objects

Only one open (galactic) cluster stands out, NGC 6709, which is large but has little central condensation. It takes an 8-inch (20-cm) or larger aperture to appreciate.

The small globular cluster (2′) NGC 6760 is located a little less than 2° west of the finder star 23 Aquilae, and is about 11th magnitude. It is obscured by the dust of the Galaxy to a considerable exent. There is one good galaxy in Aquila, in the southeastern portion. NGC 6814 is a small (2′) round face-on galaxy of about 12th magnitude which should show its bright 'arms' with a 14-inch or larger instrument. To see faint details it is often advisable to use high powers on the subject, which darkens the background sky, which is what you want. You will always be able to see fainter objects at high powers, assuming steady seeing.

Planetary Nebulae

It is in planetary nebulae, those puffs of star gas, that Aquila is outstanding. There are six easily visible in an 8-inch (20-cm) 'scope. They range from large, very dim disks (NGC 6781) to almost starlike points (NGC 6803). Others in between include NGC 6751, which is about 20 arcseconds in diameter and easy

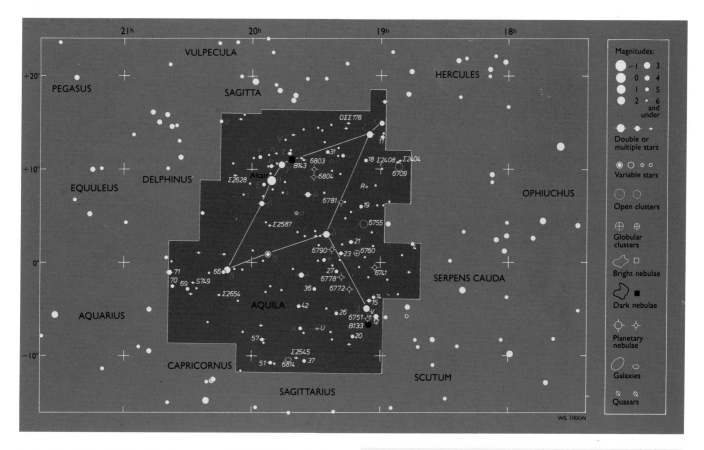

to find in a 10-inch (25-cm) telescope, and NGC 6778, which is a little smaller and fades at the edges, with a dark, obscuring dust cloud (Barnard 139) just to the north. It looks like an empty place in the sky, and was so described by the pioneer deep sky observer Sir William Herschel in the 1780s. NGC 6804 is oval, and is associated with a star of about 12th magnitude on its north-eastern edge.

Techniques for Observing Planetary Nebulae

Filters will often help define planetary nebulae, since a light pollution reduction filter reduces the skyglow background, even in a "dark sky" location. The filter reduces the auroral glow, which is always present from recombining atoms high in the Earth's upper atmosphere. An Oxygen III filter also helps some planetaries, since they often glow in the green light of ionized oxygen.

Serious planetary nebula observers often employ an eyepiece spectroscope to find small planetaries. These devices spread the light of stellar point sources into small, smeared spectra. Stars, essentially consisting of glowing gas under pressure, have a continuous spectrum. A small nebula located in the field, glows only in one or two spectral lines. Its image is not smeared out, but appears singular. This is caused by gas in the interstellar vacuum, fluorescing by excitation from the largely ultraviolet radiation of the central star embedded in each planetary. This technique is a simple application of "slitless spectroscopy".

TELESCOPIC OBJECTS IN AQUILA
Double and Multiple Stars

Name	RA	Dec.	Separation (arcseconds)	Mags.		Year
Σ 2404	18h 50.8m	+10° 59′	3.6	6.9	8.1	1957
Σ 2408	18h 52.0m	+10° 47′	2.1	7.5	8.5	1962
15	19h 05.0m	−04° 02′	38.4	5.5	7.2	1959
23	19h 18.5m	+01° 05′	3.1	5.3	9.3	1958
			11.3	13.5		1958
Σ 2545	19h 38.7m	−10° 09′	3.7	6.8	8.7	1959
			26.1	11.4		1959
χ (Chi)	19h 42.6m	+11° 50′	0.5	5.6	6.8	1958
π (Pi)	19h 48.7m	+11° 49′	1.4·	6.1	6.9	1960
Σ 2587	19h 51.4m	+04° 05′	4.1	6.7	9.4	1939
57	19h 54.6m	−08° 14′	35.7	5.8	6.5	1955
Σ 2654	20h 15.2m	−03° 30′	14.2	6.9	9.3	1951

Deep Sky Objects

Name	RA	Dec.	Type	Size	Mag.
NGC 6709	18h 51.5m	+10° 21′	Open Cl.	13′	6.7
NGC 6751	19h 05.9m	−06° 00′	Plan. Neb.	20″	12.5
B133	19h 06.1m	−06° 50′	Dust	10′ × 3′	dark
NGC 6760	19h 11.2m	+01° 02′	Glob. Cl.	6′	9
NGC 6772	19h 14.6m	−02° 42′	Plan. Neb.	1′	14pg
NGC 6778	19h 18.4m	−01° 36′	Plan. Neb.	16″	13
NGC 6781	19h 18.4m	+06° 33′	Plan. Neb.	109″	11.8 pg
NGC 6790	19h 23.2m	+01° 31′	Plan. Neb.	7″	10
NGC 6803	19h 31.3m	+10° 03′	Plan. Neb.	6″	11
NGC 6804	19h 31.6m	+09° 13′	Plan. Neb.	30″ × 60″	12.2 pg
B143	19h 40.7m	+10° 57′	Dust	80′ × 50′	dark
NGC 6814	19h 42.7m	−10° 19′	Gal. S	3′ × 3′	11

ARA

Ara, the Altar, *was associated with the Centaur in ancient times, Centaurus being the large constellation to the west of Ara and Norma. It was seen with Norma as the burning altar on which Centaurus intended to sacrifice Lupus, the wolf. The altar is the right way up for southern viewers. The stars Eta, Delta, Gamma, and Zeta mark the flame. Ara was described by Ptolemy in the 2nd century AD as a censer.*

Ara, the Altar, is a rich Milky Way constellation lying south of Scorpius. There is a fairly dense interstellar dust cloud which obscures some of the background star clouds in the northern end of the constellation. The photograph was made by mounting a camera piggyback on a larger telescope which was driven to follow the stars. A 50mm lens at f/2.8 and 100ASA transparency film were used for the 10-minutes exposure by the author at Quebrada Marquesa, Chile.

Ara is a southern-hemisphere constellation which lies almost entirely in the Milky Way, south of Scorpius' tail. It has a lantern shape, made up roughly of two parallel lines of stars. Ara reaches its highest point about 10 pm on July 5. Some of its northernmost stars can be seen as far north as New York, but to really appreciate the constellation one should be south of +30°.

This is an interesting area of our Galaxy, housing many telescopic objects, including a wonderful bright and dark nebulous area (NGC 6188). There are also, according to Hartung, nine open clusters, three globulars, a planetary nebula and a few faint galaxies seen outside the boundaries of the obscuring Milky Way. As might be expected in the Galaxy, there are many double and multiple stars awaiting the telescopic observer. To get a feel for its position, the middle of the constellation is at −53° declination, 5 degrees farther south than the great globular cluster Omega Centauri.

Multiple Stars

A few of the doubles and multiples to look for in Ara are: R Arae, a variable star which is an eclipsing binary consisting of stars of 6th and 8th magnitude separated by 3.6 arcseconds; h4876, chief star of the cluster NGC 6193, which has four components; h4901, two 8th-magnitude stars separated by 2.8 arcseconds; h4949, stars of 6th and 7th magnitude 2.2 arcseconds apart; and RmK 22, stars of 7th and 8th magnitude at 2.5 arcseconds separation.

Deep Sky Objects

There is a nice variety of deep sky objects in Ara, including the NGC 6188-93 complex, which includes NGC 6193 itself, a

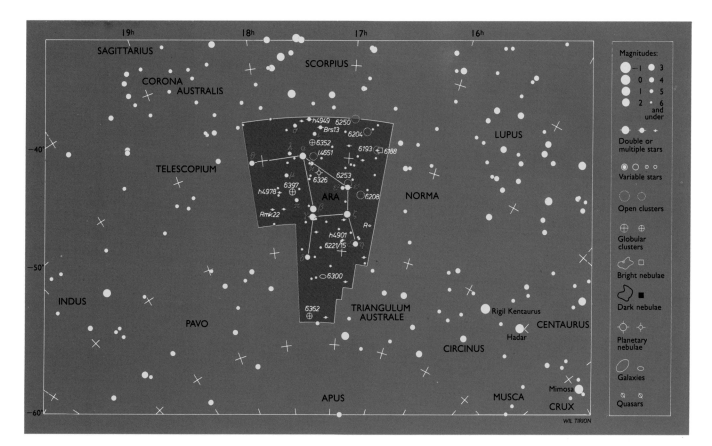

WIL TIRION

scattered star cluster involved with faint nebulosity which is spectacular in long-exposure photographs. There is a bright-edged nebulosity, which is made difficult to see by the 6th-magnitude h4876. A nebula or light pollution rejection filter will make this easier to see by reducing the continuum light of the stars while letting the nebular emission through. NGC 6326 is a small, round planetary nebula with two stars nearby. IC 4651 is an open cluster with about 80 stars brighter than 9th magnitude, and about 15 arcminutes across, demanding telescopic views at low powers.

NGC 6397

NGC 6397 is a very fine globular cluster, large with a diameter of about 20 arcminutes and easily resolved with 3-inch (7.5 cm) aperture and larger 'scopes. It is probably the closest globular cluster, at a distance of only about 8,400 light years. It is one of the best globulars for small-aperture instruments. Visually it resembles Messier 4 in Scorpius, with the brightest stars scattered across the "face" of the grouping, with no concentration in the center. The stars in 6397 are very ancient, highly evolved red giants which show their age by being low in heavy metals which are released by supernovae during their explosions in normal galactic evolution. The globulars are deficient in heavy metals presumably because they were formed before the evolutionary processes in the galactic disk. No satisfactory theory has been advanced as to how the globulars stay stable in their round form, either. Intuitively one would expect them to have either collapsed into a single body, or to have flown apart in the several billions of years since their formation.

TELESCOPIC OBJECTS IN ARA
Double and Multiple Stars

Name	RA	Dec.	Separation (arcseconds)	Mags.		Year
R	16h 39.7m	−57° 00'	3.6	6.0	8.5	1933
h4876	16h 41.3m	−48° 46'	1.6	5.6	8.9	1938
			9.6	6.8		1938
			13.4	10.4		1938
			13.9	11.3		1938
h4901	17h 01.1m	−58° 51'	2.8	7.8	7.9	1952
Brs 13	17h 19.1m	−46° 38'	5.0	5.5	8.6	1959
h4949	17h 26.9m	−45° 51'	2.2	6.0	6.7	1953
			103.0	7.6		1913
h4978	17h 50.5m	−53° 37'	12.3	6.0	9.0	1933
Rmk 22	17h 57.2m	−55° 23'	2.5	7.0	8.0	1952

Deep Sky Objects

Name	RA	Dec.	Type	Size	Mag.
NGC 6188	16h 40.5m	−48° 47'	Neb.	20' × 12'	11
NGC 6193	16h 41.3m	−48° 47'	Cl.	20'	6
NGC 6326	17h 20.8m	−51° 45'	Plan. Neb.	14"	12
IC 4651	17h 24.6m	−49° 56'	Open Cl.	12'	6.9
NGC 6352	17h 25.5m	−48° 25'	Glob. Cl.	7'	8
NGC 6362	17h 31.9m	−67° 03'	Glob. Cl.	11'	8
NGC 6397	17h 40.7m	−53° 40'	Glob. Cl.	26'	6

ARIES

Aries is an important constellation located below Andromeda, above Cetus, and west of Taurus. It is the first constellation of the ancient zodiac, where the Sun's path (the ecliptic) crossed the celestial equator during the period in which classical mythology was completed (from around 1000 BC until 420 AD). Since then this point, called the First Point of Aries, has moved owing to the Earth's precession (wobble) into western Pisces. It is also called the vernal equinox and its crossing by the Sun marks the coming of spring in the northern hemisphere (March 21). Aries is best seen in the fall, when it culminates at 10 pm on November 20. Aries has many fine double stars including the oustanding pair Gamma (γ), and has several galaxies notable in larger amateur telescopes (12-inch (30-cm) aperture or bigger).

Recently Aries was in the news for being the home of the "Aries Flasher", a peculiarly ephemeral object seen by several amateur astronomers as a slow-duration (about 1–3 seconds) bright flash located in northern Aries or southern Perseus. It appeared at slightly different places in the sky, and could not be identified as an astronomical object (because nothing known has such a period or brightness). The "flasher" was finally identified as a reflection off an artificial satellite. Certain satellite orbits have their apogee, i.e. highest point, at about 700 miles up, at which point the satellite is moving so slowly that it can appear as an almost motionless stellar point for a few minutes.

Without a telescope, Aries has only a few stars of interest, principally the triangle made up of Alpha (α), Beta (β) and Gamma (γ). This triangle is about 4° high and 4° in extent from east to west. It marks the head and neck of the ram, which is lying facing west but with its head turned facing east. The remainder of the constellation's stars are faint and scattered randomly over the animal's body. The triangle of 35, 39 and 41 Arietis was called Musca Borealis, the Northern Fly, hovering over the ram's back, but this asterism was deleted in the 1800s (the only fly left in the astronomical sky is Musca in the southern hemisphere). The ecliptic runs through southern Aries, so there are often planets passing through it.

Multiple stars

A small telescope will show many beautiful pairs of stars in Aries, and a medium-sized 'scope of around 8-inch (20-cm) aperture will resolve all those listed below. Gamma (γ) is a first-class double, with blue–white components of equal brightness, of 4.8 magnitude and separated by 7.8 arcseconds. Earlier measurements showed greater separation, so the two components are slowly closing due to orbital movement. Gamma, also called Mesarthim, was discovered to be double by Robert Hooke in 1664 while he was following a comet. It has a handy property for amateur astronomers in that the position angle (the angle of the line of separation from north to south, measured eastward from north) is 0°. That is, the two stars are lined up exactly north–south in the sky.

There are a few galaxies in Aries, but a good-sized telescope (10-inch (25-cm) or larger) is needed to see them to advantage. The best of these is NGC 772, a spiral galaxy seen in about three-quarters view, which has several arms suspected in a 12-inch (30-cm) aperture telescope. It has three fairly bright H II regions, one near the nucleus and two near the end of one of the widely spaced spiral arms. There is also a star of about 13th magnitude near the western side of the nuclear area, which should not be mistaken for a supernova.

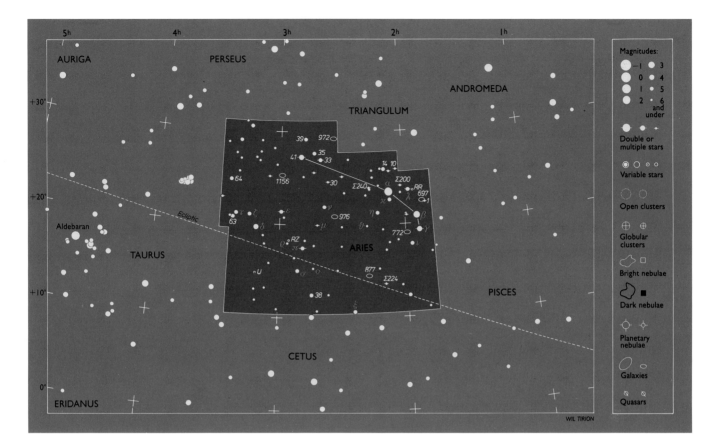

Double Star Catalogs

A	Aitken, R. G. *c.*1900, Lick Observatory.
Ar	Argelander, F. W. A. *c.*1850, German.
AC	Clark, Alvan. *c.*1860, American.
Bar	Barnard, E. E. *c.*1900.
Brs	Brisbane, T. *c.*1840, Scottish–Australian.
Burnham	S.W. 1828–1921. Double star observer.
Cor	Cordoba Observatory, Argentina.
Cp	Cape Observatory, South Africa.
Es	Espin, T. E. H., Rev. Durham *c.*1890.
H	Herschel, Sir William. *Fl.* 1780–1800, Slough.
h	Herschel, Sir John. *Fl.* 1830–60.
He	Howe, H. A. University of Denver, *c.*1890.
Hn	Holden, E. S. Lick Observatory, *c.*1895.
I	Innes, R. T. A., Johannesburg.
Jc	Jacob, W. S.
L	Lacaille, N. L. de, French astronomer, *c.*1752.
M	Messier, Charles, French astronomer, *fl.* 1775.
Mel	Melbourne Observatory.
R	Russell, H. C.
Rmk	Rumker, C. L. C. German, 1788–1862.
S	South, Sir James. English amateur.
Sa	Santiago Observatory, Chile.
Slr	Sellors.
Δ	Dunlop, J. Observer at Cape Town.
λ	Lowell Observatory. Early 1900s.
OΣ	Struve, Otto. 1819–1905. Russian.
OΣΣ	Pulkova Catalog, part II.
Σ	Struve, F. G. W. 1793–1864, German.

TELESCOPIC OBJECTS IN ARIES

Double and Multiple Stars

Name	RA	Dec.	Separation (arcseconds)	Mags.		Year
I	01h 50.1m	+22° 17′	2.8	6.2	7.4	1967
γ (Gamma)	01h 53.5m	+19° 18′	7.8	4.8	4.8	1969
λ (Lambda)	01h 57.9m	+23° 36′	37.4	4.9	7.7	1933
Σ 200	02h 01.6m	+24° 06′	8.2	8.5	9.0	1919
10	02h 03.7m	+25° 56′	0.5	5.9	7.3	1961
Σ 224	02h 10.9m	+13° 41′	5.5	8.4	8.9	1942
30	02h 37.0m	+24° 39′	38.6	6.6	7.4	1937
π (Pi)	02h 49.3m	+17° 28′	3.2	5.2	8.7	1957
			25.2	10.5		1938
ε (Epsilon)	02h 59.2m	+21° 20′	1.4	5.2	5.5	1966

Deep Sky Objects

Name	RA	Dec.	Type	Size	Mag.
NGC 697	01h 51.3m	+22° 21′	Gal. SBb	2′ × 1′	12.5
NGC 772	01h 59.3m	+19° 01′	Gal. Sb	7′ × 5′	11.1
NGC 877	02h 18.0m	+14° 33′	Gal. Sc	2′ × 2′	11.8
NGC 972	02h 34.2m	+29° 19′	Gal. Sc	3′ × 2′	11.3
NGC 1156	02h 59.7m	+25° 14′	Gal. Irr.	3′ × 2′	12.2

AURIGA

Auriga, the Charioteer, has been known thus since ancient times, and was originally portrayed complete with chariot. The brilliant star Capella represents the Charioteer's left shoulder, and was thought by the ancient Greeks to represent Amalthea, the she-goat that suckled the infant Zeus. The three small stars above Capella are known as the kids.

Auriga is a large and ancient fall and winter constellation located north of Taurus. The Galaxy runs through Auriga, providing many clusters and some faint nebulous regions. The brightest star is the zero-magnitude yellow star Capella, the sixth brightest luminary of the heavens. The constellation is almost circumpolar for mid-northern observers, and is virtually overhead at 10 pm during the first week in January.

The Goat and the Kids

The group is usually seen as a polygon, with Beta Tauri, the upper horn of Taurus, as the base (see map). The Charioteer holds three kids on his shoulder, the small stars Epsilon (ε), Eta (η) and Zeta (ζ). In Auriga we are looking outwards away from the Galactic Center in Sagittarius, therefore Auriga's star clouds are less pronounced. Capella, the Goat Star, is of 0.06 magnitude, with a spectrum similar to the Sun's. It is, however, much larger, and at a distance of 45 light years must have a luminosity of 160 Suns. Its movement in space is similar to the Hyades Cluster in Taurus, and it may be a member of that galactic cluster. Spectroscopic evidence shows Capella to consist of two stars rotating about a common center of gravity at a distance of 70 million miles with a period of 104.022 days.

Auriga is full of telescopic wonders and has several large galactic, or open, clusters which are well seen in binoculars. There is also a striking asterism, or miniature star pattern, within the polygon, in the form of two parallel lines of stars which are about one degree long. There are clusters M36 and M38, and a large faint nebula around AE Aurigae in the neighborhood, making for beautiful binocular viewing.

Zeta Aurigae is an eclipsing binary system. As seen from Earth, the brighter of zeta's (ζ) two components is the relatively small, hot, blue, B-type star. But in this view, painted from a nearby planet by intrepid interstellar artist David Hardy, the smaller star is dwarfed by the massive secondary component, a K-type orange giant which is 50 times the size of its blue companion.

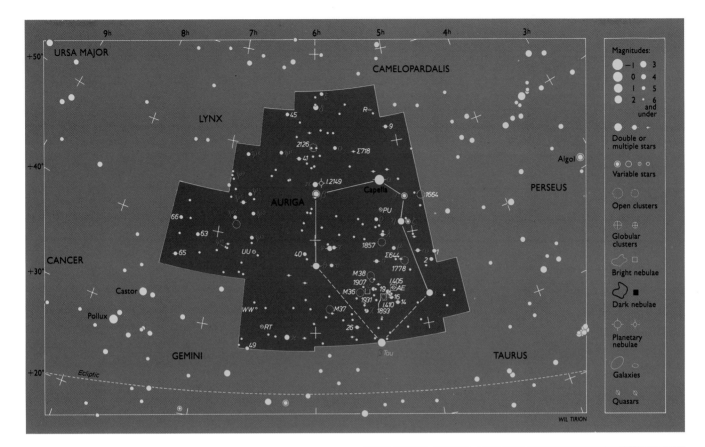

Clusters

Chief among the deep-sky wonders are the galactic clusters M36, M37 and M38. M36 is a concentrated, but irregular, group of about 60 stars, and, like the other open clusters in Auriga, is best seen with low-power eyepieces. The group resembles M6 in Scorpius, and all of its bright stars are white. M37 is one of the finest open clusters in the sky, with about 150 stars down to 12.5 magnitude. The actual diameter is approximately 25 light years and the distance from the Earth is some 4,600 light years. There are a number of yellowish or reddish giant stars in this group, giving it quite a different appearance from M36. M38 is a large open cluster which has streams of stars leading into a rather dark middle. This is a rich neighborhood, with the smaller galactic cluster NGC 1907 almost directly south.

Dust and Gas

A large (primarily photographic) nebula is IC 410, which in a small Schmidt camera photograph resembles the Rosette Nebula in Monoceros. It is red, has a small star cluster in its central area, and also possesses a darker "hole" in the center, where the material has perhaps condensed into the cluster. On the northwest side of the prominent asterism in the midst of the polygon is the AE Aurigae complex of dust and gas. AE is a small-amplitude dusty variable star, which illuminates a reflection nebula and an emission nebula around it. In a color photograph, the bluish reflection nebula is near the star, and it is overlaid with a larger reddish emission nebula glow. The result is a magenta cloud fading into the redder nebula in the area. AE is one of the "runaway" stars whose proper motion can be traced back to the Orion belt area.

TELESCOPIC OBJECTS IN AURIGA
Double and Multiple Stars

Name	RA	Dec.	Separation (arcseconds)	Mags.		Year
ω (Omega)	04h 59.3m	+37° 53′	5.4	5.0	8.0	1950
ε (Epsilon)	05h 02.0m	+43° 49′	21.2	3.0	14.0	1925
			AC 43.0	3.0	11.7	1925
			AD 46.2	3.0	12.0	1924
Σ 644	05h 10.3m	+37° 18′	1.6	6.7	7.0	1959
			AC 72.6	6.7	9.3	1903
Σ 698	05h 25.2m	+34° 51′	31.2	6.6	8.7	1951
Σ 718	05h 32.4m	+49° 24′	7.7	7.5	7.5	1955
			AC 119.4	7.5	9.2	1910
26	05h 38.6m	+30° 30′	0.2	6.0	6.3	1963
			AC 12.4	6.0	8.0	1967
			AD 33.1	6.0	11.5	1915
θ (Theta)	05h 59.7m	+37° 13′	3.6	2.6	7.1	1976
			AC 50.0	2.6	10.6	1939

Variable Stars

Name	RA	Dec.	Type	Mag. Range	Period
ε (Epsilon)	05h 02.0m	+43° 49′	Ecl. Bin.	2.92–3.83	9892 days
ζ (Zeta)	05h 02.5m	+41° 05′	Ecl. Bin.	3.7–4.0	972 days
	05h 16.3m	+49° 33′	AE Irr.	5.78–6.08	Irr.

Deep Sky Objects

Name	RA	Dec.	Type	Size	Mag.
IC 405	05h 16.2m	+34° 16′	Diff. Neb.	30′ × 19′	~9
IC 410	05h 22.6m	+33° 31′	Diff. Neb.	40′ × 30′	
NGC 1907	05h 28.0m	+35° 19′	Gal. Cl.	7′	8.2
M38 (NGC 1912)	05h 28.7m	+35° 50′	Gal. Cl.	21′	6.4
NGC 1931	05h 31.4m	+34° 15′	Diff. Neb.	3′ × 3′	~10
M36 (NGC 1960)	05h 36.1m	+34° 08′	Gal. Cl.	12′	6.0 60
M37 (NGC 2099)	05h 52.4m	+32° 33′	Gal. Cl.	24′	5.6 150
IC 2149	05h 56.3m	+46° 07′	Plan. Neb.	8″	11.2pg

BOÖTES

Boötes is a large spring and summer constellation between Ursa Major and Virgo (north and south respectively) and Corona Borealis and Canes Venatici (east and west respectively). Its major observational attractions are the zero-magnitude star Arcturus, and many beautiful double and multiple stars. Its center culminates overhead for mid-northern latitudes at midnight on April 30.

Arcturus

Boötes' main star is Arcturus, the fourth brightest star in the sky and the brightest north of the celestial equator. Its bright orange color is unmistakable in an otherwise rather empty part of the sky. It was used by the Greeks and no doubt other ancient peoples as a calendar sign when its heliacal rising (just before sunrise) indicated grape harvesting time. This brilliant stellar jewel lies at a distance of 25 light years and its spectral type is K2, telling us that it has a surface temperature of 4,200 K, 1,200 degrees cooler than the Sun. The star is, however, much larger, with an estimated diameter of 20 million miles (the Sun's is less than 1 million miles). Consequently it has a luminosity about 115 times the Sun's, although it only has four times its mass. Arcturus stands out as a star which has not remained "fixed" in the sky. Edmond Halley discovered in 1718 that it has a rapid "proper motion" across the sky of 2.28 arcseconds per year. This motion is in the southwest direction toward Virgo. It also means that in 1000 BC Arcturus was located almost 2 degrees northeast of where it is today. This rapid motion happens because the star's motion in space is almost at a right angle to, and in the opposite direction to, the Solar System's motion towards Hercules. It is now almost at its closest to us and therefore at its fastest-moving point.

You can find Arcturus by extending the handle of the Big Dipper (Ursa Major) southwards until you come to a bright orange star. It can easily be observed in the daytime with a telescope equipped with a setting-circle (first done in 1634). A brilliant orange point standing out against the blue of the sky will reward the diligent searcher.

Multiple Stars

Kappa (κ) Boötis is a bright binary pair, with stars of magnitudes 4.6 and 6.6 separated by 13.4 arcseconds. The brighter is slightly variable, and they are of spectral types A7 and F2, respectively. Iota (ι) is a wider pair, similar in color. Separated by 38.5 arcseconds, they are of magnitude 4.9 and 7.5, respectively. Pi (π) Boötis is a nice, relatively close double, with 5th- and 6th-magnitude stars at a separation of 5.6 arcseconds. Spectral categories are B9 and A5, respectively.

Zeta (ζ) Boötis is a triple star with a close pair 0.9 arcseconds apart and another star some 99 arcseconds distant. The magnitudes of the trio are 4.5, 5.0 and 10.5 (the first two are of spectral class A2). Epsilon (ε) also known as Mirak or Izar, is one of the finest colored doubles in the sky. It was discovered by Frederick Struve in 1829 and the pair are of spectral types K0 and A2, separated by 2.8 arcseconds. The orbital movement of the secondary star is very slow. Magnitudes are 2.5 and 4.9, so the smaller star is sometimes difficult when turbulent air is present. The color contrast is great, with a yellowish orange primary and the smaller star appearing bluish or green.

Xi (ξ) Boötis is an easy double for all telescopes, with a separation of 6.9 arcseconds for its 4th- and 7th-magnitude components. This system of solar-type stars is one of the closest

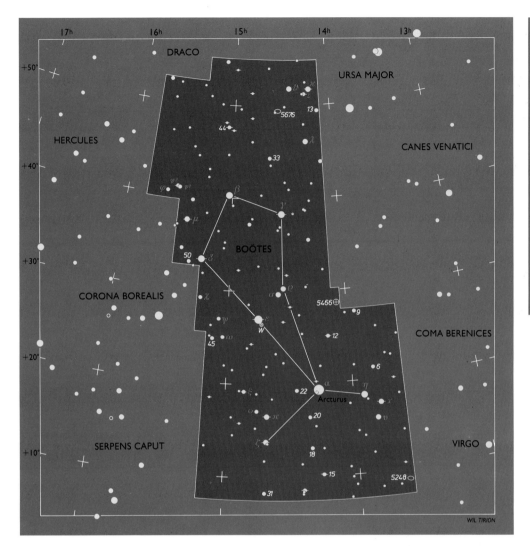

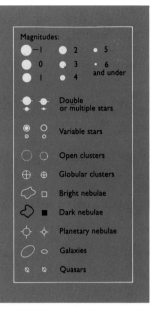

WIL TIRION

binaries to us at about 22 light years distance. Sir William Herschel discovered them in 1780: distance was greatest in 1983 and will decrease to 1.8 arcseconds by 2062 AD. The star colors are yellow and deep orange. 44 or Iota (ι) Boötis is a binary system which has stars of 5th and 6th magnitude in an elongated orbit, allowing separation to vary from less than 0.4 to 4.7 arcseconds. The stars were closest in 1969, so it will be interesting to watch them separate over the next hundred years or so. The primary is a solar-type star, and the secondary star a close eclipsing binary which varies in brightness by half a magnitude in a 6.4-hour period (much too close to be separated visually).

Mu 2 (μ_2) and Mu 1 (μ_1) Boötis form a wide pair of stars separated by 105 arcseconds. They are of spectral types F0 and G1 and have brightnesses of magnitude 4.3 and 6.5. μ_2 is a close binary of solar-type stars of magnitudes 7.0 and 7.6.

Deep Sky Objects

NGC 5466 is a 9th-magnitude globular cluster which has less condensation than many globulars. A 10-inch (25-cm) 'scope is needed to achieve resolution at the edges. NGC 5248 is a spiral galaxy of 10th magnitude, some 6.5 × 4.9 arcminutes in size. A 12-inch (30-cm) 'scope shows a circular haze with a faint offset nucleus.

TELESCOPIC OBJECTS IN BOÖTES

Double Stars

Name	RA	Dec.	Separation (arcseconds)	Mags.		Year
κ (Kappa)	14h 13.5m	+51° 47'	13.4	4.6	6.6	1968
ι (Iota)	14h 16.2m	+51° 22'	38.5	4.9	7.5	1942
π (Pi)	14h 40.7m	+16° 25'	5.6	4.9	5.8	1957
ζ (Zeta)	14h 41.1m	+13° 44'	AB 0.9	4.5	5.9	1960
			AC 9.9	4.5	10.5	
ε (Epsilon)	14h 45.0m	+27° 04'	2.8	2.5	4.9	1971
μ (Mu)	15h 24.5m	+37° 23'	2.0	7.0	7.6	1968

Deep Sky Objects

Name	RA	Dec.	Type	Size	Mag.
NGC 5248	13h 37.5m	+08° 53'	Gal. Sc	3' × 1'	10
NGC 5466	14h 05.5m	+28° 32'	Glob. Cl.	11'	9
NGC 5676	14h 32.8m	+49° 28'	Gal. Sc	3' × 1'	11.9

29

CAELUM/COLUMBA

Both Caelum, the Sculptor's Chisel, and Columba, the Dove, are recent additions to the heavens, and have no classical legends associated with them. Caelum was introduced in 1752 by the French astronomer Nicolas Louis de Lacaille, who travelled to the Cape of Good Hope in order to map the southern skies. It was originally called Caela Sculptoris, the Sculptor's Tools, but was later shortened.

Columba was introduced by the Frenchman Augustin Royer in 1679, when it bore the name Columba Noachi (Noah's Dove), representing the bird released from the Ark.

Spiral galaxy NGC 1598. This CCD picture of NGC 1598, which is located some 200 million light years away, and too faint for amateur telescopes, has been image-processed to show the variety of structure in the galaxy. The inner spiral pattern is seen in white; the orange halo is a high-contrast display of the faint outer structure, which may be the remnant of tidal interaction with a nearby galaxy (just out of frame in this view). The orange rings around the intervening stars are an artefact of the image processing. The picture was recorded in yellow light at the 160-inch (4-m) telescope at the Cerro Tololo Inter-American Observatory in Chile.

Caelum is a late fall and early winter constellation for northern observers. It lies just west of Columba, the Dove, and though it covers about 125 square degrees it is an inconspicuous group. It can be found by first locating the four-sided figure of Columba and Nu1 (v_1) to Nu4 (v_4) Eridani. Caelum is between these two asterisms. The center of Caelum is located around −38° declination, so it lies quite far south of Orion and Lepus.

Caelum

Only three double stars and one galaxy are of interest telescopically. h3650 is a nicely colored double with stars of magnitudes 7.1 and 8.3 at a distance of 3 arcseconds separation. It can easily be seen in a 3-inch (7.5-cm) refractor. Alpha (α) Caeli is a 4th-magnitude star with a faint (12.7 magnitude) companion only 6.6 arcseconds away. Gamma (γ) is a closer (2.9 arcseconds separation) pair with a primary of magnitude 4.6 and an 8th-magnitude companion. NGC 1679 is a 13th-magnitude galaxy which appears brighter. It has an irregular round shape and there are three or four faint foreground stars which are seen against the galaxy.

Columba

Columba is another small grouping, located directly south of Lepus, the first constellation south of Orion, and is therefore a winter constellation for northern observers. Visually it is characterized by a straggling line of stars stretching east–west about 20° from Delta (δ) to Beta (β). There are some good doubles, several galaxies, and one of the better globulars (NGC 1851).

Mu (μ) Columbae is one of the three "runaway" stars that have been discovered to be travelling away from the Belt of

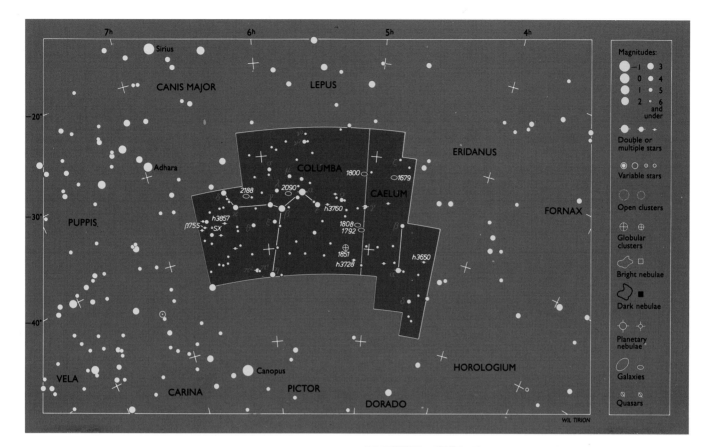

WIL TIRION

Orion area at high speed. The others are AE Aurigae and 53 Arietis. The high space velocity of 72 miles per second has carried it out of the Orion complex area for some 2.7 million years. A common origin for the three stars has been postulated, perhaps in a supernova explosion in a multiple star system. The star's proper motion is only 0.025 arcseconds, so it's not one to watch for much movement over a few years.

With smaller instruments (of 6-inch (15-cm) aperture or less), try observing h3728, which has two stars of 6th and 9th magnitude separated by 10 arcseconds. h3760 is a nice triple with two 8th-magnitude stars and a third of 10th magnitude some 26 arcseconds away. Another wide triplet is h3857, which consists of 5th-and 9th-magnitude stars, with the third of 7th magnitude. Larger-telescope owners may wish to try Burnham 755, another triple with components of 6th and 7th magnitude only 1.3 arcseconds apart (1959 measurement). The third component is of 11th magnitude and separated from the others by 21.4 arcseconds.

Columba also contains five galaxies brighter than 13th magnitude. NGC 1792 is a fairly bright, 10th-magnitude galaxy, elliptical in shape and 3 by 1 arcminutes in size. NGC 1800 is smaller and fainter at magnitude 12.9. NGC 1808 is cigar-shaped, measuring more than 7 by 4 arcminutes with a brighter nucleus and an overall magnitude of 11.4. NGC 2090 is a 12th-magnitude galaxy, covering some 4.5 by 2.3 arcminutes and classified as type Sc. NGC 2188 is an almost edge-on 12th-magnitude galaxy, some 3.0 by 0.6 arcminutes in size. NGC 1851 is a large (11-arcminute) globular cluster, easily resolved with a 10-inch (25-cm) aperture 'scope. Its integrated magnitude is 7.3 and it is some 45,000 light years away from us.

TELESCOPIC OBJECTS IN CAELUM
Multiple Stars

Name	RA	Dec.	Separation (arcseconds)	Mags.		Year
h 3650	04h 26.6m	−40° 32′	3.0	7.1	8.3	1937
α (Alpha)	04h 40.6m	−41° 52′	6.6	4.5	12.5	1933
γ (Gamma)	05h 04.4m	−35° 29′	2.9	4.6	8.1	1942

Deep Sky Objects

Name	RA	Dec.	Type	Size	Mag.
NGC 1679	04h 50.0m	−31° 59′	Gal. Sc.	1.2′ × 0.8′	13.5

TELESCOPIC OBJECTS IN COLUMBA
Multiple Stars

Name	RA	Dec.	Separation (arcseconds)	Mags.		Year
h 3728	05h 08.5m	−41° 14′	10	6.5	9.5	1951
h 3760	05h 25.9m	−35° 20′	AB 7.4	8.0	8.5	1935
			AC 2.6	8.0	10.0	
h 3857	06h 24.0m	−36° 42′	AB 12.9	5.7	10.8	1960
			AC 64.8	5.7	6.9	1960
Burnham 755	06h 35.4m	−36° 47′	AB 1.3	6.0	6.8	1959
			AC 21.4	6.0	11.5	1932

Deep Sky Objects

Name	RA	Dec.	Type	Size	Mag.
NGC 1792	05h 05.2m	−37° 59′	Gal. Sb	4.0′ × 2.1′	10.2
NGC 1800	05h 06.4m	−31° 57′	Gal. E6	1.6′ × 0.9′	12.6
NGC 1808	05h 07.7m	−37° 31′	Gal. SBa	7.2′ × 4.1′	9.9
NGC 1851	05h 14.1m	−40° 03′	Glob. Cl.	11′	7.3
NGC 2090	05h 47.0m	−34° 14′	Gal. Sc	4.5′ × 2.3′	11.8
NGC 2188	06h 10.1m	−34° 06′	Gal. SBm	3.7′ × 1.1′	11.8

CAMELOPARDALIS

Camelopardalis, the Giraffe, was introduced by the Polish astronomer Johannes Hevelius, in his star chart of 1690. It is frequently referred to as Camelopardus. The brightest stars within the constellation are only of 4th magnitude, so it is a very barren area of the sky. Though it covers 757 square degrees, there is no apparent pattern. However, the telescopic observer will find multiple stars, galaxies, an open cluster and two planetary nebulae within its boundaries.

TELESCOPIC OBJECTS IN CAMELOPARDALIS
Double and Multiple Stars

Name	RA	Dec.	Separation (arcseconds)	Mags.		Year
Σ 362	03h 16.3m	+60° 02'	AB 7.1	8.5	8.8	1955
			AC 26.1	8.5	10.5	1915
			AD 30.9	8.5	11.1	1915
			AE 35.3	8.5	9.9	1915
OΣ 67	03h 57.1m	+61° 07'	1.9	5.3	8.5	1959
Σ 485	04h 07.9m	+62° 20'	17.9	7.0	7.1	1967
11–12	05h 06.1m	+58° 58'	180.5	5.4	6.5	1924
Σ 634	05h 22.6m	+79° 14'	10.4	5.1	9.1	1943
Σ 780	05h 51.0m	+65° 45'	AB 3.8	6.9	8.1	1954
			AC 10.9	6.9	10.0	1954
			AD 18.0	6.9	13.4	1954
Σ 1127	07h 47.0m	+64° 03'	AB 5.3	7.0	8.8	1956
			AC 11.3	9.9		1956
Σ 1694	12h 49.2m	+83° 25'	21.6	5.3	5.8	1958

Deep Sky Objects

Name	RA	Dec.	Type	Size	Mag.
IC 342	03h 46.8m	+68° 06'	Gal. SBc	17.8' × 17.4'	9.1
NGC 1501	04h 07.0m	+60° 55'	Plan. Neb.	52"	12
NGC 2336	07h 27.1m	+80° 11'	Gal. Sb	6.9' × 4.0'	10.5
NGC 2403	07h 36.9m	+65° 36'	Gal. Sc	17.8' × 11.0'	8.4
NGC 2523	08h 05.0m	+73° 35'	Gal. SBb	3.0' × 2.0'	12.6pg
NGC 2655	08h 55.6m	+78° 13'	Gal. SBa	5.1' × 4.4'	10
NGC 2715	09h 08.1m	+78° 05'	Gal. Sc	5.0' × 1.9'	11.4
IC 3568	12h 32.9m	+82° 33'	Plan. Neb.	>6"	11.6

Camelopardalis is a constellation formed by many faint stars which wind around the north celestial pole. It is circumpolar for northern observers, and lies in the area between Cassiopeia and Ursa Major. It can therefore be thought of as a winter constellation north of Auriga.

Multiple Stars

Only a few of the hundreds of multiple stars in Camelopardalis can be covered here. Σ 362 is a multiple, with components of 8th, 9th and 10th magnitudes separated by 7, 26, 30 and 35 arcseconds respectively. OΣ 67 has two stars of 5th and 8th magnitude some 1.9 arcseconds apart. Σ 485 is a multiple star in the cluster NGC 1502, of which the primary is the variable star SZ Camelopardalis. 11 and 12 Camelopardalis are a wide optical double, with 5th- and 6th-magnitude components easily separated in 7 × 50 binoculars. Σ 634 is an optical pair of 5th and 9th magnitudes, their separation decreasing greatly from 34 arcseconds in 1833 to 10 arcseconds in 1943. (What do you estimate their separation is now?)

Two other triples in Camelopardalis are Σ 780 and Σ 1127. Σ 1694 is an easily observed wide pair for any telescope, with two 5th-magnitude stars separated by 21.6 arcseconds.

Deep Sky Objects

The planetary nebulae in Camelopardalis are NGC 1501, a fairly large (1-arcminute-diameter), 12th-magnitude disk with a 14.3-magnitude central star. No detail is seen in the disk with amateur-sized telescopes. IC 3568 is smaller and brighter, at magnitude 11.6 and a diameter of 6 arcseconds. It appears as a featureless puff of gas with a 12th-magnitude central star.

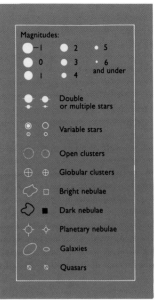

Well away from the galactic plane, there are many extragalactic objects in Camelopardalis, including one of the best galaxies for common telescopes (12-inch (30-cm) aperture and smaller), NGC 2403. This large Sc galaxy is a close 8 million light years away from us, about the same as M81 and M82. In photographs, it resembles M33, the large face-on spiral in Triangulum. In the telescope, aside from several foreground stars, one can suspect (and really see in 16-inch (40-cm) aperture instruments and up) the spiral arms. There are two prominent HII nebulous regions on opposite sides of the nucleus.

IC 342 is a very large nearby face-on spiral with low surface brightness. This may be the nearest spiral after M31 and M33, and it resembles M101 in photographs. It is best seen in astronomical binoculars (70 mm objectives or bigger) as a large faint glow about half the size of the Moon. Other noteworthy galaxies include NGC 2336, a 10.5 magnitude Sb spiral seen almost face-on, 6.9 × 4 arcminutes in size. NGC 2523 is easily seen in small telescopes. NGC 2655 is another relatively nearby spiral galaxy shining at magnitude 10 with high surface brightness some 4 arcminutes in diameter. NGC 2715 is an example of a spiral galaxy seen edge-on. It extends 4.5 by 1.2 arcminutes and is of about 12th magnitude. In small telescopes it is a featureless cigar-shaped glow.

Hevelius

Johannes Hevel was a prosperous brewer in the busy Hanseatic port of Danzig (now Gdansk), in the mid-1600s. His hobby became astronomy, and he built an observatory at his house. His first project was a lunar atlas, which contained the best maps up to that time (remember, the telescope had only been invented about 40 years previously). Many of the 250 names shown on the maps are still used today. This *Selenographia* appeared in 1647. At this time, telescope lenses were still single-element, non-achromatic, and small. They suffered from serious chromatic aberration, degrading the detail that could be seen. Hevel decided to make longer and longer telescopes, which put the offending colors so out of focus that they were no longer so offensive. His telescopes became progressively longer until the summit of his creations, a 150-foot (45-m) focus one, was hung from a 90-foot (27.5-m) mast! Naturally this was not particularly practical, as even the slightest breeze made it unusable. The mounting burned during the great Danzig fire of 1679, and Hevelius never again was a productive observer.

Cancer

The Beehive Cluster, M44 (NGC 2632), is an open star cluster located some 520 light years away. Also known as Praesepe, the Manger, it consists of some 300 stars. It is one of the nearest clusters of its type and is visible to the naked eye as a fuzzy spot. It is located 13 degrees southeast of the star Pollux in Gemini. This photograph was taken by the author with a 500mm mirror telephoto lens. The exposure was 10 minutes at f/5 on Fujichrome 100 film that was push processed.

Cancer is a small but important zodiacal constellation lying east of Gemini and west of Leo. It was the fourth constellation of the ancient zodiac, east of Aries, Taurus and Gemini, but is now the fifth since the first point of Aries has moved west into Pisces. Considering the crab's colorful mythological history, it is a particularly undistinguished memorial. But it is redeemed for the amateur astronomer because it contains an open or galactic cluster named Praesepe, or the Beehive. Cancer itself is highest in the night skies during springtime, when it culminates at 10 pm on March 1. Cancer's five brightest stars lie in a lambda (λ) form, and can be found by looking east of a line connecting Castor and Pollux in Gemini. Continuing the line to the southeast will reveal the fuzzy patch marking the Beehive. It was recorded by Hipparchus in ancient Greece, and Messier listed it as the 44th entrant in his catalogue. Praesepe lies in the middle of the constellation's lambda shape, between Gamma (γ) and Delta (δ). The constellation also contains many double and multiple stars, the famous Zeta (ζ) being the most interesting.

The Beehive

Though Praesepe is usually referred to as the Beehive, it also carries the name of the Crib associated with the Manger in Christian teachings. Certainly, M44 (NGC 2632) contains many charming doubles and triangles of stars, best seen in big binoculars or a low-power, rich-field telescope. It was first resolved into individual stars by Galileo, and, as its diameter is over a degree, it contains many hundreds of stars. According to Burnham's *Celestial Handbook* – the "bible" for dedicated double-star observers – it contains over 300 members down to 17th magnitude. The brightest member of the cluster is an A0 spectral type star,

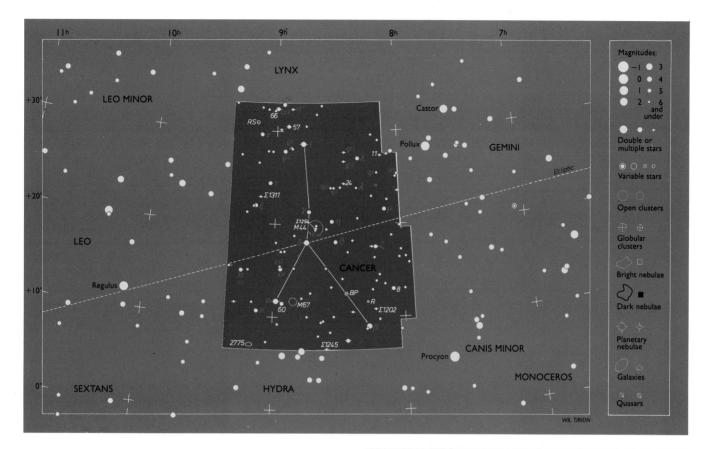

WIL TIRION

richer than our Sun in metals. Astrophysicists estimate that Praesepe is about 650 million years old, and 520 light years away in space.

Cancer also possesses another galactic cluster, M67 (NGC 2682), which has a total magnitude of 6.9, and is just beyond naked-eye visibility. To be resolved it requires binoculars, but to appreciate its magnificence, a 6- or 8-inch (15- or 20-cm) aperture telescope is needed. It is elongated in an east–west direction and there is a prominent dark space in the middle near the eastern end. This cluster is known as one of the oldest open clusters, with an age in excess of 10 billion years (10 thousand million). Its stars are evolved Main Sequence types, some of which have passed the red giant stage. The constellation's galaxies are mainly faint, but NGC 2775 is a high-surface-brightness object. With a telescope of 8-inch (20-cm) aperture, it appears as a round, 10th-magnitude glow, brighter in the middle.

Multiple Stars

Zeta Cancri, or Tegmene, is a multiple double: the main components are of magnitude 5.6 and 6.0, each being a very close double itself. Iota (ι) is a beautifully coloured double, consisting of stars of magnitude 4.2 and 6.6 separated by an easily resolvable distance of 30.5 arcseconds. It resembles Albireo in Cygnus, for the double's components are gold and pale blue in colour (spectral types G8 and A3).

Cancer also contains a number of interesting variables. R Cancri is a Mira-type variable which changes from magnitude 6.2 to 11.8 in a period of 362 days. RS Cancri is a semi-regular variable, whose magnitude ranges from 5.3 to 6.4 with a period of 120 days.

TELESCOPIC OBJECTS IN CANCER

Double and Multiple Stars

Name	RA	Dec.	Separation (arcseconds)	Mags.		Year
11	08h 08.8m	+27° 29'	3.2	6.9	10.2	1934
ζ (Zeta)	08h 12.2m	+17° 39'	AB ~1	5.6	6.0	1960
			AC 5.7	5.6	6.2	1969
24	08h 26.7m	+24° 32'	5.8	7.0	7.8	1957
Φ_2 (Phi 2)	08h 26.8m	+26° 56'	5.1	6.3	6.3	1958
Σ 1254	08h 40.4m	+19° 40'	AB 20.5	6.4	8.9	1956
			AC 63.2	6.4	8.6	1956
			AD 82.6	6.4	8.9	1956
ι (Iota)	08h 46.7m	+28° 46'	30.5	4.2	6.6	1968
57	08h 54.2m	+30° 35'	AB 1.4	6.0	6.5	1960
			AC 55.6	6.0	9.1	1953
64 (σ_3)	08h 59.5m	+32° 25'	89.6	5.6	9.4	1914
66	09h 01.4m	+32° 15'	4.6	5.9	8.0	1955
			AC 187.4	5.9	10.8	1908
Σ 1311	09h 07.4m	+22° 59'	AB 7.5	6.9	7.3	1956
			AC 27.8	6.9	12.6	1906

Deep Sky Objects

Name	RA	Dec.	Type	Size	Mag.
M44 (NGC 2632)	08h 40.1m	+19° 40'	Gal. Clus.	95'	3.1
M67 (NGC 2682)	08h 51.0m	+11° 49'	Gal. Cl.	30'	6.9
NGC 2775	09h 10.3m	+07° 02'	Gal. Sa	4.5' × 3.5'	10.33pg

Canes Venatici

Canes Venatici, the Hunting Dogs, was a grouping suggested by the Polish astronomer Johannes Hevelius in his star map of 1690. The two hunting dogs (identified as Asterion and Chara) are usually depicted as greyhounds, held on a leash by Boötes, the Herdsman. Presumably he is protecting his flocks from the marauding bears, Ursa Major and Minor: after all, the dogs appear to "chase" them round the celestial north pole!

Whirlpool Galaxy M51 is one of the best known spiral galaxies. It is really two connected galaxies, NGC 5195 (top) and NGC 5194, the spiral below. M51 is located 20 million light years away and is distinguished by its bright nucleus and spiral arms dominated by hot, young, blue stars. The photograph was taken by the 40-inch (1-m) telescope of the US Naval Observatory.

Canes Venatici is a northern constellation, at its most prominent in the spring skies. It is a medium-sized grouping located between Boötes, Ursa major and Leo. It reaches culmination at 10 pm on May 1.

The 23 stars that form the flattened isosceles triangle of Canes Venatici were once part of nearby Ursa Major: 20 of its stars are fainter than the 4th magnitude, so are quite inconspicuous. A "triangle" points southwards, with Alpha (α) its apex. Alpha, named Cor Caroli (the heart of Charles) by Edmond Halley in honor of Charles I of England, is the brightest of the grouping's stars, just over 3rd magnitude (2.9) and one of the finest telescopic doubles. Another telescopic highlight is the large globular cluster, M3 (NGC 5272). Located on the border with Boötes, it can be found by pointing the telescope to a position almost halfway between Arcturus and Cor Caroli, but a little more towards the former. It should show in the finder 'scope as a fuzzy 6th-magnitude "star". M3 begins to resolve in a 6-inch (15-cm) telescope: in a telescope of twice that aperture, it will appear as a ball of glittering points.

Galaxies

It is in extra-galactic systems that Canes Venatici is particularly well endowed. Scores of examples are easily visible with most amateur telescopes, and all are at similar distances away, approximately 20 to 35 million light years. This is close enough for the brightest stars, nebulae and dust clouds within them to allow close scrutiny by astronomers. 20 of the best telescopic objects are listed below, out of perhaps 100 easily found in 8-inch (20-cm) or larger aperture instruments.

M51 is really two objects: a fine face-on spiral (NGC 5194)

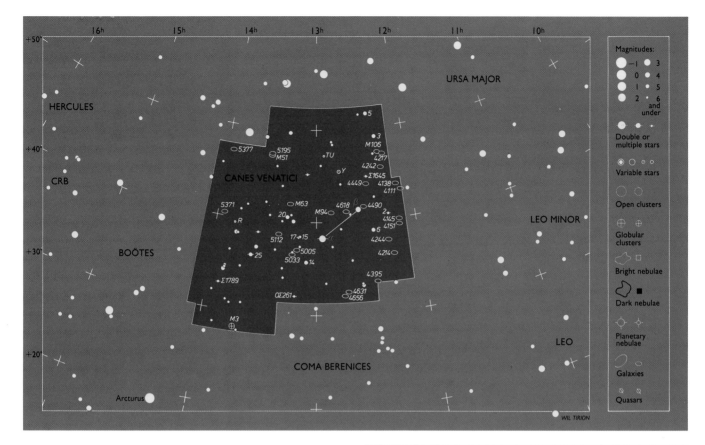

which is visually connected to the irregular NGC 5195. In small telescopes or larger binoculars, M51 looks like two fuzzy spots next to each other. In a 6-inch (15-cm) instrument, they appear different, with the spiral a softly defined disk, and the other seen as a bright spot with a brighter nucleus. In a A 10- or 12-inch (25- or 30-cm) or larger aperture instrument with medium-power eyepieces we begin to see signs of the spiral arms looking just like a revolving firework, with several small stars seen against the arms. The "bridge" that connects NGC 5194 and 5195 is a faint one, and its visibility is a good indication of good atmospheric conditions and good telescope optics.

M63 (NGC 5055) is another island universe in Canes Venatici. It is a large, bright oval surrounding a strong nucleus. The many spiral arms are only perceived as a soft glow around the nucleus, even in a 12-inch (30-cm) 'scope. In an instrument with a 16-inch (40-cm) aperture, one begins to discern the "breakup" into condensations that are apparent in photographs.

M94 (NGC 4736) is another fine spiral seen almost face-on. It has tightly wound, fairly smooth arms with only a few condensations. The nucleus is bright and a "sense" of the arms is present in 12-inch (25-cm) or larger apertures. NGC 4258 is also known as M106 and is a large, bright galaxy. It can be found in a finder or binoculars by sweeping about halfway from Beta (β) Canes Venatici to Gamma (γ) Ursa Majoris (in the "bowl" of the Great Dipper, equivalent to the "share" of the Plough). It has a fairly bright spiral arm, which can be seen extending from the body of the galaxy in a 10-inch (25-cm) aperture instrument or larger with good atmospheric conditions. Another interesting galaxy is NGC 4631, which we see as an elongated (15 × 3 arcminute) glow of 9th magnitude.

TELESCOPIC OBJECTS IN CANES VENATICI

Multiple Stars

Name	RA	Dec.	Separation (arcseconds)	Mags.	Year
2	12h 16.1m	+40° 40'	11.4	5.8 8.1	1958
Σ 1645	12h 28.1m	+44° 48'	9.9	7.4 8.0	1976
α (Alpha)	12h 56.2m	+38° 19'	19.4	2.9 5.5	1970
15 + 17	13h 10.1m	+38° 30'	284	6 6.2	1922
17	13h 10.1m	+38° 30'	1.2	6.2 11.2	1958
OΣ 261	13h 12.0m	+32° 05'	2.2	7.2 7.7	1959
25	13h 37.5m	+36° 18'	1.8	5.0 6.9	1959
Σ 1789	13h 54.1m	+32° 50'	6.5	8 8	1963

Deep Sky Objects

Name	RA	Dec.	Type	Size	Mag.
NGC 4111	12h 07.1m	+43° 04'	Gal. SO	4.8' × 1.1'	10.8
NGC 4151	12h 10.5m	+39° 24'	Gal. SB–p	5.9' × 4.4'	10.3
NGC 4214	12h 15.6m	+36° 20'	Gal. Irr.	7.9' × 6.3'	9.7
NGC 4217	12h 15.8m	+47° 06'	Gal. Sb	5.5' × 1.8'	11.9
NGC 4244	12h 17.5m	+37° 49'	Gal. Sb	16.2' × 2.5'	10.1
M106 (NGC 4258)	12h 19.0m	+47° 18'	Gal. Sb	18.2' × 7.9'	8.3
NGC 4395	12h 25.8m	+33° 32'	Gal. S	12.9' × 11.0'	11.0
NGC 4449	12h 28.2m	+44° 05'	Gal. Irr.	5.1' × 3.7'	9.4
NGC 4490	12h 30.7m	+41° 38'	Gal. Sc	5.9' × 3.1'	9.8
NGC 4618	12h 41.5m	+41° 09'	Gal. Sc	4.4' × 3.8'	10.8
NGC 4631	12h 42.1m	+32° 32'	Gal. Sc	15.1' × 3.3'	9.3
NGC 4656	12h 44.0m	+32° 10'	Gal. Irr.	13.8' × 3.3'	10.4
M94 (NGC 4736)	12h 50.9m	+41° 07'	Gal. Sb-p	11.0' × 9.1'	8.17
NGC 5005	13h 10.9m	+37° 03'	Gal. Sb	5.4' × 2.7'	9.8
NGC 5033	13h 13.5m	+36° 36'	Gal. Sb	10.5' × 5.6'	10
M63 (NGC 5055)	13h 15.8m	+42° 02'	Gal. Sb	12.3' × 7.6'	8.6
M51 (NGC 5194)	13h 29.9m	+47° 12'	Gal. Sc	11.0' × 7.8'	8.4
M51 (NGC 5195)	13h 30.0m	+47° 16'	Gal. Irr.	2.0' × 1.5'	9.6
M3 (NGC 5272)	13h 42.2m	+28° 23'	Glob. Cl.	16.2'	6.3
NGC 5371	13h 55.7m	+40° 28'	Gal. Sb+	4.4' × 3.6'	10.75

Canis major/Lepus

Canis Major, the Great Dog, *represents one of Orion's hunting dogs, and is close to the mighty hunter in the skies. Canis Major contains Sirius, the Dog Star, the brightest star in the heavens. In ancient mythology, it is more important than the constellation, as it was used as a time marker which prompted harvests and celebrations in certain cultures. Its first appearance at dawn led the ancient Egyptians to celebrate a new year and the coming of the annual flooding of the Nile.*

Lepus, *the Hare, is also an ancient constellation and its location near to Orion is highly appropriate, since in in mythology Orion was fond of hunting hares.*

Sirius, the Dog Star, and the pink nebulosity cataloged as NGC 2327 are seen in this tricolor photograph by Californian amateur Reverend Ronald Royer. Sirius, in the bottom right corner, is the brightest star in the sky. It is also one of the closest stars, at a distance of 8.6 light years. NGC 2327 (upper right) is a large, diffuse nebula which reaches across the border of Canis Major into Monoceros.

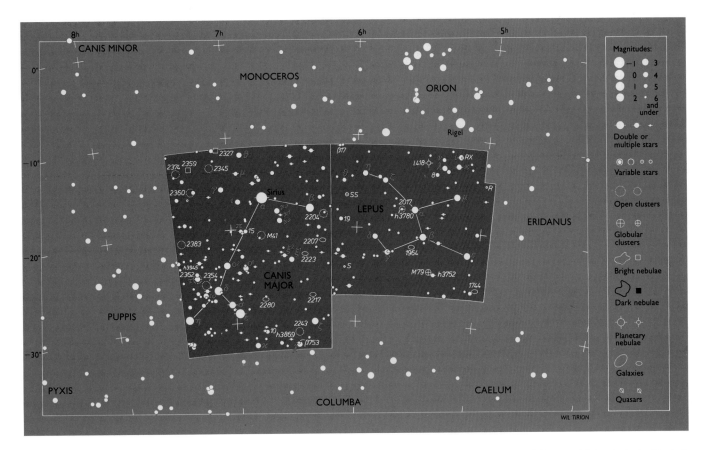

Canis Major is Orion's companion in the winter heavens for northern-hemisphere observers. Lepus the Hare is included here for convenience. Both are south of the celestial equator and therefore well seen by observers in southern latitudes. Lepus reaches the meridian first, culminating at 10 pm about January 15 (the same as Orion). It is recognized by a prominent parallelogram of six stars forming two lines, the bottom one being a little curved. Alpha (α) and Beta (β) are approximately the same 3rd-magnitude brightness. Canis Major can hardly be missed, since it contains the brightest fixed star after the Sun, Sirius. The brilliant blue–white star (−1.5 magnitude) is not its only attraction, however, since the Milky Way passes through the southeastern part of the constellation, providing clusters and some faint nebulae. The Great Dog culminates at 10 pm on about February 7.

Dog Star Doubles

Canis Major has many doubles of note, the first being Sirius itself. The famous white dwarf star, Sirius B, was discovered by Alvan G. Clark while testing an 18.5-inch (46-cm) lens in 1862. Its presence had been predicted by Bessel about 1835 but nobody saw it before Clark. The enormous density of the dwarf has been remarked upon, but superdense matter is now an accepted part of the "astrophysical zoo" of quasars, black holes and other peculiar states of matter. The companion (magnitude 8.5) is difficult to see, mainly because of its proximity to the brilliant primary. It has a period of 50 years, and the distance varies from 3.7 to 11.4 arcseconds. It was farthest in 1974 and will be closest in about 1996. The most important factors in seeing Sirius B are: to observe when the stars are on the meridian, and when the atmospheric steadiness, or seeing, is

excellent with fine, clean optics. Other multiples include Mu (μ), Epsilon (ε) and h3945.

Deep Sky Objects

Canis Major contains many deep sky objects. Its galactic clusters are superb examples, and we seem to see them with less interstellar obscuration than those clusters seen in northern summertime. M41 (NGC 2287) is visible to the naked eye, located where you would find the Dog's heart. It contains several fairly bright stars and multiples. The cluster is almost half a degree in diameter, so is best seen with low powers. NGC 2362 is a beautiful cluster of several dozen stars gathered around 4th-magnitude Tau (τ), which is a wonderful triple star. Although rather low for some northern observers, this cluster is a neglected showpiece of the skies.

NGC 2327 is a large nebula at the south end of a great complex which stretches north across the border with Monoceros. This is a conspicuous object in a rich-field telescope, especially with a nebular filter added. It is an interesting photographic subject, and a detached portion resembles an eye with a star for the pupil. 78 Canis Majoris is reported by Hartung to be a reddish star imbedded in a small nebula which is thought to be of the reflection type. It is not plotted in all atlases, but is depicted just southeast of NGC 2362, in the renowned *Atlas of the Heavens*, from the Czechoslovakian Observatory at Skalnate Pleso.

Lepus

Lepus is directly under Orion's feet and contains several doubles, some faint galaxies, a planetary nebula (IC 418), and a good globular cluster, M79. Starting with the doubles, Kappa (κ) is a 4.5 and 7.4 magnitude pair separated by 2.6 arcseconds, both hot white stars. h3752 is a triple – with a blue-colored component that contrasts its warmer-colored companions. h3780 is a small cluster of at least six stars, named NGC 2017. They are of various colors, making this an interesting object. Gamma (γ) is a relatively nearby (26 light years) binocular double star with 3rd- and 6th-magnitude components, gold and white in color.

R Leporis is a variable star and one of the reddest, and is easily seen in a telescope. It is a long-period variable like Mira, and changes from magnitudes 5.5 to 11.7 and back in 432 days. J. R. Hind of London discovered it in 1845 and ever since it has been called "Hind's Crimson Star". The surface temperature is about 2,600K and the spectrum shows strong carbon absorptions. R is found by extending a line from Alpha (α) through Mu (μ) and continuing an equal distance to R. Look carefully, as it may be near minimum! The star reaches a maximum brightness around 17 September 1990.

M79 was actually discovered by Messier's colleague Méchain in 1780, and is a globular cluster about 50,000 light years distant. In small telescopes it remains unresolved, but shows a few stars around the edges in an 8-inch (20-cm) aperture. A 12-inch or (30-cm) or larger instrument will show the object richly resolved into a tight ball of faint stars. IC 418 is a small but bright planetary nebula, appearing as a blue disk about 12 arcseconds in diameter, with an 11th-magnitude central star.

TELESCOPIC OBJECTS IN CANIS MAJOR
Multiple Stars

Name	RA	Dec.	Separation (arcseconds)	Mags.		Year
Burnham 753	06h 28.7m	−32° 22'	1.3	5.9	7.9	1942
h3869	06h 32.6m	−32° 02'	24.9	5.7	7.7	1930
ν₁ (Nu 1)	06h 36.4m	−18° 40'	17.5	5.8	8.5	1926
Sirius	06h 45.1m	−16° 43'	var	−1.5	8.5	1960
μ (Mu)	06h 56.1m	−14° 03'	AB 3.0	5.3	8.6	1944
			AC 88.4	5.3	10.5	1912
			AD 101.3	5.3	10.7	1912
ε (Epsilon)	06h 58.6m	−28° 58'	7.5	1.5	7.4	1951
h3945	07h 16.6m	−23° 19'	26.6	4.8	6.8	1959

Deep Sky Objects

Name	RA	Dec.	Type	Size	Mags.
NGC 2217	06h 21.7m	−27° 14'	Gal. SBa	4.8' × 4.4'	10.4
NGC 2243	06h 29.8m	−31° 17'	Open Cl.	5'	9.4
M41 (NGC 2287)	06h 46.0m	−20° 44'	Open Cl.	38'	4.5
NGC 2327	07h 04.3m	−11° 18'	Diff. Neb.	20'	11?
NGC 2359	07h 18.6m	−13° 12'	Diff. Neb.	8' × 6'	faint
NGC 2360	07h 17.8m	−15° 37'	Open Cl.	13'	7.2
NGC 2362	07h 18.8m	−24° 57'	Open Cl.	8'	4.1

TELESCOPIC OBJECTS IN LEPUS
Multiple Stars

Name	RA	Dec.	Separation (arcseconds)	Mags.		Year
κ (Kappa)	05h 13.2m	−12° 56'	2.6	4.5	7.4	1959
h3752	05h 21.8m	−24° 46'	AB 3.2	5.4	6.6	1953
			AC 61.2	5.4	9.1	1898
h3780	05h 39.3m	−17° 51'	AB 0.8	6.4	7.9	1947
h3780c	05h 39.3m	−17° 51'	AC 89.2	6.4	8.5	1914
(in cluster NGC 2017)			AE 76.1	6.4	8.4	1915
			AF 128.8	6.4	8.1	1915
			CD 1.5	8.5	9.2	1946
γ (Gamma)	05h 44.5m	−22° 27'	AB 96.3	3.7	6.3	1957
			BC 45.0	6.3	10.9	1832
Burnham 17	06h 08.4m	−11° 09'	AB 3.1	6.8	10.8	1935
			AC 9.0	6.8	11.8	1933

Variable Star

Name	RA	Dec.	Type	Mag. Range	Period
R	04h 59.6m	−14° 48'	Mira LP	5.5–11.7	432.13 days

Deep Sky Objects

Name	RA	Dec.	Type	Size	Mag.
NGC 1744	05h 00m	−26° 01'	Gal. SBc	6.8' × 4.1'	11
M79 (NGC 1904)	05h 24.5m	−24° 33'	Glob. Clus.	8.7'	9.9
IC 418	05h 27.5m	−12° 42'	Plan. Neb.	12"	11pg

M41 is a beautiful open star cluster located some 1600 light years from Earth. Visible to the naked eye, it contains about 100 stars. This photograph, which clearly shows the different colors of the stars, was taken by the author with a 10-inch (26-cm), f/10 Schmidt–Cassegrain telescope from Silverado, California. The 10-minute exposure on Fuji RD400 film was pushed one stop in processing.

CANIS MINOR/MONOCEROS

Canis Minor, the Little Dog, was the second of Orion's hunting dogs, and is always associated with him and the larger dog in mythology. It was accorded only two stars by Ptolemy, Procyon (**α**) and Beta (**β**). Procyon literally means "before the dog", referring to its rising slightly before Sirius. **Monoceros,** the Unicorn, has no mythological attachment to the legendary unicorn. It was formed at an unknown time in the past, and appears on a map by Bartschius in 1624 and on a Persian globe considerably earlier.

Hubble's Variable Nebula *(NGC 2261) is a triangular cloud of dust lit by the star at its apex, R Monocerotis. In the early years of this century, the great American astonomer Edwin Hubble discovered that both star and nebula are variable, but that they do not vary together. The nebula was the first object to be photographed with the 200-inch (5-m) Hale Telescope when it opened on Mount Palomar in 1948. This picture was recorded at optical wavelengths by a CCD camera mounted on a telescope at the Whipple Observatory, Arizona.*

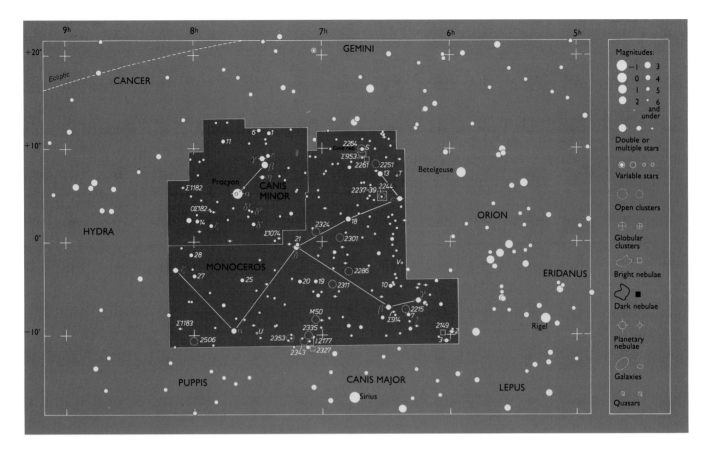

Canis Minor is a tiny constellation which has one bright star, Procyon. It is, like Sirius, a nearby star, only 11 light years away. Canis Minor is highest at 10 pm on February 15. Monoceros, the Unicorn, is included with Canis Minor for convenience. It is a large winter constellation, located largely within the triangle formed by Betelgeuse in Orion, Sirius to the south, and Procyon to the east.

Canis Minor

Canis Minor has a few doubles, but no deep sky objects prominent in amateur-sized telescopes. Procyon is a binary, which like Sirius has a white dwarf neutron star companion. However, the small star is fainter (11th magnitude) and closer (mean separation 5 arcseconds) than Sirius B, and was only found by Schaeberle with the Lick 36-inch (90-cm) refractor in 1896.

Monoceros

The winter portion of the Milky Way runs diagonally down through Monoceros. We are looking outwards along the Orion Arm of our galaxy, away from the center in Sagittarius. Monoceros has a few scattered stars, with no discernible pattern, and can be recognized more by the large "empty" area within the above-mentioned triangle.

Monoceros has many clusters, and several nebulae as well as many multiple stars, including the remarkable triple Beta (β). Beta comprises a close double, with components of magnitude 4.7 and 5.2, separated by 2.8 arcseconds, and another 5th-magnitude star some 7.3 arcseconds away. S Monocerotis is a slightly variable blue supergiant with an 8.5 magnitude companion some 3.0 arcseconds distant. S, or 15 Mon, is at the north

end of the "Christmas Tree" cluster, a group of largely B stars (young) imbedded in dense nebulosity which glows from their presence. Just to the south of the second brightest star is the Cone Nebula, a wonderful mass of dark material which juts upward toward the star. At a distance of 2,600 light years, the Cone is at least 6 light years long. This area is still the site of star formation within the cocoon of dust and gas surrounding several protostars. All of this object is invisible in small telescopes except as a slight haze around the stars, although some people have seen the Cone with a 16-inch (40-cm) f/5.5 and a nebular filter.

The Rosette Nebula

Another large area of star formation, clustering, and gas is the formation NGC 2244 and its surrounding gas cloud called the Rosette Nebula. In long exposure photographs this great cloud and its stars appear to be nestled in a "hollowed-out" part of the surrounding interstellar glow. It is as if the glowing cloud condensed out of the more evenly distributed material of the area, as it may well have done. The Rosette can be seen as a soft glow surrounding the distinctive parallelogram of the star cluster in 20 × 80 binoculars or a rich-field telescope. A nebular or light pollution rejection filter will as usual make it easier to see.

This is one of many sites in the Milky Way where "Bok globules" are found. These are small, dark, and usually spherical condensations of matter. It would appear that each, if massive enough, can become a star through gravitational contraction until the center reaches the temperature and pressure needed to trigger the hydrogen–helium–carbon conversion cycle in the core of the new star.

South of M50 (see below) is an interesting large nebulous

region, suited to photographic rather than visual observation, although the brighter parts can be seen in an 8-inch (20-cm) telescope. This is IC 2177 and its associated clusters NGC 2335, 2343, and Cr465 and 466. There are two main parts to the nebula, a 2°-long north–south curtain of nebulosity which crosses the border into Canis Major, and the smaller eye-like vdB 93, a small nebula surrounding a star. There is a horizontal dust lane through this nebula which makes the whole thing look much like an eye with the pupil the star. This entire nebula has been given the appellation the Seagull Nebula because of the curved wings of nebulosity. Hans Vehrenberg, the German astrophotographer, calls it "the Eagle" in his *Atlas of Deep Sky Splendors*, 3rd edition. At least a 300-mm lens is needed to see much detail, although it appears on a 50-mm photo by the author as a small streak with a couple of spots of nebulosity. In color photographs this nebula appears the typical hydrogen II red of the 6563-Angstrom hydrogen alpha line.

Monoceros has another interesting nebula, known as Hubble's Variable Nebula, or NGC 2261. This small but fairly bright object surrounds the variable star R Monocerotis. It appears like a small comet with the star as the nucleus. The star and nebula vary in brightness from about 10th to 13th magnitude in an irregular cycle. This is apparently a new star encased in a nebulous cocoon of dust and gas, since it is a brighter object at infrared wavelengths than in the visible. M50 (NGC 2323) is a large star cluster in southern Monoceros, with an integrated magnitude of 6.3. It consists of about fifty stars in an area about 10 arcminutes in diameter. M50 is a good cluster for small instruments, and is located halfway between Sirius and Procyon in the night skies.

TELESCOPIC OBJECTS IN CANIS MINOR
Multiple Stars

Name	RA	Dec.	Separation (arcseconds)		Mags.		Year
Σ 1074	07h 20.5m	+0° 24′	AB	0.6	7.4	7.8	1958
			AC	12.8	7.4	12.5	1924
			AD	15.3	7.4	12.0	1922
			AE	53.7	7.4	9.9	1919
Procyon	07h 39.3m	+5° 14′	AC	119.0	0.4	11.6	1958
OΣ 182	07h 52.7m	+3° 23′		1.0	7.5	8.0	1958
Σ 1182	08h 05.4m	+5° 50′		4.5	8.0	10.0	1944

TELESCOPIC OBJECTS IN MONOCEROS
Double and Multiple Stars

Name	RA	Dec.	Separation (arcseconds)		Mags.		Year
8	06h 23.8m	+4° 36′	AB	13.4	4.5	6.5	1934
			AC	93.7	4.5	12.7	1911
Σ 914	06h 26.7m	−7° 31′		21.1	6.4	8.7	1938
β (Beta)	06h 28.8m	−7° 02′	AB	7.3	4.7	5.2	1955
			AC	10	4.7	6.1	1955
			AD	25.9	4.7	12.2	1932
			BC	2.8	5.2	~6	1973
S (in cluster NGC 2264)	06h 41.0m	+9° 54′	AB	3.0	4.7	8.5	1957
Σ 953	06h 41.2m	+8° 59′		7.1	7.2	7.7	1932
Σ 1183	08h 06.5m	−9° 15′	AB	30.9	6.0	8.7	1935
			BC	1.2	8.7	13.1	1936
			BD	14.0	8.7	14.9	1917
ζ (Zeta)	08h 08.6m	−2° 59′	AB	32	4.3	10.0	1936
			AC	66.5	4.3	7.8	1936

Deep Sky Objects

Name	RA	Dec.	Type	Size	Mag.
NGC 2237 NGC 2238 NGC 2239	06h 32.3m	+5° 03′	Diff. Neb.	80′ × 60′	~6
NGC 2244	06h 33.4m	+4° 03′	Open Cl.	24′	4.8
NGC 2261	06h 39.2m	+8° 44′	Refl. + Em. Neb.	1′ × 2′	10
NGC 2301	06h 51.8m	+0° 28′	Open Cl.	12′	6.0
M50 (NGC 2323)	07h 03.2m	−8° 20′	Open Cl.	16′	5.9
IC 2177	07h 05.1m	−10° 42′	Diff. Neb.	120′ × 40′	≈10
NGC 2506	08h 00.2m	−10° 37′	Open Cl.	7′	7.6

The Rosette Nebula is a shell of gas surrounding the NGC 2244 star cluster. The two brightest stars in the cluster heat and ionize the gas in the nebula, causing it to emit the distinctive red light of excited hydrogen. The stars in the cluster are believed to be very young, perhaps less than 500,000 years old. Both the nebula and star cluster are some 4,500 light years away. This color image was made from three black-and-white filtered plates at the 101-inch (2.5-m) Du Pont Telescope at Las Campanas, Chile.

Capricornus

Globular Cluster M30. M30 plays a lonely role as the only prominent deep-sky object in the constellation of Capricornus. As this photograph shows, it consists of a dense core of stars with a less dense periphery. The photograph was taken at the Anglo-Australian Observatory at Epping, New South Wales.

Capricornus is a medium-sized constellation which follows Sagittarius in the early autumn skies (for northern hemisphere observers). It reaches culmination about 10 pm on September 1. The constellation appears as an inverted triangle, but some amateurs have described it as a "Bikini Bottom". Though these descriptions are open to interpretation, Capricornus is easy to identify, located south of Aquarius and north of Piscis Austrinus. Capricornus contains five stars brighter than the 4th magnitude: the brightest is Alpha (α) Capricorni, a naked-eyed double. The others include: Delta (δ) with a visual magnitude of 2.87; Beta (β), magnitude 3.08; Gamma (γ), or Nashira, magnitude 3.68; and Zeta (ζ), magnitude 3.74.

Double Stars

Alpha Capricorni is a naked-eye double; it is one of the most complex systems visible in the night sky. The components are known as α_1 and α_2, some 376 arcseconds (over 6 arcminutes apart) and not physically associated. In other words, their double appearance is an optical illusion, as α_1 is 490 light years distant and α_2 is 36 light years distant. They are of magnitude 4.2 and 3.6 respectively, and both are themselves double. To complicate matters yet further, the fainter component of α_2 is itself double!

Beta (β), also called Dabih, is a wide double, but as both components share the same proper motion – that is, their observed motion through space relative to the celestial sphere is the same – they are probably connected by mutual gravitational attraction. Dabih's main components are of 3rd and 6th magnitude and separated by 205 arcseconds. Looking at Beta you'll see the bright star as white and the 6th-magnitude companion as bluish in comparison. This is also a complex

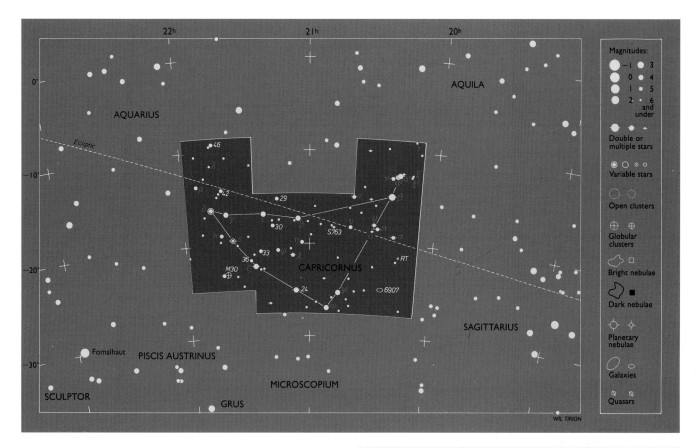

system, as the brighter component is a spectroscopic triple, and there is a faint double star between the two components.

Among the other doubles in Capricornus are Omicron (o), which consists of a fine white pair of magnitudes 6.1 and 6.6, separated by 22 arcseconds. Tau (τ) is a binary system with a period of 200 years, the components separated by 0.3 arcseconds and very similar in brightness (magnitudes 5.8 and 6.3). Pi (π) consists of magnitude 5.3 and 8.9 stars separated by 3.2 arcseconds.

Mention must also be made of the semi-regular variable RT Capricorni, which has a magnitude range from 6.5 to 8.1 with a period of about 395 days. There are two other variables in Capricornus: RR, in the range 7.8 to 15.5, and RS, 7.0 to 9.0.

Deep Sky Objects

This constellation is oddly bereft of much in the way of deep sky objects, with only a small galaxy and the medium-quality globular cluster M30 available to most amateur telescopes. NGC 6907 is a barred spiral which we see almost face-on, appearing as a round hazy spot in a 10-inch (25-cm) telescope, with a brighter nucleus. Messier discovered the globular cluster that he cataloged as number 30 in August 1764. His small Gregorian reflector with an equivalent modern aperture of about 2 inches (5-cm) did not resolve the "nebula" into stars. This was done first by Sir William Herschel's far superior telescopes 19 years later, when he remarked on the lines and streams of stars in the group. It is 4 arcminutes in diameter, extending to 9 arcminutes in long exposure photographs, and can be resolved at the edges with a modern 4-inch (10-cm) telescope. The cluster makes a long isoceles triangle to the southeast with 34 and 36 Capricorni.

TELESCOPIC OBJECTS IN CAPRICORNUS

Multiple Stars

Name	RA	Dec.	Separation (arcseconds)	Mags.		Year
α (α₁, α₂)			377.7	4.2	3.6	1924
α₁ (Alpha 1)	20h 17.6m	−12° 30′	AB 44.3	4.2	13.7	1960
			AC 45.4	4.2	9.2	1932
			DC 29.3	9.2	13.9	1905
α₂ (Alpha 2)	20h 18.1m	−12° 33′	AB 6.6	3.6	11.0	1959
			AD 154.6	3.6	9.3	1909
			BC 1.2	9.3	11.3	1959
β (Beta)	20h 21.0m	−14° 47′	AB 205.3	3.4	6.2	
			BC <1″	6.2	10.0	
π (Pi)	20h 27.3m	−18° 13′	3.2	5.3	8.9	1955
o (Omicron)	20h 29.9m	−18° 35′	21.9	6.1	6.6	1955
τ (Tau)	20h 39.3m	−14° 57′	0.4?	5.8	6.3	1959
S 763	20h 48.4m	−18° 12′	AB 15.8	6.7	8.6	1950
			CD 9.4	10.3	10.5	1903

Deep Sky Object

Name	RA	Dec.	Type	Size	Mag.
NGC 6907	20h 25.1m	−24° 49′	Gal. SBb	3.4′ × 3.0′	11.30v
M30 (NGC 7099)	21h 40.4m	−23° 11′	Glob. Cl.	11.0′	7.5

47

CARINA/VOLANS

Carina (the Keel) was part of the huge ancient constellation Argo Navis (the Ship Argo). It was delineated by Ptolemy of Alexandria around 200 AD and was then composed of 45 stars. The ship was later dismembered by Nicolas Louis de Lacaille into Carina, Vela (the Sails) and Puppis (the Poop deck). It would be natural for the Greeks to make this area a ship, since it rises only partially above the Mediterranean and crosses it from east to west as seen from the coast of Greece.

Volans, the Flying Fish, was composed by Bayer in 1603 to accompany the ship Argo.

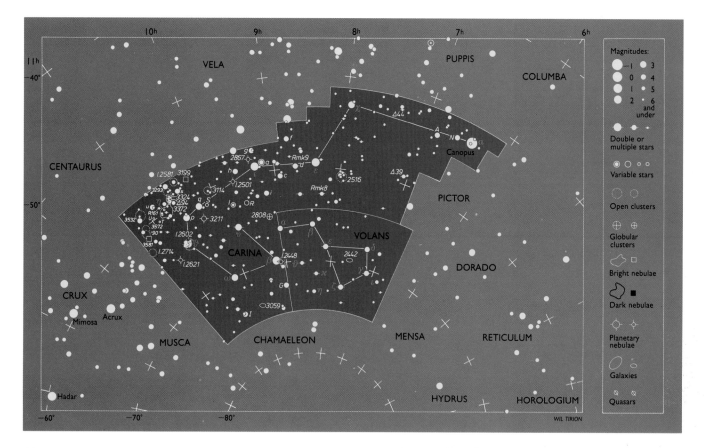

Carina is a large, important constellation which is visible to southern-hemisphere observers much of the year. It is about as close to the southern celestial pole as Cassiopeia is to the northern one, and therefore will be visible during some part of every night for observers from about −30° southwards. It is, however, at its highest at 10 pm on February 1. Carina's shape roughly parallels the rich southern Milky Way, and is loaded with good deep sky objects for common telescopes or binoculars. Volans is a small constellation between Carina and the south celestial pole.

The celesitial wonders of Carina would take many pages to describe completely. Here I will attempt to cover "the very best of the best". The rich Milky Way passing through the Keel contains many bright galactic clusters and a nebula rivalled only by the Great Nebula in Orion. Canopus, Alpha (α) Carinae, is the second-brightest fixed star (magnitude −0.72), and is visible from the latitudes of the southern parts of the United States, shining like a beacon near the horizon straight south of Sirius. It lies near the western end of the constellation, and leads the rest of the long constellation rising in late winter. The middle of the whole group is at its highest at 10 pm on March 10.

Canopus, or Alpha Carinae, is the bright star a little off center in this picture. The fuzzy patch in the bottom left corner is our neighboring galaxy, the Large Magellanic Cloud or LMC in Dorado. Taken on April 1, 1987, the photograph shows the most brilliant supernova in 400 years, SN 1987a, as the brighter of the two bright spots in the LMC (the other bright spot is the Tarantula Nebula). The picture is by Robert McNaught with a 55-mm lens on a 6 × 7-cm Pentax. The exposure was 63 minutes at f/4 using Ektachrome 400 film.

Canopus is an Egyptian-sounding name, but we get it from the ancient Greeks, including Eratosthenes, whose Κάνωπος transliterates directly into our name. It is a huge blue–white star of spectral class A9, lying at a distance of 74 light years with a luminosity of 1,200 Suns. Some of the best doubles and multiples are described in the table below.

Deep Sky Objects

The star clusters and nebulae of Carina are not to be missed. Even with the naked eye, the brightest clusters are impressive, as is the Eta Carinae region. With binoculars one can see the nebula surrounding Eta, and in "astronomical" glasses (70 mm or larger objectives) there are many fine objects to observe. NGC 2516 is a large cluster, best in binoculars or a low-power telescope because it's almost a degree in diameter. There is a red star in the center, along with several multiples using higher magnifications. NGC 2808 is a globular cluster so bright that it can be seen with the naked eye under good conditions. A 6-inch (15-cm) 'scope begins to resolve it, and it appears as a richly concentrated ball of stars in a 10-inch (25-cm) instrument. NGC 3114 is a first-class galactic cluster containing about 100 stars, again needing a large field of view. IC 2602 is another naked-eye cluster surrounding Theta Carinae, and somewhat resembling M7 in Scorpius in size and shape.

NGC 3199 was discovered by John Herschel during his stay near Cape Town and is a bright nebula situated in a field of scattered stars. There is dark material surrounding it, forming a "bay" on the northeast side. NGC 3324 can be described as a fairly bright cloud situated in a rich star field, and is at its brightest near an 8th-magnitude O-type star.

Eta Carinae

It is the Eta Carinae region which serves as the centerpoint of this magnificent constellation. Eta (ε) is a giant nebular-type variable star encased in a bright orange cloud. This star has a history of great variability, having reached magnitude −0.8 in 1843, but sinking to less than 6th by 1868. Its brightness is affected by material being expelled from the star and/or dust clouds condensing around the star. The nebula takes the form of three enormous fan-shaped areas with dark lanes between. In the telescope, the main area containing Eta itself is brightest, and the dark lanes set it off with very definitive borders. The distinctively shaped Keyhole Nebula (NGC 3372) is the most famous dark zone seen near Eta, and it is more prominent to the eye than in long-exposure photographs. The whole area is a delight to the visual observer, and each increase in telescopic aperture is rewarded by more fascinating detail. NGC 3532 is another of Carina's large galactic clusters. It, too, is visible to the unaided eye and presents a large, elongated group, with the 6th-magnitude orange star X Carinae at the east end. NGC 3581 is a prominent member of a small group of nebulae in the same area as NGC 3532 and several other galactic clusters (including NGC 3572). At least an 8-inch (20-cm) telescope is needed to appreciate the clumps of nebulosity in this area.

Carina also contains several planetary nebulae accessible to amateur instruments. IC 2448 is an 8-arcsecond diameter, 12th-magnitude object. NGC 2867 is at 10th magnitude and presents an 11-arcsecond round blue disk. NGC 3211 is a bit fainter at 12th magnitude with a 12-arcsecond diameter disk.

Volans

Volans is almost devoid of deep sky objects prominent in amateur telescopes. There are three bright doubles worth looking for (see table). There is also the galaxy NGC 2442, a face-on barred spiral with low surface brightness, whose arms can begin to be glimpsed in a 12-inch (30-cm) telescope.

TELESCOPIC OBJECTS IN CARINA
Multiple Stars

Name	RA	Dec.	Separation (arcseconds)	Mags.		Year
Δ 39	07h 03.3m	−59° 11′	1.7	6.0	7.1	1952
Δ 44	07h 20.4m	−52° 19′	9.5	6.0	6.6	1955
Rmk 8	08h 15.3m	−62° 55′	3.9	5.3	8.0	1943
Rmk 9	08h 45.1m	−58° 44′	AB 4.1	6.9	7.0	1951
			AC 50.9	6.9	11.0	1913
			AD 61.4	6.9	10.8	1913
υ (Upsilon)	09h 47.1m	−65° 04′	5.0	3.1	6.1	1943
Δ 94	10h 38.8m	−59° 11′	14.5	4.7	8.1	1932
R 161	10h 49.4m	−59° 19′	1.0	6.2	7.4	1960

Variable Star

Name	RA	Dec.	Type	Mag. Range	Period
η (Eta)	10h 45.1m	−59° 41′	Irr. S Dor.	−0.8–7.9	Irr.

Deep Sky Objects

Name	RA	Dec.	Type	Size	Mag.
NGC 2516	07h 58.3m	−60° 52′	Open Cl.	30′	3.8
NGC 2808	09h 12.0m	−64° 52′	Glob. Cl.	13.8′	6.3
NGC 3114	10h 02.7m	−60° 07′	Open Cl.	35′	4.2
NGC 3199	10h 17.1m	−57° 55′	Diff. Neb.	22′ × 22′	~8?
NGC 3211	10h 17.8m	−62° 40′	Plan. Neb.	12″	12pg
IC 2581	10h 27.4m	−57° 38′	Open Cl.	8′	4.3
NGC 3293	10h 35.8m	−58° 14′	Open Cl.	6′	4.7
NGC 3324	10h 37.7m	−58° 14′	Diff. Neb.	16′ × 14′	~11?
IC 2602	10h 43.2m	−64° 24′	Open Cl.	50′	1.9
NGC 3372 η (Eta) Car. Nebula	10h 43.8m	−59° 52′	Diff. Neb.	120′ × 120′	6
NGC 3532	11h 06.4m	−58° 40′	Open Cl.	55′	3.0
NGC 3581	11h 12.1m	−61° 18′	Diff. Neb.	?	12?

TELESCOPIC OBJECTS IN VOLANS
Double Stars

Name	RA	Dec.	Separation (arcseconds)	Mags.		Year
γ (Gamma)	07h 08.8m	−70° 30′	13.6	4.0	5.9	1941
ε (Epsilon)	08h 07.9m	−68° 37′	6.1	4.4	8.0	1922
θ (Theta)	08h 39.1m	−70° 23′	45.0	5.3	10.3	1917

Deep Sky Objects

Name	RA	Dec.	Type	Size	Mag.
NGC 2442	07h 36.4m	−69° 32′	Gal. SBb	6.0′ × 5.5′	11.22

The giant Eta Carinae Nebula (NGC 3372) is some 300 light years across, twenty times the size of the Orion Nebula. Although 9000 light years away, it stretches across 2° of sky (about 4 Moon breadths). It is lit by a considerable number of very heavy and very hot stars, some of which shine 5 million times as brightly and weigh over 100 times as much as our Sun. Two million years ago, the Carina Nebula was a huge, dense and dark molecular cloud. The dark dust lanes we see today are the remnants of that cloud. The large naked-eye clusters in the picture are NGC 3532 (nearest to the nebula) and IC 2602, a very bright group which includes Theta (θ) Carinae. The photograph was taken by Australian amateur Gordon Garradd.

CASSIOPEIA

The constellation of Cassiopeia is one of the most distinctive, and is one of the many ancient groupings to which a legend is attached. Cassiopeia was married to King Cepheus; their daughter was Andromeda. Cassiopeia's boasting about her own and her daughter's beauty so enraged Poseidon that he sent a sea monster to kill Andromeda, but she was saved by the hero Perseus, whom she later married. Appropriately enough, husband, wife, daughter and son-in-law are all located in roughly the same part of the sky. The Queen is usually represented in a throne or chair shaped by the six most prominent stars of the group.

NGC 281 is a large, fairly bright diffuse nebula. It resembles the famous North America Nebula in Cygnus minus the Florida peninsula. It glows red in color photographs because the hydrogen in the nebula is excited by radiation from the hot OB star in the cloud. The photograph was taken by Californian amateur Rick Hull with a 12.5-inch (32-cm) f/4 telescope. The exposure was 40 minutes on hypered Konica 400 film.

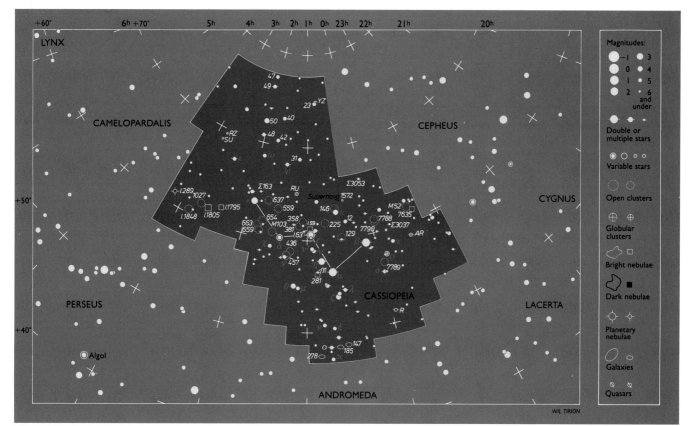

WIL TIRION

*C*assiopeia is a large fall constellation which includes a portion of the Milky Way, making it rich in telescopic objects. It occupies the area between the north celestial pole and Andromeda. Because of its northern position, the group will be above the horizon most of the night for any observer north of +30° latitude. It culminates at 10 pm on November 10. Cassiopeia's five brightest stars form a flattened "W" or "M" shape, making it one of the most distinctive and best known constellations in the sky.

Deep Sky Objects

There are many good doubles and multiples (see table) in Cassiopeia, but its main attraction is galactic clusters. It has 49 known open clusters, a couple of small planetary nebulae, but no known globulars. There are many galaxies, and two near the southern border with Andromeda are companions to M31, the Great Galaxy in Andromeda.

NGC 147 and 185 are about a degree apart, just inside the southern border of Cassiopeia. They are both about 12th-magnitude and appear as fuzzy spots with ill-defined edges. NGC 185 is slightly more concentrated, and has a dark absorption feature in large telescope photographs. These dwarf galaxies contain a few million solar masses and lie about 250,000 light years from the large M31 spiral. These are largely population II objects; that is they contain relatively old stars with little free hydrogen left for stellar creation.

There are several nebulous areas, but these are better photographic objects than visual ones and are best seen in larger amateur telescopes (12-inch (30-cm) aperture or above).

Of the many open clusters, the following stand out: NGC 457 is classified in Dreyer's catalog as "bright, large, pretty rich", having a diameter of 13 arcminutes and containing 100 stars of 8th magnitude and fainter. The 5th-magnitude star Phi (Φ) is next to the cluster. M103 (NGC 581) contains about 40 stars with a total diameter of 6 arcminutes, and is located a third of the distance from Delta (δ) to Epsilon (ε). NGC 663 is a very rich cluster in the same neighborhood in which several Struve catalog doubles are located. M52 (NGC 7654) is a large (13-arcminute diameter) scattered but rich cluster of the Pleiades type. Nearby, some 36 arcminutes to the southwest, is the Bubble Nebula, NGC 7635. This object shows a complete spherical shell of gas in large instrument photographs, but only the diffuse area near the bright star was apparent to the author in a 22-inch (55-cm) f/8 reflector. See what you can see after you find M52! NGC 7789 was discovered by Caroline Herschel (William's sister and assistant) near the end of the 1700s. It is a very rich galactic cluster located between Sigma (σ) and Rho (ρ) Cassiopeiae. There are roughly 1,000 members of the group and it's a striking sight in a 10-inch (25-cm) at × 70 magnification. There is a wide double on each side of the cluster, adding interest to this field.

NGC 281 is a large, triangular-shaped nebulous cloud, with a dark intrusion on the left side. It is fairly bright in an 8-inch (20-cm) telescope with low power, and a nebular filter helps show the boundaries more sharply. This object photographs easily and appears bright red on color film.

IC 59 and IC 63 are faint nebulosities in the neighborhood of the middle star of the "W", Gamma (γ). These wisps are fairly easily photographed, but are difficult visually because of the glare of the bright star. A 10-inch (25-cm) aperture with a fast focal ratio of f/6 or below ought to show these nebulae. Be sure to use enough power or be careful to set the telescope so that the bright star is out of the field of view. IC 63 will probably be the easier to spot because it is more concentrated and is comet shaped with the head toward Gamma. They are both within half a degree of the bright star. The nebulae appear to be illuminated or excited to fluoresence by the bright star.

Eclipsing Binary

The eclipsing binary star RZ Cassiopeia is one of the better examples of its type and can be observed through its cycle during one evening. It starts at its "normal" 6.4 magnitude and then in about 2 hours fades to 7.8. It then rises back to full brightness in 2 hours. After 1 day 4h 41m the cycle repeats. There is also a slight secondary eclipse, which is too small to see visually. RZ is 2½ degrees northeast of Iota (ι) Cass.

Supernova Remnants

A couple of years after the catastrophic explosion of a star as a supernova, the shell of outflowing gas has expanded so much that it becomes thin and transparent. But the ejected material remains visible as a nebula which continues to collide with interstellar gas, creating heat and a distinctive optical spectrum, X-rays and radio waves. It is by these means that supernova remnants are detected, and Cassiopeia A, illustrated opposite, is one of the most spectacular of the 135 known radio supernova remnants.

TELESCOPIC OBJECTS IN CASSIOPEIA

Multiple Stars

Name	RA	Dec.	Separation (arcseconds)		Mags.		Year
Σ 3053	00h 02.6m	+66° 06'	AB	15.2	5.9	7.3	1958
			AC	98.5	5.9	10.8	1912
λ (Lambda)	00h 31.8m	+54° 31'		0.5	5.3	5.6	1959
η (Eta)	00h 49.1m	+57° 49'	AB	11	3.4	7.5	1959
			AC	158.9	3.4	11.3	1922
			AD	159.6	3.4	11.5	1921
			AE	190.6	3.4	8.9	1921
			AF	281.7	3.4	...	1913
			AG	339.2	3.4	8.8	1915
Burnham 1	00h 52.8m	+56° 38'	AB	1.4	7.8	9.8	1936
			AC	3.8	7.8	8.8	1936
			AD	8.9	7.8	9.3	1936
			AE	15.7	7.8	12.0	1914
			CD	7.6	8.8	?	1936
Σ 163	01h 51.3m	+64° 51'	AB	34.8	6.8	8.8	1936
			AC	114.8	6.8	10.1	1908
ι (Iota)	02h 29.1m	+67° 24'	AB	2.2	4.6	6.9	1971
			AC	7.2	4.6	8.4	1968
			BC	9.4	6.9	8.4	1937
			CD	207.2	8.4	...	1956
AR	23h 30.0m	+58° 33'	AB	1.1	4.9	9.3	1947
			AC	75.7	4.9	7.1	1922
			AE	43.4	4.9	8.9	1918
			AF	67.3	4.9	8.9	1905
			AG	67.0	4.9	9.1	1918
			CD	1.4	7.1	8.9	1956
			CH	26.9	7.1	12.9	1880
Σ 3037	23h 46.1m	+60° 28'		2.7	7.1	8.6	1956
σ (Sigma)	23h 59.0m	+55° 45'	AB	3.0	5.0	7.1	1958
			AC	109.9	5.0	...	1909

Deep Sky Objects

Name	RA	Dec.	Type	Size	Mag.
NGC 185	00h 39.0m	+48° 20'	Gal. E0	11.5' x 9.8'	9
NGC 278	00h 52.1m	+47° 33'	Gal. E0p	2.2' x 2.1'	11
NGC 281	00h 52.8m	+56° 36'	Diff. Neb.	35' x 30'	~8
NGC 457	01h 19.1m	+58° 20'	Open Cl.	13'	6.4
M103 (NGC 581)	01h 33.2m	+60° 42'	Open Cl.	6'	7.4
NGC 654	01h 44.1m	+61° 53'	Open Cl.	5'	6.5
NGC 663	01h 46.0m	+61° 15'	Open Cl.	16'	7.1
IC 289	03h 10.3m	+61° 19'	Plan. Neb.	>34"	12pg
NGC 7635	23h 20.7m	+61° 12'	Refl. Neb.	15' x 8'	12+
M52 (NGC 7654)	23h 24.2m	+61° 35'	Open Cl.	13'	6.9
NGC 7789	23h 57.0m	+56° 34'	Open Cl.	16'	6.7

Supernova remnant Cassiopeia A. The most impressive astronomical object in Cassiopeia, Cas-A is barely visible at optical wavelengths, even in large professional telescopes. At radio wavelengths it is the brightest object in the whole sky. This false-color radio image was recorded at a wavelength of 6 cm by the Very Large Array (VLA) radio telescope at Socorro, New Mexico. It shows Cas-A as a spherical, expanding cloud of gas produced by the catastrophic explosion of a massive star approximately 300 years ago.

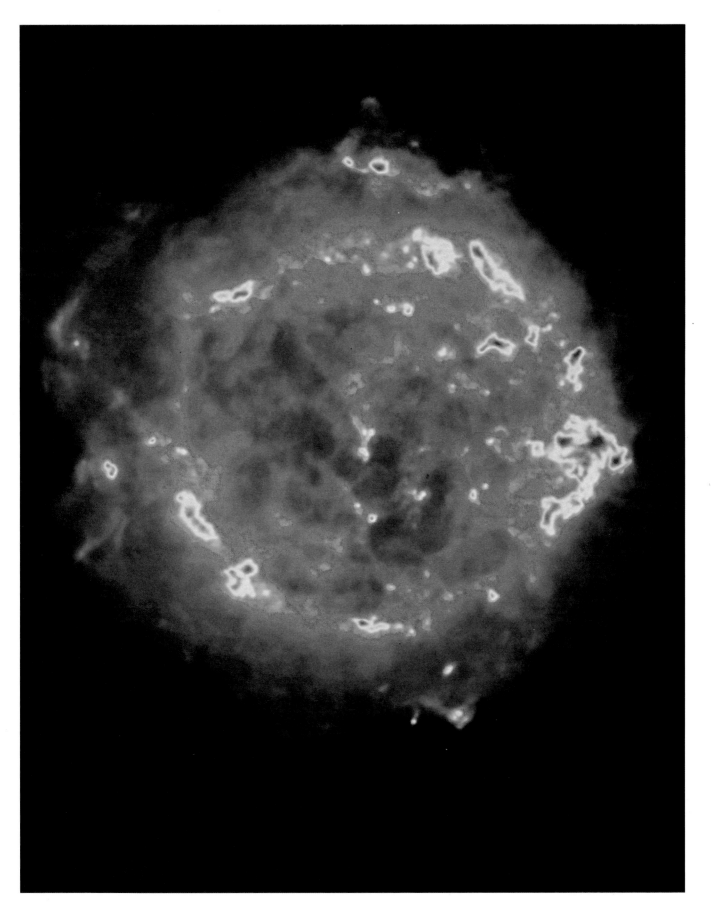

CENTAURUS

Though Centaurus, the Centaur, is one of the most prominent of all the southern constellations, there seems to be no legend directly attached to its heavenly appearance. The concept of the half-man, half-beast comes from the ancient Greeks, but unlike the Sagittarius figure, the Centaur is not portrayed as being warlike. Rather, he was full of wisdom and was perceived as a teacher.

Omega Centauri is the largest and richest globular cluster in our sky. It looks like a 4th-magnitude star to the naked eye, and resolves into pinpoint stars with a 3–4 inch (75–100mm) aperture telescope. The photograph, by Jack Marling, was made from the University of Hawaii's Mauna Kea Observatory with the 24-inch (60-cm) Cassegrain telescope. Only 10 minutes was needed at f/9 on hypered Fujichrome 400; the film was then developed to a negative to increase contrast.

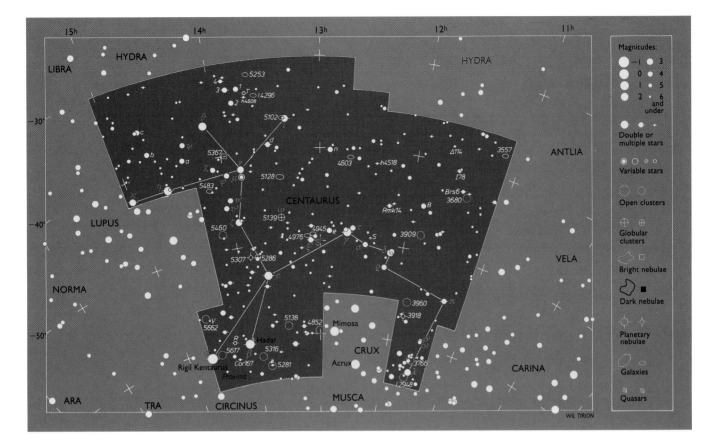

Centaurus is one of the major "Milky Way" constellations, through which the plane of our Galaxy passes. The northern boundary is at −30° latitude, so part of Centaurus can be seen well up into northern latitudes, but the southern boundary at −65° is well below the horizon except for those south of +20°. It is a long constellation, stretching from near 11 hours of Right Ascension in the west, to just over 15 hours at its easternmost extent. Centaurus can be considered a spring constellation in the northern hemisphere, but it signifies the coming of fall for southern observers, where the seasons are "reversed". Crux, the Southern Cross, is set within Centaurus, and used to be part of the Centaur. Centaurus culminates at 10 pm around May 1.

Centaurus is the constellation of superlatives. It contains the third brightest star in the sky (Alpha Centauri), the best globular cluster (Omega Centauri), the nearest star (Proxima Centauri) and a great number of telescopic objects of interest. The peculiar galaxy Centaurus A (NGC 5128) is also one of the brightest extragalactic radio objects.

Multiple Stars

Alpha (α) is a famous double star with yellow components of 0.0 and 1.2 magnitudes, in an 80-year orbit, during which the separation varies from 2 to 22 arcseconds. The last closest approach occurred in 1955 and the components are approximately at their widest in 1990. Hartung says the stars are easily visible in broad daylight with a telescope of almost any aperture. Proxima is an 11th-magnitude red dwarf in a huge orbit around Alpha which brings the extremely faint (its luminosity is 1/13,000 of the Sun) star a little closer to the Sun than Alpha during part of its orbit. The whole Alpha Centauri system is 4.3 light years distant.

Proxima is also a flare star which undergoes flaring episodes which cause it to brighten from 0.5 to 1.0 magnitudes every couple of years. More double and multiple stars are listed in the table.

Clusters

Centaurus claims 20 open or galactic clusters, the best of which are listed in the table. NGC 3766, which contains about 60 stars, some 12 arcminutes in diameter, has a number of highly colored stars, and the whole object is good for small-aperture telescopes. NGC 5617 lies 80 arcminutes west of Alpha and is a small but fairly rich cluster with about 50 stars from 8th magnitude down. The brightest and largest globular cluster in the entire sky is Omega (ω) Centauri (NGC 5139). It is a large ball of stars that covers about the same area of sky as the full Moon, and can be fully resolved in anything over a 4-inch (10-cm) telescope. Although mapped in the *Almagest* of Ptolemy, it was discovered to be a cluster by Halley from St Helena in 1677. Most northern observers see Omega at a low altitude, which causes the stars to enlarge and blur. Southern observers see the true glory of thousands of tiny points resolved down to the core.

NGC 5286 is another globular cluster worth observing. It resolves in a 6-inch (15-cm) telescope and is magnificent in a 10- or 12-inch (25- or 30-cm). There is a yellow star preceeding it to the north named M Centauri, which is a spectroscopic binary star. There are several nebulous areas in Centaurus (west of Crux), and much of the famous Coalsack dark nebula lies in Centaurus, but none are worth much attention except NGC 5367. It is a small, 10th-magnitude nebula, which may be of the bipolar dust-type – light illuminates the nebula in two opposite

Supernova in galaxy NGC 5253. This short-exposure photograph, tinted blue, shows only the central part of galaxy NGC 5253, and as a result makes clearly visible the supernova that occurred in the galaxy in 1972. The supernova, classified as SN 1972e, is the bright star-like object immediately below the galaxy's center.

directions. An 8th-magnitude planetary nebula should be mentioned, NGC 3918, a small (10-arcseconds) diameter disk that Hartung calls a "vivid pale blue".

Where not obstructed by our Galaxy, the constellation of Centaurus has a nice selection of galaxies, some of which are southern members of the Coma–Virgo cloud. Two are of special interest to amateur observers. NGC 4945 is a bright streak, a spiral seen edge-on, resembling a smaller version of NGC 253 in Sculptor. A 10-inch (25-cm) telescope will show the dark dusty mottling along the galaxy. Centaurus A, or NGC 5128, is one of the most curious galaxies in the sky. Far enough north to be seen by many US observers, it has been of great interest to professional astronomers since Herschel first sketched it in the 18th century. It appears as a relatively bright, round haze which has a well-defined broad dust band across the middle. This is an extraordinary feature, as is the intense radio source occupying two lobes outside, and perpendicular to, the dust lane. The best photographs begin to resolve the brightest supergiant stars in the dusty area, but the ball – perhaps composed of fainter, redder stars – will resist resolution until the Hubble Space Telescope observes it in the early 1990s. A supernova in NGC 5128 reached about 12th magnitude in the dust band area before fading in 1986. NGC 5253, an elliptical-shaped galaxy in the north part of the constellation, should be monitored regularly, since it has produced two bright supernovae in the past 100 years. In 1895 and 1972 two bright supernovae burst forth which reached 7.2 magnitude. These super-violent explosions outshone the galaxy itself by about 10 times, and had absolute magnitudes of −20, 13 billion times the solar output!

TELESCOPIC OBJECTS IN CENTAURUS

Multiple Stars

Name	RA	Dec.	Separation (arcseconds)	Mags.		Year
Brs 6	11h 28.6m	−42° 40′	13.1	5.2	7.9	1947
178	11h 33.6m	−40° 35′	1.0	6.2	6.2	1959
Δ 1114	11h 40.0m	−38° 07′	17.0	6.7	9.5	1934
Rmk 14	12h 14.0m	−45° 43′	2.9	5.6	6.8	1954
h4518	12h 24.7m	−41° 23′	10.0	6.3	9.6	1959
ξ₂ (Xi 2)	13h 06.9m	−49° 54′	25.1	4.3	9.4	1933
Q	13h 41.7m	−54° 34′	5.3	5.3	6.7	1956
h4608	13h 42.3m	−33° 59′	4.2	7.4	7.5	1952
N	13h 52.0m	−52° 49′	18.0	5.4	7.6	1954
3	13h 51.8m	−33° 00′	7.9	4.5	6.0	1954
Cor 167	14h 15.0m	−61° 42′	2.8	6.6	8.4	1956
α (Alpha)	14h 39.6m	−60° 50′	var.	0.0	1.2	
κ (Kappa)	14h 59.2m	−42° 06′	3.9	3.1	11.2	1960

Deep Sky Objects

Name	RA	Dec.	Type	Size	Mag.
NGC 3766	11h 36.4m	−61° 37′	Open Cl.	12′	5.3
NGC 3909	11h 49.6m	−48° 15′	Open Cl.	...	~10?
NGC 3918	11h 50.3m	−57° 11′	Plan. Neb.	12″	8.4 pg
NGC 4945	13h 05.4m	−49° 29′	Gal. SBc	20′ × 4.4′	9.4
NGC 5128	13h 25.5m	−43° 01′	Gal. S0p	18.2′ × 14.5′	7
NGC 5139	13h 26.8m	−47° 29′	Glob. Cl.	36.3′	3.65
NGC 5253	13h 39.9m	−31° 39′	Gal. E5	4.1′ × 1.7′	10.5
NGC 5286	13h 46.4m	−51° 22′	Glob. Cl.	9.1′	7.6
NGC 5316	13h 53.9m	−61° 52′	Open Cl.	14′	6.0
NGC 5367	13h 57.7m	−39° 59′	Dipol. Neb.	4′ × 3′	10
NGC 5617	14h 29.8m	−60° 43′	Open Cl.	10′	6.3

Centaurus A (NGC 5128) is located some 16 million light years away and is the nearest active galaxy to Earth. As this painting illustrates, it looks like a giant spherical galaxy with a dark dust band across its middle. But some astronomers believe it is a spiral galaxy and that the dust lane is a disk of dust, yet to be formed into stars, which surrounds the galaxy's core and which we see edge-on. The third brightest radio source in the sky, with an enormous, two-lobe radio structure that completely dwarfs the optical galaxy, Centaurus A is an astronomical mystery waiting to be solved.

CEPHEUS

Cepheus is a large, far-northern constellation north and east of Cygnus and between Draco and Cassiopeia. The Milky Way crosses its southern area and a spur of the Galaxy reaches northward towards the North Celestial Pole. It has several fairly bright stars with an easily identifiable figure. There are some wonderful low-power fields where the Galaxy crosses the constellation, and many good doubles will reward the keen searcher. In the deep sky arena, Cepheus contains several clusters, planetary nebulae, and nebulous patches, as well as galaxies in unobscured areas. The center culminates at 10 pm around November 1.

Multiple Stars

Struve 320 (Σ 320) is a fine yellow and blue double star of 5.7 and 8.8 magnitudes with 4.6 arcseconds separation. Σ 460 is a good test for a 6-inch (15-cm) telescope, with stars of magnitude 5.5 and 6.3 separated by 0.9 arcseconds. Kappa (κ) is an easy blue–white (B9 spectrum) pair, magnitudes 4.4 and 8.0, at 7.4 arcseconds separation. Σ 2790 is a beautiful blue-and-orange double with magnitude 5.8 and 10.0 stars 5.0 arcseconds apart. Beta (β) is a pair of white stars, magnitude 3.3 and 7.9 separated by 13 arcseconds. Kruger 60 is an interesting double because of its proxmimity to the solar system (12.9 light years) and the fact that the dimmer star is a flare star, exhibiting 2–3 magnitude irregular brightenings from its normal 11.3 magnitude. Omicron (o) is a yellow double, magnitudes 4.9 and 7.1, at 3.2 arcseconds.

Cepheus contains two stars of unusual character. Mu (μ) is a red Mira-type pulsating star with a period of 730 days and a variation in magnitude of between 3.4 and 5.1. Mu (μ) is called "Herschel's Garnet Star" because it is one of the reddest stars visible to the naked eye. Delta Cephei (δ) is the stereotype

TELESCOPIC OBJECTS IN CEPHEUS
Multiple Stars

Name	RA	Dec.	Separation (arcseconds)	Mags.		Year
Σ 13	00h 16.2m	+76° 57'	0.8	7.0	7.3	1961
Σ 320	03h 06.1m	+79° 25'	4.6	5.6	8.8	1934
Σ 460	04h 10.0m	+80° 42'	0.9	5.5	6.3	1966
OΣ 457	21h 55.5m	+65° 19'	1.4	5.9	8.1	1954
Σ 2873	21h 58.2m	+82° 52'	AB 13.7	7.0	7.3	1975
			AC 145.1	7.0	....	1921
ξ (Xi)	22h 03.8m	+64° 38'	AB 7.7	4.4	6.5	1974
			AC 96.8	4.4	12.6	1925
Σ 2893	22h 12.9m	+73° 18'	28.9	6.2	8.3	1967
Kruger 60	22h 28.1m	+57° 42'	2.4	9.8	11.3	1961
δ (Delta)	22h 29.2m	+58° 25'	AB 20.4	var.	13.0	1934
			AC 41.0	var.	7.5	1972
OΣ 482	22h 47.5m	+83° 09'	3.5	4.7	9.4	1940
Σ 2950	22h 51.4m	+61° 42'	AB 1.7	6.1	7.4	1960
			AC 39.3	6.1	10.7	1959
OΣ 486	23h 03.4m	+60° 27'	33.9	6.7	9.3	1920
o (Omicron)	23h 18.6m	+68° 07'	3.2	4.9	7.1	1961

Variable Stars

Name	RA	Dec.	Mag. Range	Period	Type
δ (Delta)	21h 29.2m	+58° 25'	3.48 4.37	5.366 days	Cepheid
μ (Mu)	22h 43.5m	+58° 47'	3.43 5.1	730 days	SRc

Deep Sky Objects

Name	RA	Dec.	Type	Size	Mag.
NGC 7822	00h 03.6m	+68° 37'	Diff. Neb.	60'	12?
NGC 40	00h 13.0m	+72° 32'	Plan. Neb.	~40"	10
NGC 188	00h 44.4m	+85° 20'	Open Cl.	14'	8.1
NGC 6939	20h 31.4m	+60° 38'	Open Cl.	8'	7.8
NGC 6946	20h 34.8m	+60° 09'	Gal. Sc	11.0' × 9.8'	8.8
NGC 7023	21h 01.8m	+68° 12'	Diff. Neb.	18' × 18'	10
IC 1396	21h 39.1m	+57° 30'	Diff. Neb.	170' × 140'	12+
NGC 7139	21h 45.9m	+63° 39'	Plan. Neb.	78"	13
NGC 7354	22h 40.4m	+61° 17'	Plan. Neb.	20"	12.9
NGC 7538	23h 13.5m	+61° 31'	Diff. Neb.	5' × 10'	11?

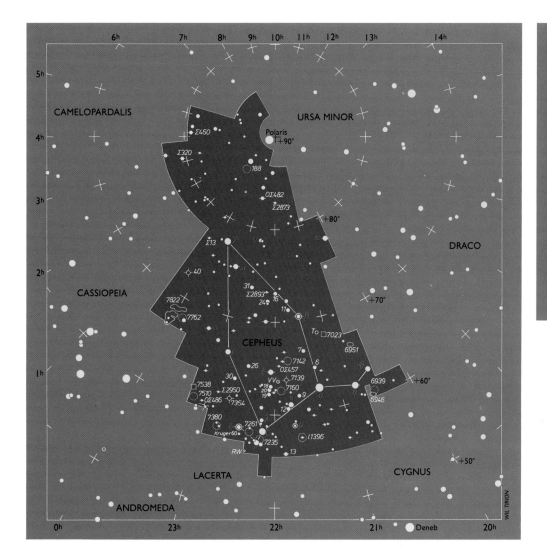

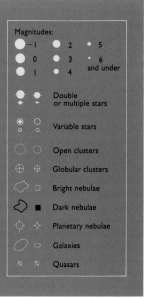

cepheid variable star. Its variation was discovered by the gifted deaf-mute astronomer John Goodricke of York in 1784. Harvard College Observatory astronomers determined that a period–luminosity relationship existed in this type of star by photographic photometry undertaken from 1890 to 1912. This means that the period of light variation is directly related to the absolute magnitude of these stars. So a measure of the apparent brightness can be used as a distance indicator. This "yardstick" was used by Hubble and Humason at Mt Wilson in the 1920s to determine that M31 was really an island universe or galaxy, lying isolated in space 2 million light years away, and not a nebula within our Galaxy.

Deep Sky Objects

Scattered around the King are telescopic objects of great variety. NGC 188 is a rather faint but interesting open cluster. This is the nearest cluster to the north celestial pole, and is known to be very, very old. Its stars are evolved yellow giants which are 10–12 billion years old! This is older even than the globular clusters as determined by elemental abundances and other spectral data. NGC 6939 is a rich but rather faint galactic cluster situated on the edge of our Galaxy's obscuration. We know this because only 38 arcminutes southeast (less than a low-power field) is

NGC 6946, a nearby low-surface-brightness Sc galaxy. In the telescope a softly glowing round haze is visible with a brighter nucleus. Evidence of the arms is seen in 16-inch (40-cm) and larger 'scopes. This galaxy is productive in supernovae, but they are a bit difficult to identify visually because of the screen of faint Galactic stars through which we are looking. NGC 7023 is a good example of a dusty cocoon nebula. Here a recently formed star (or stars) lights up an envelope of dust and gas. NGC 40 is a medium-bright (10th-magnitude) glow, which begins to show some dark material silhouetted against the glow with 10-inch (25-cm) and larger 'scopes. NGC 40 is a bright (10th magnitude), large (40 × 60 arcseconds), blue planetary with an obvious central star of 11.6 magnitude. NGC 7354 is a 20 arcsecond diameter planetary nebula, which appears brighter than its 13th-magnitude listing. NGC 7822 is a large photographic nebula near the open cluster NGC 7762. IC 1396 is also primarily photographic, a huge red nebula quite easy to photograph. There are dust lanes which the author has seen in a 16-inch (40-cm) f/5 with a nebular filter. IC 1396 can be captured on film with a modest photographic setup such as a 135-mm or similar focal-length lens, in about a 10-minute exposure at f/3.5 with one of the superfast films that have become available recently, like Konica 3200, Fuji 1600, and Kodak Ektar 1000.

CETUS

Cetus is a large group prominent in the equatorial skies in fall. Its 1231 square degrees rank it fourth in size of all the constellations. It lies in a star-poor region of sky east of Aquarius and south of Pisces. The center is on the meridian at 10 pm about November 1. Cetus has no very bright stars, but its form is fairly easy to follow if you have a dark sky and use the star map opposite.

For telescopic observers there are the usual quota of double and multiple stars, as well as an interesting planetary nebula, and a good number of galaxy systems. Also, the prototype long-period pulsating red giant variable star, Mira, is present.

Mira, "the Wonderful"

Mira, "the Wonderful", has been known as a variable star since 1596, when the Dutch astronomer David Fabricius noted an apparent nova in its place. It was observed to fade and then later reappear, and every maximum since 1638 has been recorded. The average period from one maximum to another is 331 days, the range in brightness being from about magnitude 2.5 to 9.3. The star changes size and color (and therefore temperature) as it slowly pulsates. At maximum it is cool and large, being an estimated 400 million miles in diameter, or over 400 times that of the Sun. Mira is about 220 light years from the Sun. There also appears to be a very close companion (<1 arcsec) which is a blue subdwarf but with about twice Mira's mass. It can be seen only with a large telescope and only when the red star is near minimum.

Multiple stars

Gamma (γ) stands out among the many doubles in Cetus. It is a slow binary pair, of 3.5 and 7.3 magnitudes at a separation of 2.7 arcseconds. The colors are white and yellow, sometimes described as blue and yellow. The blue is probably illusory and due to the yellowness of the fainter star. Any good telescope should be able to divide this pair, providing enough magnification (power) is used. Σ 91 is another fine double, with 7.4 and 8.2 stars separated by 4.2 arcseconds. 42 is a close, contrasting color pair (G8-A7 spectra) of 6th and 7th magnitude which were 1.5 arcseconds apart in 1961. The smaller star is an extremely close (0.1 arcsecond), almost equally bright pair. 37 Ceti is a bright, wide double, also blue and gold, 5th and 8th magnitudes, at a distance of 49.7 arcseconds. Σ 147 is a couple of white stars of magnitudes 6.1 and 7.4 separated by 2.1 arcseconds in 1959. Burnham makes the remark that the distance is decreasing. What distance apart do you see the components now?

Omicron (o), the famous variable star Mira, is a multiple star, with a 9th-magnitude companion at 118.7 arcseconds (it is an optical companion only).

Deep Sky Objects

Cetus contains quite a few galactic systems, including the large but rather faint nearby NGC 45, NGC 247, and IC 1613. These objects are best seen in a pair of large astronomical binoculars (15 or 20 x 80 or larger) or with a rich-field telescope (defined as f/5 or faster, with a power of about x10 per inch of aperture). NGC 247 appears as a large, faint stain on the sky with such an instrument, brighter toward the south. It is a large, nearby member of the South Galactic Pole group of galaxies, which includes NGC 300, 253, 55, 45, and 7793 in Sculptor. This loose grouping has been characterized as the nearest group of galaxies there is beyond the Local Group, which is centered on our Milky

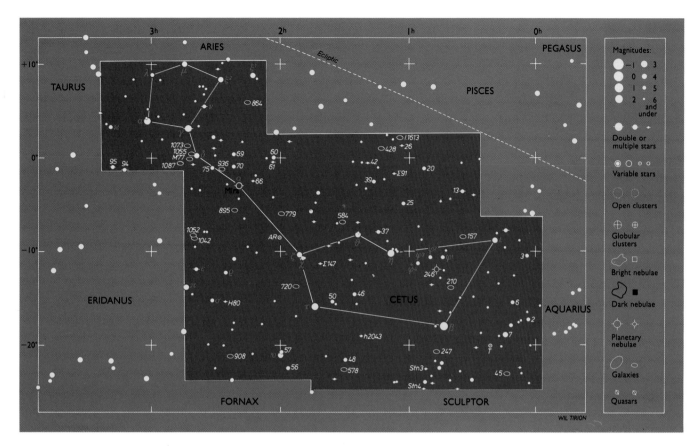

Way Galaxy. 247 is seen at a high inclination, and has a curious darkening of the northern part, shown in phtographs to be due to either a dark cloud of intervening matter or an area in the galaxy which has low stellar density. There are in 247 several H II regions that are almost stellar in appearance and visible in large amateur telescopes. These are located at the north end, about halfway down to the nucleus on the west side, with a group of 3 nebulae just south of the nucleus on the west side. There is a fairly bright star (probably of about 11th-magnitude) at the southern limit of the galaxy, which is a foreground object. NGC 247 requires a clear, dark sky to be found, but is worth the search! IC 1613 is an irregular dwarf galaxy and a member of the Local Group. It has two major concentrations which are visible in 12-inch (30-cm) or larger telescopes, providing you know exactly where to look. A much brighter and easier object is the face-on spiral M77. It is simply found about 1° southeast of Delta (δ) Ceti. This is a "Seyfert" galaxy, one of a class with an active nucleus that is brighter than normal. Current thinking is that there may be a massive black hole at the center and that the disturbance observed in visual and radio wavelengths is radiation from matter being torn·apart as it joins the rapidly rotating accretion disk and is sucked into the black hole's gravity well. M77 shines at 9th magnitude and has a fainter set of arms outside the fairly bright ones visible in a 10-inch (25-cm) 'scope.

One of the author's favorite objects is NGC 246, a fairly large round planetary nebula containing three stars of about the same brightness, one of which is the central star. There is a dark spot near the centre which can be seen with large amateur telescopes. An oxygen or deep sky filter helps show the faint disk against the sky background.

TELESCOPIC OBJECTS IN CETUS
Multiple Stars

Name	RA	Dec.	Separation (arcseconds)		Mags.		Year
Stn 3	00h 52.2m	−22° 37′	AB	1.8	7.6	8.3	1959
			AC	32.6	7.6	11.9	1908
Stn 4	00h 53.2m	−24° 47′		5.4	6.5	8.5	1952
26	01h 03.8m	+01° 22′	AB	16.0	6.2	8.6	1926
			AC	107.2	6.2	12.7	1909
Σ 91	01h 07.2m	−01° 44′		4.2	7.4	8.2	1972
37	01h 14.4m	−07° 55′		49.7	5.2	8.7	1931
42	01h 19.8m	−00° 31′		1.5	6.5	7.0	1961
h2043	01h 22.5m	−19° 05′		5.0	6.5	8.8	1952
Σ 147	01h 41.7m	−11° 19′		2.1	6.1	7.4	1959
61	02h 03.8m	−00° 20′	AB	43.0	5.9	14.5	1975
			AC	83.0	5.9	11.8	1909
66	02h 12.8m	−02° 24′	AB	16.5	5.7	7.5	1975
			AC	172.7	5.7	11.4	1908
Mira	02h 19.3m	−02° 59′	AB	73.1	var	12.0	1911
			AC	118.7	var	9.3	1925
H 80	02h 26.0m	−15° 20′	AB	12.2	5.9	8.9	1923
			AC	105.8	5.9	10.8	1922
γ (Gamma)	02h 43.2m	+03° 14′		2.7	3.5	7.3	1955

Variable Star

Name	RA	Dec.	Type	Range	Period
Mira (ο)	2h 19.3m	−02° 58′	Mira LP	2.0 10.1	332 days

Deep Sky Objects

Name	RA	Dec.	Type	Size	Mag.
NGC 45	00h 14.1m	−23° 11′	Gal. S	5.8′ × 8.1′	10.4
NGC 157	00h 34.8m	−08° 24′	Gal. Sc	4.3′ × 2.9′	10.4
NGC 246	00h 47.0m	−11° 53′	Plan. Neb.	225″	8.0pg
NGC 247	00h 47.1m	−20° 46′	Gal. S−	20.0′ × 7.4′	9.3
IC 1613	01h 04.8m	+02° 07′	Gal. Irr.	12.0′ × 11.2′	9.3v
NGC 428	01h 12.9m	+00° 59′	Gal. Scp	4.1′ × 3.2′	11.3
NGC 578	01h 30.5m	−22° 40′	Gal. Sc	4.8′ × 3.2′	10.9
M77 (NGC1068)	02h 42.7m	−00° 01′	Gal. Sbp	6.9′ × 5.9′	8.8
NGC 1087	02h 46.4m	−00° 30′	Gal. Sc	3.5′ × 2.3′	11

CHAMELEON/OCTANS

The constellations of Chameleon, the Chameleon, and Octans, the Octant, were proposed in the 17th and 18th centuries, respectively, and so do not have any classical legends attached to them. **Chameleon** was originated by Johann Bayer (1572–1625) in 1604.

Octans was proposed by Lacaille in 1752 and commemorates the invention of the instrument by John Hadley, a renowned English instrument maker, in 1730. The octant or "reflecting quadrant" allowed very small angles to be measured, and so replaced the astrolabe and cross-staff in navigation.

Chameleon and Octans are small constellations grouped together for convenience. They contain few objects of telescopic interest, although Octans contains a star which is very close to the south celestial pole, the faint "pole star" Sigma Octantis. Both constellations are circumpolar and consequently visible all night on any night for southern-hemisphere observers. Chameleon is directly above the pole at 10 pm on March 30.

Chameleon

Chameleon contains few stars, the brightest of which are of 4th magnitude. They are not designated in order of brightness like most constellations, with Gamma (γ) being the brightest star, presently at magnitude 4.11. Alpha (α) and Theta (θ) make a wide, naked-eye "double" easily distinguished by the contrasting colours of its stars (white and orange).

Chameleon contains two bright, close double stars. Delta (δ) has two yellow-coloured components of 6th magnitude, separated by a mere 0.6 arcseconds, making it very difficult to resolve. Epsilon's (ε) components were measured as being 0.9 arcseconds apart in 1941 and closing, so they may be a difficult objects to split in the 1990s. The components are magnitude 5.4 and 6.0 and blue–white in color.

Chameleon also contains two variable stars. R Chameleonis is a Mira-type variable that has a magnitude range of 7.5 to 14.2 over a period of 335 days. RS Chameleonis is a short-period variable similar to Algol in Perseus, in that its range is 6.0 to 6.7

Chameleon. This photograph of nebulosity in Chameleon was taken by the 48-inch (1.2-m) UK Schmidt Telescope at the Siding Spring Observatory in New South Wales, Australia.

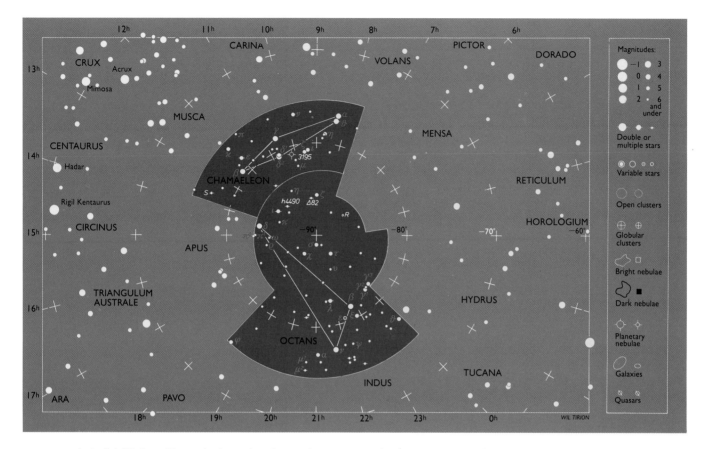

over a period of 1.67 days. The only deep sky object of note is the planetary nebula, NGC 3195, which is 38 arcseconds in diameter but at magnitude 12 requires a telescope with at least a 4-inch (10-cm) aperture to be appreciated.

Octans

Octans also consists of a few scattered stars not designated in order of magnitude. The brightest is Nu (ν) at magnitude 3.2, the only star above fourth magnitude. The southern pole is located about 1° from Sigma (σ) Octantis, which is a 5th-magnitude star of spectral type F0. As it is only 120 light years distant, its proper motion is appreciable: in 1900 it was only 45 arcseconds from the southern pole. On the author's trips to the southern hemisphere, telescopic polar alignment was performed by using the almost-right-angled triangle of the stars Tau (τ), Chi (χ), and Sigma itself, with Sigma's position subtending a right angle with respect to the others. The pole is just off the point made by Sigma. A rougher, but easier to find, approximation is that the pole is near the midpoint but slightly (about 2°) south of a line connecting the 3rd-magnitude stars Beta (β) Hydrae and Gamma (γ) Chameleonis.

Octans also contains a number of variable stars, three of which (R, U and S Octantis) are Mira-type or long-period variables. This means they are late spectral-type stars with periods ranging from 80 to as much as 1000 days, though these are not constant, nor are their magnitude ranges. Their spectra exhibit emission lines and it is suspected that many of the stars are binary systems. R Octantis has a magnitude range of 6.4 to 13.2 over 406 days; U Octantis, 7.1 to 14.1 over 303 days; and S Octantis, 7.3 to 14.0 over 259 days.

Octans has a few doubles of note and only one small galaxy, NGC 2573, which is very difficult to find. Mu (μ) consists of two stars (magnitudes 7.1 and 7.6) separated by a distance of 17.4 arcseconds. Lambda (λ) is a nice color-contrasting pair of magnitudes 5.4 and 7.7 at a separation of 3.1 arcseconds.

TELESCOPIC OBJECTS IN CHAMELEON

Multiple Stars

Name	RA	Dec.	Separation (arcseconds)	Mags.		Year
δ (Delta)	10h 45.3m	−80° 28′	0.6	6.1	6.4	1946
ε (Epsilon)	11h 59.6m	−78° 13′	0.9	5.4	6.0	1941
S (h4590)	13h 33.3m	−77° 34′	22.4	6.0	9.5	1931

Deep Sky Objects

Name	RA	Dec.	Type	Size	Mag.
NGC 3195	10h 09.5m	−80° 52′	Plan. Neb.	38″	12

TELESCOPIC OBJECTS IN OCTANS

Double Stars

Name	RA	Dec.	Separation (arcseconds)	Mags.		Year
Δ 82	09h 33.1m	−86° 01′	15.7	7.4	8.0	1940
h4490	12h 02.3m	−85° 38′	25	6.1	10.4	1940
μ₁ (Mu 1)	20h 41.7m	−75° 21′	17.4	7.1	7.6	1940
λ (Lambda)	21h 50.9m	−82° 43′	3.1	5.4	7.7	1946

CIRCINUS

Circinus, the Compasses, was another constellation introduced by Nicolas Louis de Lacaille in 1752. It celebrates that most important navigational tool, which had allowed pioneers to travel to southern latitudes. It is usually portrayed as a pair of compasses, despite its singular lack of a definite shape.

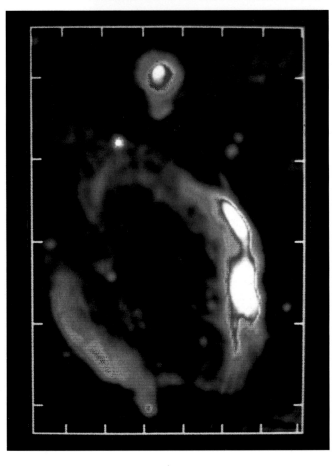

Circinus is a small, undistinguished constellation that can be found just east of Centaurus. The easiest way to locate it is to follow the line made by Alpha (α) and Beta (β) Centauri, also known as "the Pointers". Circinus covers only 93 square degrees of sky, and is orientated north–south across the southern Milky Way. There is no notable figure formed by its stars. Its principle star is Alpha (α), located directly south of Alpha Centauri, and at magnitude 3.2 the only member of Circinus above 4th magnitude. It is an autumn constellation for southern-hemisphere observers, culminating at 10 pm on June 1. It contains several fine doubles and one small, but bright, planetary nebula.

Double Stars

Alpha (α) Circini is an interesting double star with components of magnitude 3.2 and 8.6 about 15.7 arcseconds apart. Their separation has stayed the same for a long time, but the position angle (the apparent position of one with respect to the other, measured in degrees eastwards from the north position) has changed. This suggests we are seeing the orbit of B "flat on". Δ169 is a color-contrasting pair, with stars of magnitude 6.2 and

Circinus X-1, the bright spot at the top of this false-color radio image, is believed to be a binary star system, one part of which is so compact that it may be a neutron star or black hole. It is a source of variable X-ray emissions. The elliptical radio nebula in the lower part of the picture may be produced by the accumulation of energetic particles and plasma emitted by Circinus X-1 during its flaring activity. This 1986 picture, at a wavelength of 36 cm by R. F. Haynes and colleagues at Australia's Molonglo Observatory Synthesis Telescope, was the first observation of the nebula.

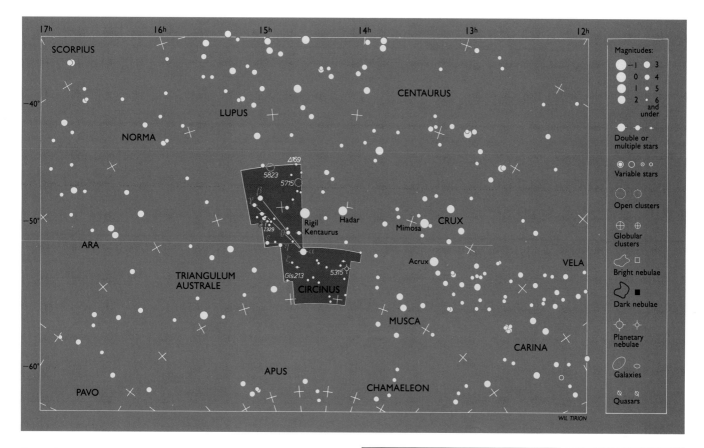

7.6 (B2 and K0 spectral classes) at 68 arcseconds distance. Gamma (γ) is a spectacular double, with magnitude 5.1 and 5.5 stars separated by 0.9 arcseconds in 1949, and closing ever since. Gamma is actually a binary with a period of around 180 years.

Circinus also contains a couple of variable stars. AX Circini is a Cepheid whose magnitude ranges from 5.6 to 6.1 in 5.3 days. Theta (θ) Circini is an irregular variable, whose magnitude changes from 5.0 to 5.4.

Deep Sky Objects

NGC 5315 appears as a small, disk-shaped object, differing from a star only because of its bluish–green colour in low-power eyepieces. A high-power eyepiece will show a fairly bright, featureless disk about 5 arcseconds in diameter. The central star is listed at magnitude 11.4. NGC 5823 is a galactic star cluster containing about 80 stars and is appreciated only with a telescope of 12-inch (30-cm) aperture or greater.

TELESCOPIC OBJECTS IN CIRCINUS
Multiple Stars

Name	RA	Dec.	Separation (arcseconds)	Mags.		Year
α (Alpha)	14h 42.5m	−64° 59′	15.7	3.2	8.6	1951
Δ 169	14h 45.2m	−55° 36′	68	6.2	7.6	1938
Gls213	15h 01.3m	−67° 59′	5.2	7.1	9.2	1943
γ (Gamma)	15h 23.4m	−59° 19′	0.9	5.1	5.5	1949

Deep Sky Objects

Name	RA	Dec.	Type	Size	Mag.
NGC 5315	13h 53.9m	−66° 31′	Plan. Neb.	5″	13pg
NGC 5823	15h 05.7m	−55° 36′	Open Cl.	10′	7.9

Naming the Constellations

When European explorers headed southwards across the equator, the southern skies presented new vistas to be grouped into constellations. In his *Almagest,* the Alexandrian astronomer Ptolemy had listed 48 constellations, most drawn from classical mythology. Most are retained on modern maps, a few suitably amended. However, the far southern stars remained hidden, and it was only natural that new shapes would be drawn up. Johann Bayer introduced 11 southern constellations in his *Uranometria* of 1603. Nicolas Lacaille added a further 14 in 1752.

During the 18th century, however, many astronomers felt it necessary to bless ever fainter groups of stars with increasingly obscure names. They did not only restrict themselves to southern skies. Some of the more bizarre include Taurus Poniatowskii (Poniatowski's Bull), Sceptrum Brandenburgicum (the Sceptre of Brandenburg) and Officiana Typographica (the Printing Press). Some of the more cumbersome names were mercifully shortened, particularly those suggested by Lacaille: Mensa was Mons Mensae, Table Mountain ; Pyxis was Pyxis Nautica, the Mariner's Compass.

In 1933, the International Astronomical Union (the world body that governs astronomy) decided to standardize the constellations, and rationalized them to a grand total of 88 members. These 88 constellations form the basis of this book.

COMA BERENICES

Coma Berenices is a cluster of stars, located between Boötes, Ursa Major and Leo. It is a rather faint spring constellation, which culminates at 10 pm on May 1, virtually at the zenith for most northern observers.

Like Canes Venatici, Coma Berenices is a treasure-trove of galaxies, lying on the outer edges of the rich collection of galaxies in the Virgo cluster. At a dark site, with steadily held binoculars, many galaxies will be revealed as fuzzy spots in and around the stars. A rich-field telescope will show dozens of these objects, although an 8-inch (20-cm) aperture is needed to see any character in individual examples. A globular cluster worth finding is M53 (NGC 504), about a degree northeast of Alpha (α). It is a compact, rich object in a 10-inch (25-cm) telescope.

Among the doubles and multiples in Coma, two pairs and a triple are some of the best. 24 Comae is a nicely colored contrasting pair, consisting of gold and blue stars (spectral types K2 and A7 respectively). 32 and 33 Comae are a nice pair for binoculars, also contrasting in colors, with 6th-magnitude components. 35 Comae is a triple system, with a nicely colored contrasting pair (5th and 7th magnitudes, separated by 1 arcsecond) accompanied by a 9th-magnitude companion 28.7 arcseconds away.

Six of the Best

Six of the brightest galactic systems in Coma will be described out of perhaps 30 that are easily seen with telescopes of 8-inch (20-cm) aperture. M98 (NGC 4192) is a large spiral seen almost edge-on, about 3 by 9 arcminutes in size and of 10th magnitude. It is easily located about half a degree west of the star 6 Comae. M100 (NGC 4321) has been called the brightest galaxy in the Virgo Cluster. It appears as a large haze 6.9 by 6.2 arcminutes across, with a bright nucleus. In 14-inch (35-cm) or larger aperture telescopes, two major arms are seen wrapped around the nucleus. M100 has produced several supernovae, with such events taking place in 1901, 1914, 1959 and 1984. A typical supernova at this distance reaches about 12th magnitude, easily seen in an 8-inch (20-cm) or larger aperture telescope.

M99 (NGC 4254) is a wide-open, face-on spiral with two prominent arms which become evident in a 16-inch (40-cm) telescope. M88 (NGC 4501) is another compact spiral similar in structure to the Great Galaxy in Andromeda, M31. It appears as a grey-coloured ellipse with no structure apparent until it is seen in very large telescopes. There is a wide double star just to the south and also a closer pair seen against the southern part of the galaxy with larger telescopes. These are actually foreground objects in our own Galaxy at distances less than 10,000 light years away (M99 is about 40 million light years distant).

A Needle and a Black Eye

The famous edge-on galaxy, NGC 4565, is also called the "Needle Galaxy". It is found by panning the telescope east from the wide double star 17 Comae until you come to the galaxy about 1.5 degrees east. The unmistakably thin, edge-on shape is 16 by 3 arcminutes wide, with a 13th-magnitude star visible just above the nuclear area. The dark dust lane is only really apparent where it crosses the nuclear bulge.

M64 (NGC 4826) is known as the "Black Eye" galaxy, and is an early-type Sb with none of the lumpiness seen in later classifications. The galaxy is seen as an ellipse, with no structure except for a dark spot seen against the glow of the galaxy on the north-

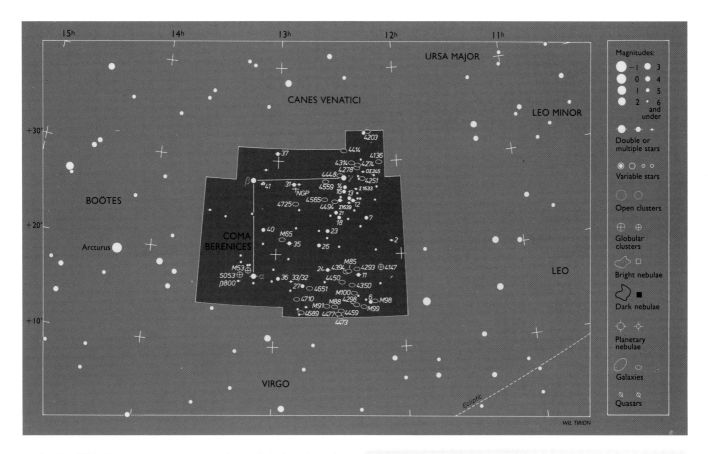

WIL TIRION

east side. This is an enormous complex of dark, obscuring material concentrated on this side of the galaxy. It can be seen in a 6-inch (15-cm) aperture telescope, although larger instruments will show much more detail.

The Coma Cluster

Far beyond the spattering of bright galaxies described above is the Coma Cluster of Galaxies. This highly concentrated grouping of over 1,000 galaxies lies about 10 times the distance to the Coma–Virgo objects so far discussed, at about 400 million light years away. The brightest of these is NGC 4889, a giant elliptical system of apparent magnitude 13.4, and located about 2.3 degrees west of Beta (β) Comae. In large amateur telescopes (14-inch (35-cm) and larger), many of the fainter galaxies become visible as the tiniest, faintest fuzzballs imaginable, right at the edge of vision.

TELESCOPIC OBJECTS IN COMA BERENICES

Multiple Stars

Name	RA	Dec.	Separation (arcseconds)	Mags.		Year
2	12h 04.3m	+21° 28'	15.8	5.9	7.4	1917
Σ 1633	12h 20.7m	+27° 03'	9.0	7.0	7.1	1958
12	12h 22.5m	+25° 51'	AB 35.0	4.8	11.8	1935
			AC 65.2	4.8	8.3	1972
Σ 1639	12h 24.4m	+25° 35'	4.6	7.0	12.8	1960
17	12h 28.9m	+25° 55'	145.	5.3	6.6	1928
24	12h 35.1m	+18° 23'	20.3	5.2	6.7	1958
32 + 33	12h 52.2m	+17° 04'	95.2	6.3	6.7	1922
35	12h 53.3m	+21° 14'	AB ~1.0	5.1	7.2	1959
			AC 28.7	5.1	9.1	1958

TELESCOPIC OBJECTS IN COMA BERENICES continued

Deep Sky Objects

Name	RA	Dec.	Type	Size	Mag.
NGC 4147	12h 10.1m	+18° 33'	Gl. Clus.	4.0'	10.2
M98 (NGC 4192)	12h 13.8m	+14° 54'	Gal. Sb	9.5' × 3.2'	10
NGC 4203	12h 15.1m	+33° 12'	Gal. Ep	3.6' × 3.3'	10.6
NGC 4251	12h 18.1m	+28° 10'	Gal. E7	4.2' × 1.9'	11.6
M99 (NGC 4254)	12h 18.8m	+14° 25'	Gal. Sc	5.4' × 4.8'	9.8
NGC 4274	12h 19.8m	+29° 37'	Gal. Sb	6.9' × 2.8'	10.4
NGC 4278	12h 20.1m	+29° 17'	Gal. E1	3.6' × 3.5'	10.2
NGC 4293	12h 21.2m	+18° 23'	Gal. Sap	6.0' × 3.0'	11.1
NGC 4298	12h 21.5m	+14° 36'	Gal. Sc	3.2' × 1.9'	11.3
NGC 4314	12h 22.6m	+29° 53'	Gal. SBa	4.8' × 4.3'	10.5
M100 (NGC 4321)	12h 22.9m	+15° 49'	Gal. Sc	6.9' × 6.2'	9.4
NGC 4350	12h 24.0m	+16° 42'	Gal. E7	3.2' × 1.1'	11.1
M85 (NGC 4382)	12h 25.4m	+18° 11'	Gal. Ep	7.1' × 5.2'	9.2
NGC 4414	12h 26.4m	+31° 13'	Gal. Sc	3.6' × 2.2'	10.2
NGC 4448	12h 28.2m	+28° 37'	Gal. Sb	4.0' × 1.6'	11.1
NGC 4450	12h 28.5m	+17° 05'	Gal. Sb	4.8' × 3.5'	10.1
NGC 4459	12h 29.0m	+13° 59'	Gal. E2	3.8' × 2.8'	10.4
NGC 4477	12h 30.0m	+13° 38'	Gal. SBa	4.0' × 3.5'	10.4
NGC 4494	12h 31.4m.	+25° 47'	Gal. E1	4.8' × 3.8'	9.8
M88 (NGC 4501)	12h 32.0m	+14° 25'	Gal. Sb	6.9' × 3.0'	9.5
NGC 4548	12h 35.4m	+14° 30'	Gal. SBb	5.4' × 4.4'	10.2
NGC 4559	12h 36.0m	+27° 58'	Gal. Sc	10.5' × 4.9'	9.8
NGC 4565	12h 36.3m	+25° 59'	Gal. Sb	16.2' × 2.8'	9.5
NGC 4651	12h 43.7m	+16° 24'	Gal. Scp	3.8' × 2.7'	10.7
NGC 4689	12h 47.8m	+13° 46'	Gal. Sb	4.0' × 3.5'	11
NGC 4725	12h 50.4m	+25° 30'	Gal. SBb	11.0' × 7.9'	9.2
M64 (NGC 4826)	12h 56.7m	+21° 41'	Gal. Sb	9.3' × 5.4'	8.5
M53 (NGC 5024)	13h 12.9m	+18° 10'	Glob. Cl.	12.6'	7.7
NGC 5053	13h 16.4m	+17° 42'	Glob. Cl.	10.5'	9.8

CORONA AUSTRALIS

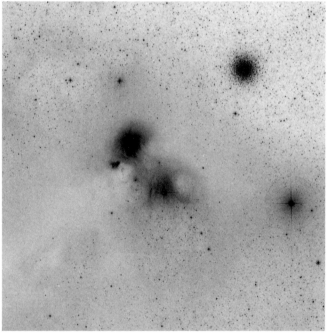

NGC 6726/6727 and NGC 6729 form the complex of light and dark nebulosity at the center of this negatively printed photograph. The globular cluster at top right is NGC 6723, which is just across the Corona Australis border in Sagittarius. The upper patch of black nebulosity is NGC 6726/6727. The lower black patch, shaped like a wispy comet, is NGC 6729. The photograph was taken on blue-sensitive emulsion with the 48-inch (1.2-m) UK Schmidt Telescope.

Corona Australis is a small constellation east of the tail of Scorpius and south of Sagittarius. Its stars visible to the naked eye mark an ellipse that is orientated from the northeast to the southwest, with part of the Milky Way running through its western portions. This is a summer constellation for northern-hemisphere observers, culminating at 10 pm on August 1. It contains a number of nice doubles and globular clusters, as well as a dark dust nebula, NGC 6729, similar to Hubble's Variable Nebula in Monoceros.

Multiple Stars

h5014 is an interesting binary system. Its classification comes from Sir John Herschel's extensive study of southern clusters, nebulae and binary stars undertaken from 1834 to 1838 at the Cape of Good Hope. It is therefore the 5,014th double in his survey which was published in 1847. It consists of a pair of 5.7 magnitude stars in binary motion which take 190 years to complete one orbit. The stars have closed from 1.8 arcseconds in 1943, though they were resolved with a telescope of 4-inch (10.5-cm) aperture in 1962. The nearby, but somewhat obscured, globular cluster NGC 6541 is in the same field as h5014. Kappa (κ) is an easy bright double, made up of stars of magnitude 5.9 to 6.6 some 21.4 arcseconds apart. Gamma (γ) is another binary, with 4.8 and 5.1 magnitude stars about 2.7 arcseconds apart and a period of about 120 years.

Deep Sky Objects

The complex of light and dark nebulosity comprising NGCs 6726, 6727 and 6729 is the most remarkable telescopic object in Corona Australis. The figure-8 shape of the nebulae NGC 6726

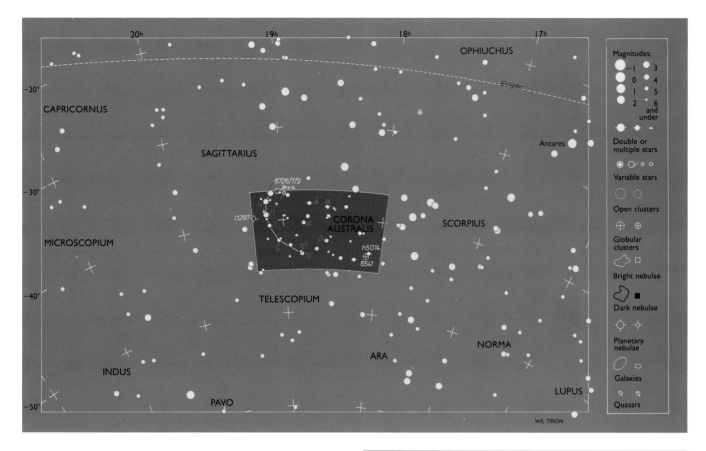

and 6727 surrounds two stars, one of which is a variable, TY Corona Australis. This variable star changes magnitude erratically from 8.8 to about 12.5 and the nebula generally follows. There is also the comet-like nebula NGC 6729, which has the variable star R Cor. Aus. in its "nucleus" and also follows the erratic changes of brightness of the star. These are all young nebular variables which are apparently still accreting matter from the surroundings (see box). However, other astronomers subscribe to the theory that suggests that they are much older, and in the final stages of their life are blowing away the cloud of material surrounding them, out of which they were born. Whichever theory is correct, the dark, dusty objects that await the observer are worthy of attention. There are many examples of new stars that have accreted enough mass for nuclear reactions to start in their centers, blowing off material after ignition. Many of these stars appear to be rotating very fast, and the nebular material blowing off seems to have striae or streaks which follow the same direction as the equator of the star. The best example of this is the streaks in the Merope Nebula around that fast-spinning star in the Pleiades. That star may be more advanced than these still-dusty stars in Corona Australis, however. Infrared techniques are advancing rapidly in astronomy, and it is infrared and the longer-wavelength microwave astronomy that are two of the hot topics in astronomy today. These are the wavelengths that most effectively penetrate these dust clouds, so advances can be expected in the study of new stars as new techniques and equipment become avalable.

There is also a planetary nebula, IC 1297, a 2 arcsecond diameter blue point of 11th magnitude.

Nebular Variables

Nebular variables are very young stars that are still condensing and have not started to shine by thermonuclear reactions. They represent the final stages of development of protostars before they arrive on the Main Sequence. Most nebular variables are F, G or K spectral type giants, surrounded by vast regions of dust and gas and varying irregularly in brightness. As well as the nebulae in Corona Australis, the most prominent regions where they may be found are in the Orion Nebula. As they undergo contraction after thermonuclear ignition, a fierce stellar wind is blown off and in this way much material is lost. They rotate very rapidly, throwing off material at speeds of up to 180 miles (300 kilometers) per second.

TELESCOPIC OBJECTS IN CORONA AUSTRALIS
Multiple Stars

Name	RA	Dec.	Separation (arcseconds)	Mags.		Year
h5014	18h 06.8m	−43° 25'	1.8	5.7	5.7	1943
κ (Kappa)	18h 33.4m	−38° 44'	21.4	5.9	6.6	1936
Brs 14	19h 01.1m	−37° 04'	12.7	6.6	6.8	1951
γ (Gamma)	19h 06.4m	−37° 04'	AC 2.7	4.8	5.1	1943

Deep Sky Objects

Name	RA	Dec.	Type	Size	Mag.
NGC 6541	18h 08.0m	−43° 42'	Glob. Cl.	13'	6.6
NGC 6726	19h 01.7m	−36° 53'			
NGC 6727			Diff. Refl. Neb. surrounding TY and R Cor. Aus.		
NGC 6729					
IC 1297	19h 17.4m	−39° 37'	Plan. Neb.	2"	11.5

CORONA BOREALIS/SERPENS CAPUT

Corona Borealis, the Northern Crown, represents a crown given by Dionysus to Ariadne, the daughter of Minos of Crete. The Greeks referred to the distinctive star pattern as Corona: the Borealis (meaning northern) was added later on. Ptolemy recognized eight naked-eye stars in his Almagest.

Serpens Caput, the Head of the Serpent, is the upper half of the constellation Serpens, found to the west of Ophiuchus. The serpent's tail is east of Ophiuchus, and will be dealt with later. Serpens Caput is one of Ptolemy's original constellations.

TELESCOPIC OBJECTS IN CORONA BOREALIS
Multiple Stars

Name	RA	Dec.	Separation (arcseconds)	Mags.		Year
Σ 1932	15h 18.3m	+26° 50'	1	7.3	7.4	1961
η (eta)	15h 23.0m	+30° 17'	0.6	5.6	5.9	1960
ζ (Zeta)	15h 39.4m	+36° 38'	6.3	5.1	6.0	1973
Σ 2011	16h 07.6m	+29° 00'	2.4	7.8	10.4	1941
Σ 2022	16h 12.8m	+26° 40'	2.5	6.4	10.0	1958
σ (Sigma)	16h 14.7m	+33° 52'	AB 6.2	5.6	6.6	1962
			AC 8.7	5.6	13.1	1935
			AD 71.0	5.6	10.6	1933

Variable Stars

Name	RA	Dec.	Type	Range		Period
R	15h 48.6m	+28° 09'	RCB	5.71	14.8	Irr.
T	15h 59.5m	+25° 55'	Nova Rec.	2.0	10.8	Irr.

Abell 2065 "Corona Cluster of Galaxies" center is at 15h 22.5m, +29° 40'.

TELESCOPIC OBJECTS IN SERPENS CAPUT
Multiple Stars

Name	RA	Dec.	Separation (arcseconds)	Mags.		Year
5	15h 19.3m	+1° 46'	AB 11.2	5.1	10.1	1958
			AC 127.2	5.1	9.1	1924
Σ 1950	15h 30.0m	+25° 30'	3.2	8.1	9.6	1954
δ (Delta)	15h 34.8m	+10° 32'	3.9	4.2	5.2	1962

Deep Sky Objects

Name	RA	Dec.	Type	Size	Mag.
M5 (NGC 5904)	15h 18.6m	+2° 05'	Glob. Cl.	17.4'	5.75
NGC 6027 (group)	15h 59.2m	+20° 45'	Gals.	2.2' × 1.2'	13–15

Corona Borealis is an ancient grouping set between Boötes to the west and Hercules to the east. Directly to its south is the Head of the Serpent, Serpens Caput. Serpens is a larger grouping but has only a scraggly line of stars to mark its figure. Both constellations are on the meridian at 10 pm on about June 15.

Corona Borealis

Corona Borealis contains some fine double stars, two interesting variable stars and, for those with really big telescopes, one of the most concentrated clusters of galaxies known (Abell 2065). Eta (η) is a bright, close binary star which has a period of 41.6 years. During the 1990s it will have a separation of almost exactly 1 arcsecond. The components are of magnitude 5.6 and 5.9, which combined total a visual magnitude of 5.

The variable star R Coronae Borealis is an object of interest which can be monitored by binoculars. It remains near maximum (about 6th magnitude) most of the time, then irregularly drops rapidly to nearly 12th magnitude. Recovery may begin almost immediately or wait sometimes for several years before it slowly begins. Some minima reach 14th magnitude. The variations are explained in theory by the ejection of clouds of carbon (chemically, the same as soot!) which obscure the light until the material is reabsorbed or blown away. T Coronae Borealis is the best-known example of another rare variable class, the recurrant nova. T generally remains at about 10th magnitude, but twice in the past 150 years (1866 and 1946) it has suddenly blazed up to almost 2nd magnitude! The outbursts happen in a matter of hours, and a rapid decline then begins, returning the star to its normal 10th magnitude in about 20 days. Current theory explains this bizarre behavior as the instabilities of a close mass-

72

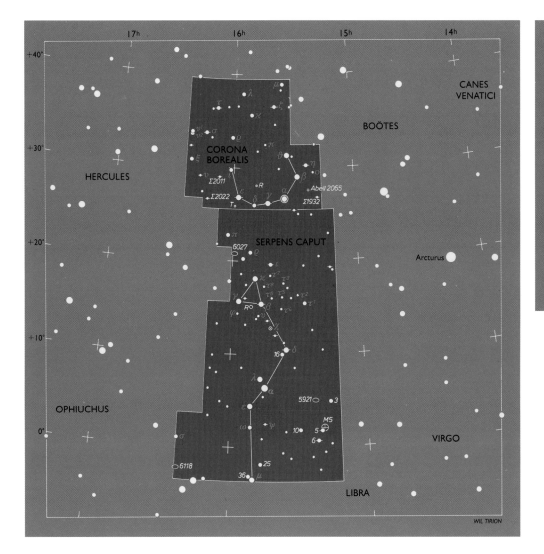

exchanging binary star resolving themselves and then the process beginning again.

Abell 2065 is a very rich cluster of galaxies from 16th magnitude downwards, so is only visible to amateurs with larger telescopes. A 16-inch (40-cm) instrument at fairly high power will begin to show dozens of "faint fuzzies" to the dark-adapted eye. There are about 400 members known, which concentrate within half a degree of sky. Distance estimates vary as the "yardstick" used, but about 1 billion, or 1,000 million, light years can be approximated.

Serpens Caput

Serpens Caput has a few doubles of interest, but its major claim to fame is the wonderful globular cluster M5 (NGC 5904). M5 is one of the premier globulars in the sky, and it is easily found near the star 5 Serpentis, only 22 arcminutes away. The cluster is located most easily by finding the stars 109 and 110 Virginis to the west of M5. Start at the brilliant star Arcturus in Boötes, go southeast to Xi Boötis. 10 degrees straight south of Xi is 109 Virginis. Extend a line from 109 to 110 directly east and project it the same distance again, and you will be on the cluster's position. In a finder scope or binoculars it looks like a bright fuzzy star, with the star 5 Serpentis just below it. During a really dark, calm

observing night, M5 and the star combine to be fairly easily visible to the naked eye. The cluster begins to resolve with a 3-inch (7.5-cm) aperture and is a glorious ball of stars when fully resolved.

5 Serpentis is a 5th-magnitude star with a dusky, 10th-magnitude companion at 11 arcseconds distance. Delta (δ) is a fine object for small telescopes, with 4.2- and 5.2-magnitude stars at 3.9 arcseconds distance (1962) and opening. There is an interesting grouping of galaxies which is a challenge for deep sky observers even with 12-inch (30-cm) or larger aperture telescopes. This is the NGC 6027 group, sometimes known as Stephan's Sextet. There are actually only five objects, with one appearing to be greatly tidally distorted. Dark sky and fairly high powers are needed to resolve the group since it is only about 1 arcminute wide and less than 2 arcminutes high. With a 16-inch (40-cm) f/5 Newtonian I was able to see five components, the southern one being very faint. The sixth galaxy, which is just a wisp on the 200-inch plate reproduced in Burnham's Celestial Handbook on page 1793, was completely invisible. These galaxies are from 14th to 16th magnitude, so are difficult to see in a 12-inch (30-cm) aperture telescope. The distance to this remote grouping is listed as 200×10^6 light years.

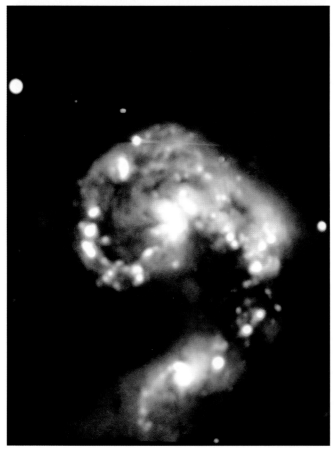

Corvus is a smallish spring grouping for northern observers. It lies south of the west part of Virgo, and is easily recognized by a trapezoidal figure made by its principal stars, which are around 3rd magnitude in brightness. Crater is a small grouping west of Corvus, and is included here for convenience. It is marked by four 4th-magnitude stars making another fainter trapezoid about 15° to the west of Corvus. The border between Corvus and Crater reaches the meridian at 10 pm about April 20.

Corvus

Several nice doubles are present in Corvus, and since this is "galaxy country" (the Coma–Virgo cluster is nearby), there are many present, although most are rather smaller and fainter than in Virgo. Σ 1604 is a nice triple star, with a 6th-magnitude and two 9th-magnitude campanions at 10 and 19 arcseconds separations, respectively. The third member of the system is an optical companion, lying in the same direction of the sky as we observe it, but at a different distance. Delta (δ) is a nice easy pair, with somewhat contrasting colors. Σ1669 consists of two 6th-

The Antennae is the nickname of interacting galaxies NGC 4038 and NGC 4039. They provide a good test of calculations of tidal distortions produced when galaxies collide. Each galaxy has a tail of tidally removed stars and gas that stretches well beyond the field of view. The bright, slightly blue condensations are sites of new star formation triggered by the interaction of the galaxies. The picture is a true-color composite of three frames taken with a CCD camera mounted on the 84-inch (2.1-m) telescope at the Kitt Peak National Observatory, Arizona.

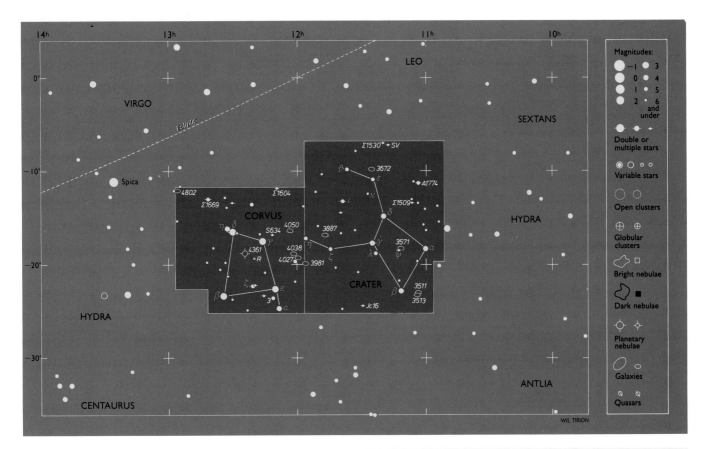

WIL TIRION

magnitude white stars at 5.4 arcseconds separation and a third star, magnitude 10.3 at 59.0 arcseconds separation.

The Antennae

One of the oddest objects in the sky is the galaxy known as the Antennae, which is NGC 4038 colliding with NGC 4039. Long exposures show two fine "tails" of matter being thrown radially out from the cataclysm in the center. Telescopically, this object looks like a doughnut with a bite taken out of it. It has fairly high surface brightness, so is interesting in any 'scope with an aperture of 6 inches (15cm) and upwards. NGC 4361 is one of the brightest large planetary nebulae in the sky, and sits just above the center of the trapezoid of Corvus. It appears as a large (80 arcsecond diameter) round, almost featureless, gray-colored object, with a fairly prominent 13th-magnitude central star.

There are a number of galaxies of the Coma–Virgo Cluster in the northeast part of Corvus. These include NGC 4782-3, two galaxies which share a common envelope of faint stars. This 12th-magnitude pair makes a triangle with 4792 (14th mag.) and 4794 (14th-mag.), and there are other extragalactic systems scattered around the area.

Crater

Crater has only a few doubles of interest, which are listed in the table. NGC 3511 is a fairly bright galaxy seen almost edge-on, and NGC 3672 is slightly brighter, classified as Sb in Hubble's system, with many tightly wound spiral arms. NGC 3887 is another spiral galaxy which is a fairly bright 11th magnitude. Its Revised New General Catalog description is: "Spiral, slightly elliptical, brighter middle, very knotty, high surface brightness."

TELESCOPIC OBJECTS IN CORVUS
Double and Multiple Stars

Name	RA	Dec.	Separation (arcseconds)	Mags.		Year
Σ 1604	12h 09.5m	−11° 51′	AB 9.9	6.8	9.3	1970
			AC 19.1	6.8	9.2	1959
S634	12h 11.4m	−16° 47′	5.5	7.2	8.4	1960
δ (Delta)	12h 29.9m	−16° 31′	24.2	3.0	9.2	1958
Σ 1669	12h 41.3m	−13° 01′	AB 5.4	6.0	6.1	1973
			AC 59.0	6.0	10.3	1930

Deep Sky Objects

Name	RA	Dec.	Type	Size	Mag.
NGC 4027	11h 59.5m	−19° 16′	Gal. Scp	3.0′ × 2.3′	11.1
NGC 4038	12h 01.9m	−18° 52′	Gal. Scp	2.6′ × 1.8′	10.7
NGC 4050	12h 02.9m	−16° 22′	Gal. SBb	3.1′ × 2.2′	12
NGC 4361	12h 24.5m	−18° 46′	Plan. Neb.	80″	10.3pg

TELESCOPIC OBJECTS IN CRATER
Double Stars

Name	RA	Dec.	Separation (arcseconds)	Mags.		Year
A1774	11h 03.2m	−11° 18′	3.7	5.6	10.6	1951
Σ 1509	11h 06.5m	−13° 24′	32.9	7	9	1925
Σ 1530	11h 19.7m	−06° 54′	7.7	7.5	8	1955
γ (Gamma)	11h 24.9m	−17° 41′	5.2	4.1	9.6	1955
Jc 16	11h 29.8m	−24° 29′	8.2	5.8	8.8	1954

Deep Sky Objects

Name	RA	Dec.	Type	Size	Mag.
NGC 3511	11h 03.2m	−23° 05′	Gal. Sc	5.4′ × 2.2′	11.6
NGC 3672	11h 25.0m	−09° 48′	Gal. Sb	4.1′ × 2.1′	11.5
NGC 3887	11h 47.1m	−16° 52′	Gal. Sc	3.3′ × 2.7′	11.0

CRUX/MUSCA

Crux is the smallest constellation in the sky. It covers only 68 square degrees but is a rich trove of celestial treasures. For amateur astronomers of the northern temperate zones, where it is forever below the horizon, Crux symbolizes the exotic tropical southern skies. The first view of the Southern Cross after a long airplane flight or even from the jet's window is unforgettable. My first view was from the Philippines: there was distant lightning, and above the tropical shower clouds was the cross. I had already been an amateur astronomer for 15 years that night in 1962, and seeing the cross for the first time was a thrill which has remained vividly in my memory. It may be considered an autumnal constellation for southern-hemisphere dwellers, culminating at 10 pm on May 1. The southern Milky Way is concentrated here, and there are several clusters, many multiple stars, and part of the remarkable Coal Sack dust cloud, which is silhoutted in front of the brilliant Milky Way in the region.

The Southern Cross can be seen from parts of the United States that have latitudes below +30°. The center of Crux has a declination of −60°.

Musca is a larger group just toward the south pole from Crux. It also has the Milky Way passing through its northern half, and therefore contains a number of interesting stars, clusters, and NGC 5189, a curious gas/dust nebula. Musca is grouped with Crux as a matter of photographic convenience.

Crux

Alpha Crucis, or Acrux (α) is a bright double star 370 light years from Earth with components of magnitude 1.4 and 1.9 only 4.4 arcseconds apart. The colors are white and blue–white, and there is a third star of 4th magnitude 90.1 arcseconds distant.

Gamma (γ) is an optical double, with the bright-orange primary and a 6th-magnitude white companion 111 arcseconds away. Beta (β) is another multiple, comprising a 1st-magnitude primary and an 11th-magnitude companion some 44 arcseconds distant. A red star, the 7th-magnitude EsB 365, is the third component, and its color contrasts beautifully with the blue–white primary. Mu (μ) is a wide double easy for any telescope (magnitudes 4.3, 5.3; separation 34.9 arcseconds).

The open cluster NGC 4103 is situated in a brilliant part of the Milky Way and is surrounded by several bright stars. It is made up of about 25 fairly bright stars. NGC 4349 is a somewhat larger open cluster, easily found about halfway between Acrux and Epsilon (ε). It has many colored stars and has a diameter of 16 arcminutes.

The Jewel Box

The telescope wonder of Crux Australis must be the Kappa (κ) Crucis open cluster NGC 4755, known since John (son of William) Herschel's time as the Jewel Box. This is a concentrated cluster of bright stars which is a good object in any instrument from binoculars upwards. The brighter stars are blue and red giants, giving beautiful – if not brilliant – colors to the points of light. These are enormously bright stars which are evolving rapidly and burning their hydrogen at a prodigious rate. Their luminosities are equivalent to that of many thousands of Suns, the brightest two being over 80,000 times more luminous than our star! The distance to the cluster is calculated to be about 7,500 light years. This Jewel Box sits on the north edge of the Coal Sack dark nebula, which spreads its inkiness down into Musca. Even with the naked eye, a three-dimensionality is discernible which is

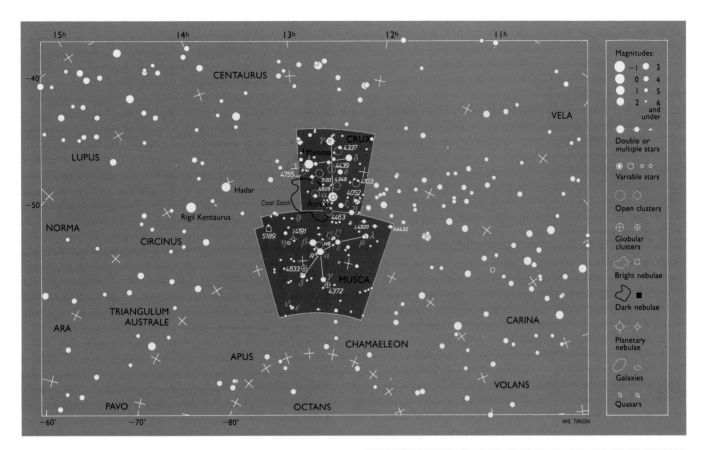

heightened by the use of binoculars. The sense is that we are looking into a dark cavity, hollowing out the Milky Way around it. Actually, the Coal Sack is a relatively nearby absorbing dust cloud at about 500 light years.

Musca

Musca shares part of the bright Milky Way with Crux, and has several telescopic objects worthy of attention. Herschel 4432 is a nice pair of yellow–white suns, magnitude 5.4 and 6.6 at 2.3 arcseconds separation and L4920 consists of stars of magnitudes 5.2 and 7.4 some 1.8 arcseconds in separation. Beta (β) Muscae is a white double with magnitude 3.7 and 4.0 stars orbiting at 1.4 arcseconds in 1955. The pair is opening: what distance do you estimate now? Theta (θ) is a fine color-contrasting double of magnitudes 5.7 and 7.3, separated by 5.3 arcseconds. The secondary star is classified as a WC6 star, meaning it is cool and has strong carbon bands in its spectrum. The color provides a nice contrast with the white (B0) primary.

There are two bright globular clusters in Musca, which might be even more prominent were there not so much obscuration by dust in the vicinity. NGC 4372 is the better of them, with a large (18 arcminute) diameter but only 12th-magnitude stars, owing to dust blocking out several magnitudes of their light. The cluster may be as close as 15,000 light years. H6 is an open or galactic cluster, with about 70 stars within a 5 arcminute diameter. NGC 5189 is a peculiar nebula whose classification is in doubt. It has internal structure and several stars are involved. Hartung says there is a single prism image which is typical of planetary nebulae, but other descriptions suggest it is more like a figure 8 or reflection nebula.

TELESCOPIC OBJECTS IN CRUX
Double and Multiple Stars

Name	RA	Dec.	Separation (arcseconds)	Mags.		Year
α (Acrux)	12h 26.6m	−63° 06′	AB 4.4	1.4	1.9	1955
			AC 90.1	1.4	4.9	
γ (Gamma)	12h 31.2m	−57° 07′	AB 110.6	1.6	6.7	1919
			AC 155.2	1.6	9.5	1879
β (Beta)	12h 47.7m	−59° 41′	AB 44.3	1.3	11.2	1901
			AC 369.9	1.3	7.3	1853
μ (Mu)	12h 54.6m	−57° 11′	34.9	4.3	5.3	1952

Deep Sky Objects

Name	RA	Dec.	Type	Size	Mag.
NGC 4052	12h 01.9m	−63° 12′	Open Cl.	8′	8.8pg
NGC 4103	12h 06.7m	−61° 15′	Open Cl.	7′	7.4pg
NGC 4349	12h 24.5m	−61° 54′	Open Cl.	16′	7.4
Tr 20 (H7)	12h 39.7m	−60° 36′	Open Cl.	8′	10.1pg
NGC 4755	12h 53.6m	−60° 20′	Open Cl.	10′	4.2

TELESCOPIC OBJECTS IN MUSCA
Double and Multiple Stars

Name	RA	Dec.	Separation (arcseconds)	Mags.		Year
h4432	11h 23.4m	−64° 57′	2.3	5.4	6.6	1947
L4920	11h 51.9m	−65° 12′	1.8	5.2	7.4	1940
β (Beta)	12h 46.3m	−68° 06′	1.4	3.7	4.0	1955
θ (Theta)	13h 08.1m	−65° 18′	5.3	5.7	7.3	1952

Deep Sky Objects

Name	RA	Dec.	Type	Size	Mag.
NGC 4372	12h 25.8m	−72° 40′	Glob. Cl.	18.6′	7.8
H6	12h 37.9m	−68° 28′	Open Cl.	5′	10.7pg
NGC 4833	12h 59.6m	−70° 53′	Glob. Cl.	13.5′	7.3
NGC 5189	13h 33.5m	−65° 59′	Plan.Neb.(?)	153″	10.3

CYGNUS

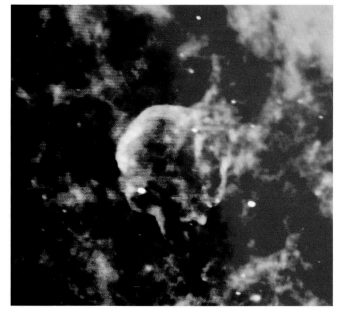

The Cygnus Loop is an enormous, wispy shell of gas and dust more than 3° in diameter, the remnant of a supernova explosion that occurred some 20,000 years ago. This image, made from data recorded by the IRAS infrared astronomical satellite, combines infrared emission at wavelengths of 20 microns (blue), 60 microns (green) and 100 microns (red). The shell of dust, heated by the shock wave from the supernova, is most prominent at 60 microns and appears yellow–green. The brightest part of the Cygnus Loop, the Veil Nebula, is visible in 80-mm diameter binoculars.

Cygnus is a large and important summer constellation in which a portion of our Galaxy is prominent as a diffuse collection of stars known as the "Cygnus star cloud". It is located north of Aquila and east of Lyra, and so far north that its Alpha (α), the star Deneb, is circumpolar for everyone living north of 45° north latitude. The brighter stars of Cygnus form a large cross, known popularly as the "Northern Cross". The Swan is seen with wings outstretched forming the "bar" of the cross, flying south down the Milky Way. The distant 1st-magnitude star Deneb signifies its tail and the beautiful double star Albireo the beak.

The naked eye appearance of Cygnus is impressive, with Argelander, a 19th-century German astronomer, ascribing no less than 146 members visible to the unaided eye. The Cygnus star cloud is a bright part of the Galaxy, and on a fine night the observer can see the Great Rift just east of the body of the swan, as well as a dark cloud, known as the northern Coal Sack, just north of Deneb. Throughout this region there are a great number of colored stars, perhaps best visible in a rich-field telescope, or astronomical binoculars, with a power of ×20 or ×30.

It has been calculated that in this region of the sky the combination of telescope size and eyepiece power that would show a visual observer absolutely the greatest number of stars in one field is a 4.25-inch (10.6-cm) f/4.8 instrument, with a power of about ×18. This is considered to be the ultimate rich-field instrument.

Multiple Stars

Cygnus is home to so many double, multiple and interesting stars, as well as nebulae and clusters, that it would take a good-

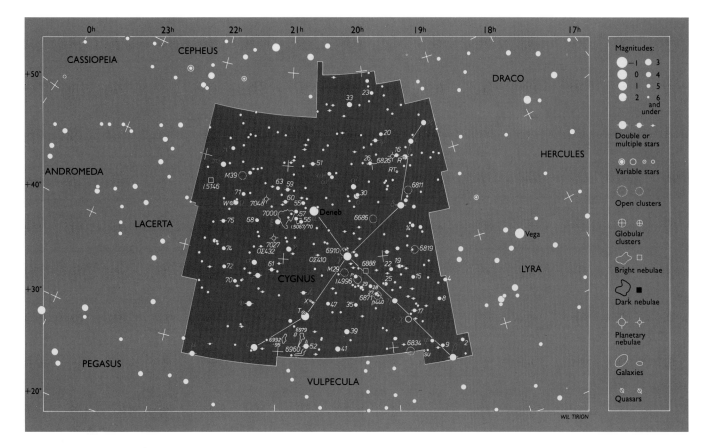

sized book to catalog them all; so our celestial tour will present the highlights, limited as we are to a few pages. One of the most celebrated double stars in the sky is Albireo, or Beta (β) Cygni. Gold and blue components of magnitude 3.1 and 5.1 are easily separated at a distance of 34.4 arcseconds with almost any telescope. The colors seem more vivid with an aperture smaller than 8 inches (20cm); perhaps too bright an image desensitizes the eye. It is a lovely object with any telescope. This pair of stars is 380 light years distant, so each is many times brighter than our Sun, which would appear to be of 10th magnitude at that distance! Delta (δ) is a fine double star which is something of a challenge, owing to the difference in magnitudes of the stars, 2.9 and 6.3. It is a binary of long period, which appears to be approximately at its widest opening of about 1.8 arcseconds in the late 20th century. The stars are both blue–white, and it requires steady seeing conditions to resolve cleanly. OΣ 390 is a triple star which has stars of magnitudes 6.6 and 8.9 at 9.7 arcseconds separation with a third component, 10.6, at 16.4 arcseconds.

61 Cygni

61 Cygni is another famous double star, notably because the primary component was the first star to have its parallax measured, by Bessel in 1838. Parallax is defined as the change in the apparent position of an astronomical body caused by the motion of the Earth around the Sun. The nearer the star to the Earth, the greater the amount of parallax. The exceedingly tiny angle of 0.294 arcseconds shows that the star is only 11.1 light years away, making it one of the 20 nearest stars. Close observations also show that there is a third companion, too faint and too

close to observe directly, but its presence was betrayed by its effect on the proper motion of 61A. This small body (61C) has only the mass of eight Jupiter-sized bodies, so it could be a large planet, or a very small, perhaps non-luminous, star. The B star is currently 28.4 arcseconds away, and the two bright stars A and B are red dwarfs of magnitudes 5.2 and 6.0. Mu (μ) is a bright yellow combination of magnitude 4.8 and 6.1 stars now separated by perhaps 2 arcseconds. The close passage of both stars took place visually in 1926 at 0.9 arcseconds and periastron (their closest distance in space) was in 1962. The period of the pair is about 500 years.

Deep Sky Objects

There are 28 open clusters in Cygnus, and 11 planetaries, but no globular clusters and no extragalactic systems, due to the Milky Way obscuration. NGC 6819 is a rich galactic cluster, containing 150 stars from 11th magnitude and fainter. It is almost exactly 5 degrees south of Delta (δ), and best approached with telescopic apertures of 8 inches (20 cm) and above. NGC 6866 is another rich cluster of brighter stars, about 50 in number from 10th magnitude and fainter. NGC 6866 is found just north of the half-way point between Gamma (γ) and Delta (δ). The two Messier clusters in Cygnus, M29 (NGC 6913) near Gamma and M39 (NGC 7092) north-west of Deneb, are both rather sparse groups of fairly bright stars, but can be seen to good advantage with binoculars and are good large binocular objects. The best two planetaries in Cygnus are NGC 6826, a medium-sized (25 arcseconds) but very bright (magnitude 8.8) disk with an 11th-magnitude central star, and NGC 7027, an elliptical, bright blue–green ovoid of the 10th magnitude.

The North America Nebula

Besides the planetaries, Cygnus abounds in nebulosities of various kinds. There are nebulous patches around Gamma (γ), which can be faintly seen and easily photographed. There is also the North America Nebula, or NGC 7000, discovered by Wolf of Heidelberg on the first "modern" long-exposure, wide-field photographs of the region in the early 1890s. This is easier to photograph than to see well, but with large binoculars or a low-power rich-field telescope the "continental" shape can be traced out reasonably well. 7×50 binoculars will show it on a really clear, dark night, and the region definitely looks brighter than the surroundings with the well-adapted naked eye. With a 10-inch (25-cm) or larger telescope (especially with a deep sky filter to remove auroral glow) the whole continent with the charming cluster NGC 6997 can be traced.

Another interesting object, which comes into its own with a 10-inch (25-cm) or larger 'scope, is NGC 6888. This is an oval of nebulosity which apparently was created by the expulsion of gas by the Wolf-Rayet star at its center. Use of a nebular filter makes this object stand out against the background and suppresses the light from the bright stars in and around the nebulosity.

The Cygnus Loop

Perhaps the most spectacular object in Cygnus, at least in photographs, is the supernova remnant NGC 6960 and NGC 6992. This is known by various names, commonly the Cygnus Loop for the whole object, or the Veil Nebula for NGC 6992. Europeans seem fond of the title Cirrus Nebula because of the resemblance to cirrus clouds. Whatever you like to call it, this object is both fascinating and beautiful. It can be seen quite well in binoculars of at least 50-mm diameter, better with the 20 × 80 or 15 × 80 astronomical binoculars which have become popular in recent years. In a larger telescope, especially with the addition of a nebular filter, the strands of nebulosity can be traced just as in the long-exposure photographs. Recently, I used a 22-inch (55-cm) f/8 Cassegrain reflector, with a Daystar 300 filter and 32-mm ocular, and the nebula looked exactly like it does in photographs. It appeared at its best above 52 Cygni where the nebula narrows and looks tubular, and over in its eastern portions, where the loop could be followed for about a degree. Fast focal ratios and the use of a good filter are required for observers with medium-sized telescopes to obtain the best views.

TELESCOPIC OBJECTS IN CYGNUS
Double and Multiple Stars

Name	RA	Dec.		Separation (arcseconds)	Mags.		Year
β (Beta) (Albireo)	19h 30.7m	+27° 58'		34.4	3.1	5.1	1967
16	19h 41.8m	+50° 32'		39.3	6.0	6.1	1976
δ (Delta)	19h 44.9m	+45° 07'		1.8(?)	2.9	6.3	1960
ψ (Psi)	19h 55.6m	+52° 26'	AB	3.2	4.9	7.4	1958
			AC	21.2	4.9	13.6	1958
			AD	165.4	4.9	10.2	1908
OΣ 390	19h 55.1m	+30° 12'	AB	9.7	6.6	8.9	1849
			AC	16.4	6.6	10.6	1849
OΣ 410	20h 39.6m	+40° 35'	AB	0.8	6.8	7.1	1959
			AB×C	69.0	6.8	8.9	1939
Burnham 440	20h 06.4m	+35° 47'	AB	6.9	6.8	11.8	1943
λ (Lambda)	20h 47.4m	+36° 29'		0.7 (1961)	4.8	6.1	1961
59	20h 59.8m	+47° 31'	AB	20.2	4.7	9.6	1951
			AC	26.7	4.7	11.5	1921
			AD	38.3	4.7	11.0	1913
61	21h 06.3m	+38° 45'		28.4	5.2	6.0	1968
OΣ 432	21h 14.3m	+41° 09'		1.4	7.8	8.2	1957
υ (Upsilon)	21h 17.9m	+34° 54'	AB	15.1	4.4	10.0	1958
			AC	21.5	4.4	10.0	1958
μ (Mu)	21h 44.1m	+28° 45'	AB	1.7 (1967)	4.8	6.1	1967
			AC	48.6	4.8	11.5	1924

Deep Sky Objects

Name	RA	Dec.	Type	Size	Mag.
NGC 6819	19h 41.3m	+40° 13'	Open Cl.	6'	7.3
NGC 6826	19h 44.9m	+50° 31'	Plan. Neb.	25"	8.8
NGC 6866	20h 03.7m	+44° 00'	Open Cl.	8'	7.6
NGC 6888	20h 12.0m	+38° 21'	Diff. Neb.	20' × 10'	11
M29 (NGC 6913)	20h 23.9m	+38° 32'	Open Cl.	7'	6.6
NGC 6960	20h 45.7m	+30° 43'	SNR	70' × 6'	11
NGC 6992/5	20h 56.4m	+31° 42'	SNR		
IC 5067-70	20h 48.6m	+44° 22'	Diff. Neb.	80' × 70'	11+
NGC 7000	20h 58.7m	+44° 20'	Diff. Neb.	120' × 100'	9
NGC 7027	21h 07.1m	+42° 14'	Plan. Neb.	18" × 11"	10.4pg
M39 (NGC 7092)	21h 32.2m	+48° 26'	Open Cl.	32'	4.6

The North America Nebula (NGC 7000) is named for its uncanny resemblance to the terrestrial continent. Immediately to its right – in mid-Atlantic, so to speak – is the Pelican Nebula (IC 5067–5070). The bright star on the right is Deneb, or Alpha Cygni, a very remote and luminous white supergiant. The tricolor photograph was made by Californian amateur astronomer the Reverend Ronald Royer.

Delphinus/Equuleus

Both Delphinus, the Dolphin, and Equuleus, the Foal are ancient constellations and were duly recorded by Ptolemy in the Almagest. Poseidon, god of the sea, placed the image of a dolphin in the sky in gratitude for the dolphin's help in wooing his wife, the mermaid Amphitrite. Alpha (α) Delphini is named Sualocin, while Beta (β) is called Rotanev – perhaps it comes as no surprise to learn they were originated by Nicolaus Venator, the assistant to the Italian astronomer Guiseppe Piazzi !

Equuleus is associated with the legend of Mercury giving Castor as a gift.

*D*elphinus and Equuleus are grouped together here for convenience. They are both late-summer equatorial constellations which are located east of Aquila and west of Aquarius. They are straight south (on the meridian) for northern-hemisphere observers at 10pm on September 9. Delphinus has one of the most distinctive shapes, that of a slightly flattened diamond, or a kite, with a couple of fainter stars as a tail. This is only about 10° east of the 1st-magnitude star Altair in Aquila. Equuleus is the elongated triangle left and below Delphinus. I look at it as the space between Delphinus, and Enif, the yellow 2nd-magnitude star marking the southwest extent of Pegasus. Delphinus has a few deep sky objects, but Equuleus has only a few doubles of note.

Delphinus

Delphinus has two small planetary nebulae: NGC 6891 is 7 x 15 arcseconds in extent, round with a bluish color and of 10th magnitude. The other is NGC 6905, a larger, elliptical object, slightly dimmer and with diffuse edges. There are also two globulars in Delphinus. One, NGC 7006, is thought to be one of the most remote globular clusters, lying in intergalactic space at a distance of 150,000 light years. It appears as a small glow, brighter in the center. At this distance the individual stars are much too faint to resolve in amateur-sized telescopes. This cluster can be found by centering Gamma (γ) Delphini in the eyepiece and then turning off the clock drive for exactly 18 minutes. Or, just find Gamma and move the scope east in RA for 18 minutes. The other globular is a much closer object: NGC 6934 is about 9th magnitude if you sum the total brightness of all its stars, and resolves with a 10 inch (25cm) aperture, at least around the edges. There is a fairly bright star in the field which contrasts well with the cluster.

Many good doubles are available in these edge-of-the-Milky-Way constellations. One of the better ones in the sky is Gamma (γ) Delphini. As with so many other Gammas that are fine doubles (Gamma Aquarii, Andromedae, Aerietis, Virginis, etc.), this pair is a great small-telescope object. It is made up of magnitude 4.5 and 5.5 stars about 10 arcseconds apart, both of which are resolved with almost any instrument. The fainter star has been seen by some past observers as green. The spectral classes are K2 and F8, indicating quite different colors. What do you see? Beta (β) Delphinae is also a double, a close binary with a rather short period of 26.65 years. The cigar-shaped orbit of the secondary star takes it 0.65 arcseconds away, but at closest (which happens twice in an orbit) the separation is an almost irresolvable 0.2 arcseconds. The last minimum separation was in 1985, so it will be opening again rapidly during the 1990s.

Equuleus

Equuleus has no notable deep sky objects but does have a number of doubles. 1 Equulei or Epsilon (ε) is really a multiple group. The AB pair is a binary with a period of 101 years, closest at 0.1 arcseconds in 1920, and open at 1.1 arcseconds in 1970. These are magnitude 6.0 and 6.3 stars. There is a 7th-magnitude C star at 10.7 arseconds and a D component of 12th magnitude 74.8 arcseconds away from the A star. 2 Equulei is a nice pair, both 7th magnitude, at 2.8 arcseconds separation. Delta (δ) is a fast binary system with a period of 5.70 years. Its separation is always less than 0.35 arcseconds, so a large telescope must be used to try to split it.

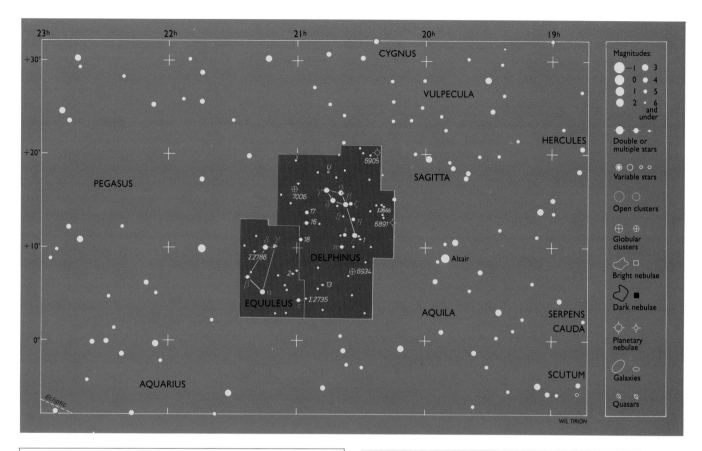

Ptolemy

Claudius Ptolemaus, known simply as Ptolemy, was the last great ancient astronomer. He lived in Alexandria, Egypt, which was the location of the great library and of what we might call a Greek university or college founded about 300 BC. He lived from about 100 to 151 AD as a subject of the Roman Empire. Ptolemy is known for several achievements in the field of astronomy. He made up a system of geometrical constructions that would account for the observed movements of the Sun, Moon, and planets on the celestial sphere. This system could not account for certain movements perfectly, however, since it had the Earth at the center, and relied on the planets and Sun and Moon travelling in circular orbits with smaller epicycles to explain some of the observed movements. However, this system did survive over 1,400 years (until Copernicus, c.1570).

Ptolemy wrote a compendium of astronomical knowledge to his period, which we now know as the *Almagest*, from its 12th-century Arabic translation. In this book, Ptolemy repeats the star catalog of Hipparchus (*c.*140 BC), who was the first great positional or astrometric astronomer. Ptolemy put these stars into 48 groups, the major constellations visible from +30° latitude. There were many stars "left over" which were classed "amorphae" or amorphous, that is without belonging to a form, which later astronomers, notably Bayer and Lacaille, organized into the remaining 40 groups.

TELESCOPIC OBJECTS IN DELPHINUS
Double and Multiple Stars

Name	RA	Dec.	Separation (arcseconds)		Mags.		Year
Σ 2665	20h 19.4m	+14° 22'		3.3	6.8	9.0	1943
1	20h 30.3m	+10° 54'		0.9	6.1	8.1	1958
β (Beta)	20h 37.5m	+14° 36'	AB	0.7	4.0	4.9	1924
			AC	22.8	4.0	12.9	1924
			AB×D	39.1		10.8	1931
γ (Gamma)	20h 46.7m	+16° 07'		9.6	4.5	5.5	1976
13	20h 47.8m	+06° 00'		1.6	5.6	9.2	1958
Σ 2735	20h 55.7m	+04° 32'		2.1	6.1	7.6	1958

Deep Sky Objects

Name	RA	Dec.	Type	Size	Mag.
NGC 6891	20h 15.2m	+12° 42'	Plan. Neb.	7" × 15"	10
NGC 6905	20h 22.4m	+20° 07'	Plan. Neb.	44" × 38"	12
NGC 6934	20h 34.2m	+7° 24'	Glob. Cl.	5.9'	8.8
NGC 7006	21h 01.5m	+16° 11'	Glob. Cl.	2.8'	10.6

TELESCOPIC OBJECTS IN EQUULEUS
Double and Multiple Stars

Name	RA	Dec.	Separation (arcseconds)		Mags.		Year
ε (Epsilon)	20h 59.1m	+04° 18'	AB	0.9	6.0	6.3	1961
			AB×C	10.7	6.0	7.1	1967
			AD	74.8	6.0	12.4	1924
2	21h 02.2m	+07° 11'		2.8	7.4	7.4	1955
δ (Delta)	21h 14.5m	+10° 00'	AB	0.3	5.2	5.3	1961
			AC	47.7	5.2	9.4	1925
Σ 2786	21h 19.7m	+09° 32'		2.5	7.2	8.3	1955

Dorado/Mensa

Dorado is a long, straggling constellation which starts at about −50° in declination and ends at −70°. It is undistinguished except for being the location of a major portion of the Large Magellanic Cloud (LMC). The LMC is the nearest galaxy to our own Milky Way, lying about 170,000 light years away. It has another, smaller, satellite, the Small Magellanic Cloud (SMC), which is slightly farther away. Dorado is a summer constellation for southerners, reaching culmination at 10pm in the first week of January. It is marked by a rambling line of stars beginning with Gamma (γ), with Alpha (α) next. These are located approximately half-way between the brilliant Canopus and 1st-magnitude Achernar in Eridanus. The line continues to Zeta (ζ) and ends with a faint triangle Beta (β), Delta (δ) and a 4th magnitude star.

Mensa, the Table, is adjacent to Dorado to the south, and is made up of several faint stars. It contains the southern third of the LMC and is otherwise undistinguished.

Double Stars

Rmk 4 is a double star with two 7th-magnitude stars at a distance of 6 arcseconds. h3683 is a binary of 550 years period and has two components of the 7th magnitude about 3 arcseconds distant. A closer pair is I 276, which has 6.7 and 6.9 magnitude stars, at a close 1.2 arcseconds in 1959.

Beta Doradonis (β) is a Cepheid variable star with a magnitude range of 3.8 to 4.7 in 9.8 days.

The Magellenic Clouds

The LMC attracts much attention, being the nearest large extragalactic system to our own. Our Galaxy is a spiral, whereas the LMC is usually called an irregular. Long-exposure photographs show a "tail" or bar, which could be the result of the gravitational interaction with the SMC and our Milky Way galaxy. The tails resemble approximately those of the NGC 4038/9 system, which is named the Antennae Galaxy (see Corvus). LMC's aggregation of stars, dust, and gas has a diameter of at least 50,000 light years and a mass of something like 25 billion Suns, about 10 per cent of the mass of our Milky Way. This must be a fairly young galaxy, because there are still great nebulous, hydrogen-rich areas called HII regions where star formation is going on at a great rate. There are also a few blue supergiants which are more luminous than anything known in our own galaxy. This means they are burning fuel (hydrogen) at a tremendous rate. It is the associations of supergiant stars and accompanying nebulosity which are the major visual telescopic features of the LMC. The Tarantula Nebula (NGC 2070) is the largest and brightest, and is perhaps the largest complex of glowing hydrogen and super-bright young stars known anywhere. NGC 2070, also known as 30 Doradonis, dwarfs the Orion Nebula, and is visible to the naked eye at the southeast end of the LMC (when the LMC is highest in the sky). In the telescope, loops and tendrils of nebulosity radiate from the central nucleus for some distance. The bright-blue supergiant central star 30 Doradonis and its attendants are easily seen, being from 9th magnitude downwards. It was on the outskirts of this nebula that the supernova of 1987 exploded on Feburary 23, reaching magnitude 2.8 by May 15. The star that exploded has been identified as the previously 12th-magnitude Sanduleak −69° 202. This was a normal, "well-behaved" blue supergiant which apparently suffered hydrogen burnout and the subsequent collapse of its

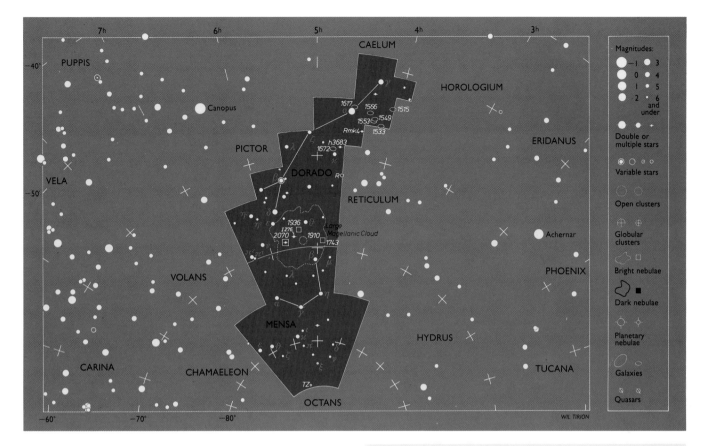

core, causing the cataclysmic explosion witnessed by us about 180,000 years after it happened. At the time of writing, almost two years later, the object has faded to about 8th magnitude, but its expanding cloud of hot gas and nuclear remnant are still an object of close scrutiny by southern-hemisphere observers.

Literally dozens of clusters, nebulae and planetaries dot the body and outskirts of the LMC.

Supernova – death of a star

A supernova is a new star which appears suddenly and rarely. The last supernova in our Galaxy happened about 300 years ago. We see them in other galaxies, and because of their remoteness, they do not appear very bright. This is a false assumption however, because supernovae are often as bright as the whole galaxy in which they appear! This means that this one explosion gives off as much energy as millions of stars. What causes this tremendous outburst of energy? Nothing less than the cataclysmic death of a large star.

To cause a supernova we first need a big star, at least 10 to 50 times more massive than the Sun. This heavy star evolves to the point where most of its hydrogen fuel has been used up, and it has a reduction of radiation. There probably is another star, a binary companion nearby which is transferring gas to the SN candidate. The atmosphere becomes too heavy for the reduced radiation to support, and a tremendous collapse occurs, which causes the necessary heat and pressure to fuse many element's atoms in the star, causing the enormous explosion.

TELESCOPIC OBJECTS IN DORADO
Double and Multiple Stars

Name	RA	Dec.	Separation (arcseconds)	Mags.		Year
Rmk 4	04h 24.2m	−57° 04′	5.9	6.9	7.3	1955
h3683	04h 40.3m	−58° 57′	3.3	7.2	7.3	1990
I276	05h 27.0m	−68° 37′	1.2	6.7	6.9	1959

Deep Sky Objects

Name	RA	Dec.	Type	Size	Mag.
NGC 1549	04h 15.7m	−55° 36′	Gal. E0	3.7′ × 3.2′	10
NGC 1553	04h 16.2m	−55° 47′	Gal. S0	4.1′ × 2.8′	9.5
NGC 1556	04h 20.0m	−54° 56′	Gal. SBb	7.6′ × 6.2″	9.4
NGC 1672	04h 45.7m	−59° 15′	Gal. SBb	4.8′ × 3.9′	11.0b
NGC 1743	04h 54.0m	−69° 12′	Neb. (LMC)	15″	13
NGC 1910	05h 18.1m	−69° 13′	Gal. Cl (LMC)	54″	10
NGC 1936	05h 22.0m	−67° 58′	Neb. +Stars	20″ × 15″	9?
NGC 2070	05h 38.7m	−69° 06′	Diff. Neb	40′ × 25′	5

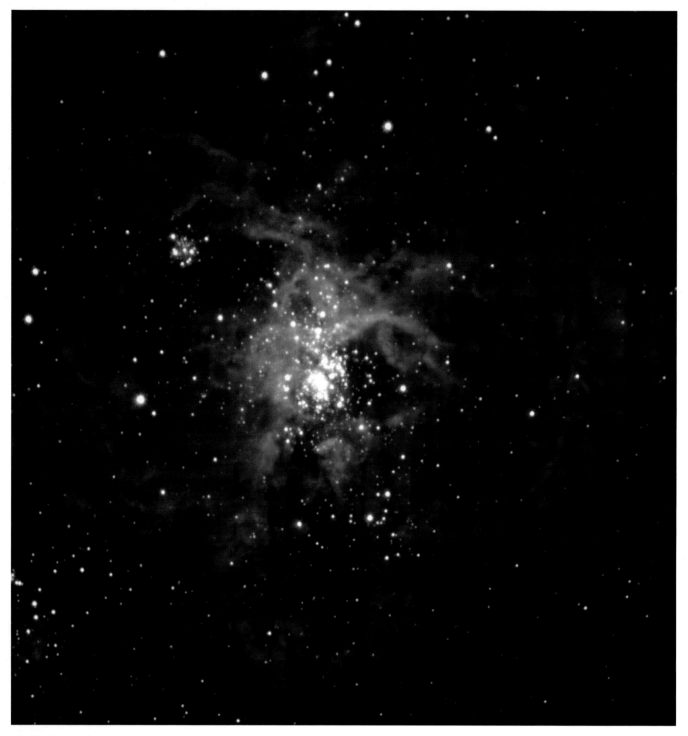

The Tarantula Nebula (NGC 2070), also known as 30 Doradonis, dominates our neighboring galaxy, the Large Magellanic Cloud. It is one of the largest and most powerful nebulae known, and its faintest extensions stretch over some 5,000 light years. This short-exposure, true-color photograph, taken with the 35-inch (0.9-m) telescope at the Cerro Tololo Inter-American Observatory in Chile, reveals the cluster of hot young stars at its center.

Large Magellanic Cloud and SN 1987a. On February 23, 1987, a little-known blue supergiant star called Sanduleak – 69° 202 blew up and became the most brilliant supernova in 400 years. For a time it rivalled the brilliance of the nearby Tarantula Nebula, as this photograph shows. The Tarantula is the diffuse pink object at the top right of the LMC. SN 1987a is the large, brilliant star immediately below it. The photograph was taken 5 weeks after the explosion, on March 29, by Australian astronomer, Robert McNaught. He used a 200-mm lens on a 6 × 7-cm Pentax; the exposure was 72.5 minutes at f/4 on Fuji 400 film.

DRACO/URSA MINOR

Draco, the Dragon, has been associated with a dragon in most western mythologies, and sometimes identified as the beast that guarded the golden apples of the garden of the Hesperides, and was killed by Hercules when he came to fetch the apples as his eleventh labor. In ancient Egyptian mythology, it was portrayed as either a hippopotamus or a crocodile.

Ursa Minor, the Little Bear, has existed for centuries, and it seems to have been formed by the Greek philosopher Thales in the 6th century BC to help mariners with their navigation.

Precession

Both Draco and Ursa Minor are important historically because of their association with the north celestial pole, a link which highlights the fact that the Earth is precessing in space. Precession is the apparent change in the position of the celestial pole with respect to the distant stellar background, and is caused by the gravitational interactions of the Sun and Moon with the Earth's equatorial bulge. In effect, the Earth "wobbles" like a spinning top, but with a complete rotation taking just under 26,000 years. This motion causes the positions of equinox to shift westward at a rate of 50.3 arcseconds per year.

Precession means that Polaris has only a temporary occupancy of the north celestial pole, a fact observed by the Greek astronomer Hipparchus around 150 BC. It will occupy this position again in 26,000 years time. In Egyptian times, Thuban (Alpha (α) Draconis) was the north polar star, then later on it was Kochab (Beta (β) Ursa Minoris). In the year 4000, the nearest star to the north pole will be Alrai (Gamma (γ) Cephei).

Because Thuban was the pole star in Egyptian times, it was important to the priests and pharaohs of the time, and was presumably revered as an object of worship. In this regard, it is sometimes said that the Great Pyramid of Cheops was built to align with Thuban, but modern measurements have called this into question because it is a few degrees "out".

Draco is a very large northern constellation, much of which is circumpolar (never setting) for observers above 30° northern latitude. It occupies the area north of Hercules, Lyra, and Cygnus. This places it above the north celestial pole for much of the night during the northern summer. Draco's head can easily be found, and is composed of a four-sided figure 10° north and a little west of zero-magnitude Vega in Lyra. The Dragon's coils enclose Ursa Minor which is the present location of the north pole star, Polaris. These constellations are grouped here for convenience. Ursa Minor is also known as the "Little Dipper" in the United States, but a clear dark night is needed to see its fainter stars. Polaris is at the end of the handle, with Beta (β) and Gamma (γ) representing the front of the bowl.

Draco

There are many doubles and multiple stars in Draco, which has 130 naked-eye stars according to the German astronomer Argelander in the last century. It also possesses one of the best planetary nebulae in the sky (NGC 6543). There are many galaxies, but only a few bright enough to be interesting in small telescopes. A few of the brighter doubles are: Eta (η), with 3rd- and 8th-magnitude stars at 4.7 arcseconds distance; 16 and 17 Draconis are a binocular pair of 5th magnitude, separated by 90 arcseconds, 17 itself has a 6th-magnitude companion 3.7 arcseconds away. Mu (μ) is a pair of equally bright, 5th-magnitude stars separated by 1.8 arcseconds, with a 13th-magnitude star 13 arcseconds away.

Among the galaxies in Draco, NGC 5907 stands out because of its 12 × 2 arcminute dimensions. It is an edge-on elliptical galaxy with dust lanes visible in large telescopes. The planetary

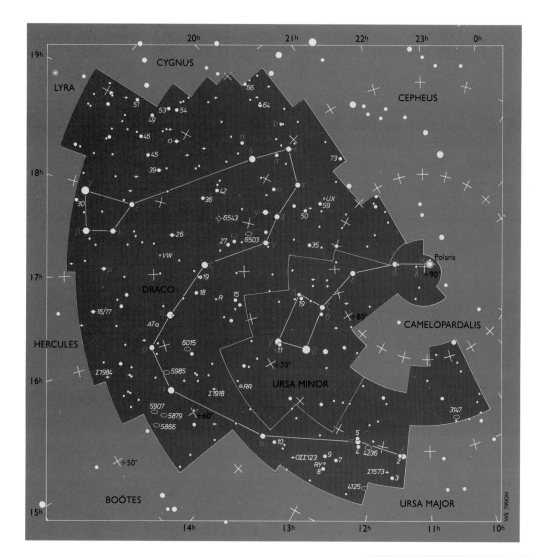

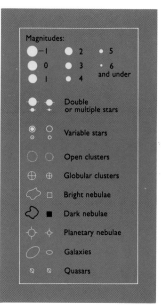

NGC 6543 appears as a vivid blue disk, of about 8th magnitude, and 18 arcseconds in diameter. There is fairly complex, but difficult to discern, internal structure, and a central star which can be seen with averted vision but not as easily directly.

Ursa Minor

Ursa Minor's telescopic interest is limited to the Cepheid-double Polaris. Polaris, the north pole star, is often thought by non-astronomers to be a bright, striking object, whereas in reality it is about 49th in rank of brightness — a fairly common, 2nd-magnitude yellow star. Polaris is within 50 arcminutes of the north celestial pole, and will continue to head towards it. In 2095 it will be at its closest, some 27 arcminutes away. The star is double, with an easily visible 9th-magnitude companion at 18 arcseconds distance. The companion is usually seen as bluish (spectral class F3), while Polaris is a spectroscopic double of F8, and slightly variable with the pulsations attributed to Cepheid variability. The star Kochab (Beta (β) Ursae Minoris) in the bowl of the Little Dipper is often mistaken for Polaris, and was in fact the star closest to the pole for the Greeks 3,000 years ago. It is of almost the same brightness and a little yellower than Polaris, and therefore can be seen a little easier than Polaris as the twilight gathers and telescopes are aligned with the pole.

TELESCOPIC OBJECTS IN DRACO
Double and Multiple Stars

Name	RA	Dec.	Separation (arcseconds)	Mags.		Year
Σ 1573	11h 49.2m	+67° 20'	11.2	7.6	8.6	1953
OΣΣ 123	13h 27.1m	+64° 44'	AB 68.9	6.7	7.0	1924
			BC 36.4	7.0	12.2	1960
Σ 1984	15h 51.2m	+52° 54'	AB 6.5	6.6	8.9	1944
			AC 17.1	6.6	12.8	1910
η (Eta)	16h 24.0m	+61° 31'	4.7	2.7	8.7	1974
16 + 17	16h 36.2m	+52° 55'	90.7	5.4	5.5	1908
17	16h 36.2m	+52° 55'	3.7	5.4	6.4	1958
μ (Mu)	17h 05.3m	+54° 28'	AB 1.8	5.7	5.7	1966
			AC 13.2	5.7	13.7	1958

Deep Sky Objects

Name	RA	Dec.	Type	Size	Mag.
NGC 4125	12h 08.1m	+65° 11'	Gal. E5p	5.1' × 3.2'	9.8
NGC 4236	12h 16.7m	+69° 28'	Gal. SB+	18.6' × 6.9'	9.6
NGC 5907	15h 15.9m	+56° 19'	Gal. Sb+	12.3' × 1.8'	10.4
NGC 6543	17h 58.6m	+66° 38'	Plan. Neb.	18"	8.8pg

ERIDANUS

TELESCOPIC OBJECTS IN ERIDANUS
Double and Multiple Stars

Name	RA	Dec.	Separation (arcseconds)	Mags.		Year
ρ	01h 39.8m	−56° 12'	10.4	5.8	5.8	1940
θ (Theta)	02h 58.2m	−40° 18'	8.2	3.4	4.5	1952
Jc 8	03h 12.4m	−44° 25'	AB 0.5	6.6	6.9	1944
			AB×C 3.5	6.6	8.9	1959
τ₄ (Tau 4)	03h 19.5m	−21° 45'	AB 5.7	3.7	9.2	1937
			AC 39.2	3.7	10.5	1955
			AD I 23.1	3.7	10.4	1879
			AE 130.0	3.7	10.4	1879
			AF 160.2	3.7	9.7	1880
f	03h 48.6m	−37° 37'	7.9	4.8	5.3	1957
32	03h 54.3m	−02° 57'	AB 6.8	4.8	6.1	1955
			AC I 65.8	4.8	11.4	1921
o₂ (Omicron 2) (40)	04h 15.2m	−07° 39'	AB 83.4	4.4	9.5	1970
			BC 7.6	9.5	11.2	1961

Deep Sky Objects

Name	RA	Dec.	Type	Size	Mag.
NGC 1187	03h 02.6m	−22° 32'	Gal. SBc	5.0' × 4.1'	10.9
NGC 1232	03h 09.8m	−20° 35'	Gal. Sc	7.8' × 6.9'	9.9
NGC 1300	03h 19.7m	−19° 25'	Gal. SBb	6.5' × 4.3'	10.4
NGC 1532	04h 12.1m	−32° 52'	Gal. Sb	5.6' × 1.8'	11.0
NGC 1535	04h 14.2m	−12° 44'	Plan. Neb.	18" × 44"	9.6pg
IC 2118	05h 06.9m	−07° 13'	Diff. Neb.	180' × 60'	....

Eridanus is one of the largest groups in the sky. It begins at the Equator, west of the top of Orion's Belt, and wanders southwest, gradually narrowing, until it ends at the brilliant star Achernar, at −57° declination. There are many small groupings along the looping progress of Eridanus, but no overall figure is apparent except for the curving path of relatively faint stars, which needs a dark night to trace southwards. Eridanus must be considered a late-fall constellation for northern observers, rising as it does before Orion by about an hour. Those living in the southern hemisphere regard it as a spring grouping, the seasons being the reverse of those in the north. The center of the constellation culminates at 10pm on December 10.

Achernar, the "End of the River" in Arabic, is of zero magnitude and the 9th brightest star in the sky. It is a blue giant star which lies about 120 light years distant in space. Only observers south of +30° north latitude are going to get a glimpse of Achernar, but those at the latitudes of southern Florida and Texas might see it in October, flashing low above the southern horizon. The star Epsilon (ε) which lies between Delta (δ) and Eta (η), is a K-type star which is the third nearest naked-eye star (after Alpha Centauri and Sirius). It's 10.7 light years away, and has an apparent magnitude of 3.73. Epsilon is a leading candidate for investigation by the Space Telescope for having planetary companions; in fact Pieter Van de Kamp at Sproul Observatory announced in 1973 that he had detected a companion with a mass of 0.05 of the Sun and a period of 25 years at 7.7 AU. This could be a Jupiter-like planet.

Multiple Stars

There are many fine double stars waiting to be seen in Eridanus.

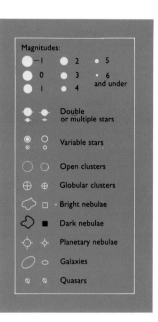

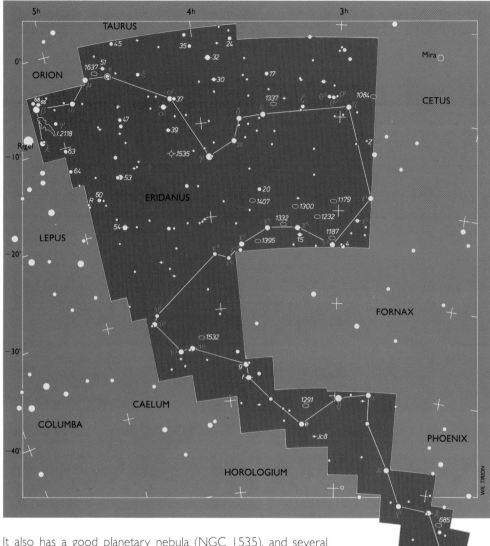

It also has a good planetary nebula (NGC 1535), and several galaxies, but most are small and relatively faint. There are no galactic or globular star clusters, and the only diffuse nebulae are two faint arcs which appear to be illuminated by Rigel in Orion.

Among the multiple stars one might hunt up is p Eridani, two yellow stars at only 21 light years' distance. It is a binary of 480 years' period, and can be split with virtually any telescope. Theta (θ) Eridani is one of the finest southern double stars, with two blue–white gems of 3rd and 4th magnitudes at an unchanging separation of 8.2 arcseconds. This is apparently a very long period binary at about 115 light years distance. Omicron 2 (o₂) Eridani, plotted as 40 Eridani on some atlases, consists of a wide double, the fainter star of which is itself a closer pair which is at its widest separation of about 10 arcseconds in 1990. This curious pair consists of two dwarf stars, one red and one white. Since the whole system is only 16 light years away, these sub-luminous stars are still relatively bright to us. The red component is unusually small, with a mass only 40 per cent that of the Sun. The white component is also tiny as stars go, only 17,000 miles in diameter! This star is the easiest white dwarf to see from the Earth, and like most of these collapsed objects has a density about 90,000 times greater than water. One cubic inch would weight almost 1½ tons here on Earth! We know that this

material is composed of atomic nuclei which have been compressed together by the enormous gravity of the object. The hydrogen and helium fuel of these stars has been used up so there is no internal radiation pushing the matter outwards. These are the compacted bodies of dying stars which will one day burn out completely, though they don't have the greater mass needed to ignite a supernova.

Deep Sky Objects

The planetary nebula NGC 1535 is one of the brighter examples of its type. It is about half an arcminute in diameter and of 9th magnitude, bluish in color. An 11th-magnitude central star is visible in larger instruments. Of the several galaxies in the table, NGC 1300 should be mentioned as an outstanding example of a barred spiral galaxy. This 11th-magnitude object has prominent arms which start at the ends of a (visually) faint bar protruding from the nucleus. Traces of the arms are visible with telescopes of 12-inch (30-cm) aperture and larger.

FORNAX/SCULPTOR/PHOENIX

Fornax, the Furnace, is a product of Lacaille's work of 1752, and presumably is a "Refiner's Fire" as mentioned in Handel's Messiah. Steel was a fairly recent development, and Lacaille wished to enshrine the furnace which made it possible in the firmament, along with the air pump or bellows, compass, octant, telescope, and other Industrial Revolutionary hardware.

Sculptor, the Sculptor, was originally named by Lacaille as the Sculptor's Workshop or Studio.

Phoenix was the mythical creature which, after being incinerated, grew again from its own ashes to fly away. It was promoted by Bayer in the 17th century.

The Fornax Cluster of galaxies is one of the nearest clusters, at a distance of 55 million light years. It contains numerous spiral, barred spiral, and elliptical galaxies of varying sizes. The photograph was taken with the 48-inch (1.2-m) UK Schmidt Telescope at the Anglo-Australian Observatory at Siding Spring, Australia.

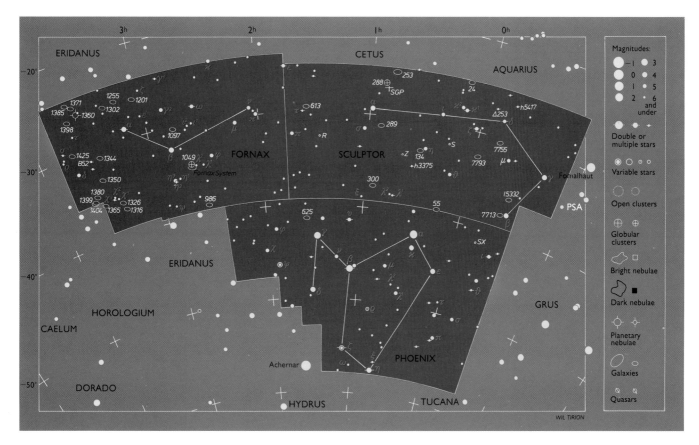

*F*ornax, Sculptor and Phoenix are grouped together here for convenience and are relatively modern southern star groups. They occupy a rather empty part of the sky as seen by the naked eye, but there are many galaxies for the telescopic observer. These are autumn constellations from the northern hemisphere, culminating in early November, low on the southern horizon. Much of Fornax is located within a bend of Eridanus, and its Alpha (α) is only of 4th magnitude. Sculptor immediately preceeds Fornax, and it too has a 4th-magnitude star as its Alpha. If you find the prominent star Beta (β) Ceti, Sculptor is the constellation just south of it. Phoenix's bright Alpha, 2.4 magnitude, marks the eye of the reincarnated bird. The north–south extent of this group is from −40° to −58° declination, so it is low or partially obscured for the majority of northern observers. Alpha Phoenicis lies almost straight south of Beta Ceti, at about −42°.

Fornax

Fornax contains a number of interesting galaxy systems which portray typical sizes and shapes for their distances. Closest is a member of the Local Group of galaxies, consisting of an elliptically shaped supercluster of stars. Known as the Fornax System, this dwarf galaxy contains several globular clusters which can be glimpsed with medium to large (10-inch (25-cm) aperture) instruments. NGC 1049 is the brightest individual member at 13th magnitude, and it is estimated that the whole group is about three times the distance to the Magellanic Clouds, or 600,000 light years.

A second grouping, but of galaxies, is found approximately 8–10 million light years away, still relatively close, galactically speak-

ing. It includes NGC 55 and NGC 253 in Sculptor, both of which are large spirals seen nearly edge-on. Both are good objects for amateur-sized telescopes.

Third, there is the Fornax Cluster of Galaxies, a concentrated grouping of 18 fairly bright and several smaller galaxies, clustered within a couple of degrees. Nine can easily be seen at once with a 1° field eyepiece on an 8-inch (20-cm) or larger telescope. NGC 1365 is one of the brighter members and is a beautiful barred spiral whose arms can be seen in a 12-inch (30-cm) or larger aperture. This is one of the brightest barred spirals in the sky (another being Messier 83). There is no satisfactory theory as to why some galaxies start their arms at the ends of straight "bars" unless the mechanism of rotation of the galaxy started after the bars came from the nuclear area. This would probably require some kind of encounter with another object some time in the past. NGC 1316 is another fairly bright elliptical about 11 minutes of RA west and a degree south of NGC 1365. It is a strong radio emitter, and is called Fornax A. The Fornax Cluster of galaxies is about 70 million light years distant.

Sculptor

Sculptor contains the south galactic pole, meaning the point through which a straight line would pass drawn at right angles to the galactic plane through the center of our Galaxy. The northern equivalent is in Coma Berenices. Several good galaxies dot the area, with the superb NGC 253 a fine object in any instrument from binoculars upwards. It appears as a thick streak in small binoculars, about half a degree long. In larger "astronomical" binoculars, some lumpiness can be seen, and in a telescope it has a mottled look. This is caused by dust silhouetted against the stars of the galaxy. There are several foreground stars as well. This is a late-type spiral system seen almost edgewise on, only about 7° from the exact edge-on position. Another large member of this South Galactic Pole Group is NGC 55, an irregular type galaxy which is also elongated and clumpy, appearing brighter at one end. I recently examined this object with a 22-inch (54-cm) f/8 reflector; it could be traced about 20 arcminutes in length, and some condensations were noted, along with a spot of obscuration near the nucleus. NGC 300 is another nearby galaxy, probably a member of the Local Group, and only about 3 million light years away. It is a spiral rather similar to Messier 33, in Triangulum, and has low surface brightness. In a 22-inch (55-cm) aperture telescope it appeared as a large smudge with a faint stellar nucleus, with several condensations (which are HII regions) in its diffuse arms. While you are in the area, you should look at the large and fairly rich globular cluster NGC 288. It can be found about one field south and a little east of NGC 253 (both can be seen at once in binoculars). It is well resolved with 8-inch (20-cm) or larger telescopes. Other galactic members of the Group are NGC 7793, NGC 247 in Cetus, and NGC 45. The average distance to these galaxies is about 7.6 million light years.

Phoenix

Phoenix is south of Sculptor and contains a few faint galaxies, NGC 625 being the best of them. It is seen almost edge-on and appears as an elliptical cloud brighter toward the center. Beta (β) Phoenicis is a fine double star, which Hartung says is widening. It is made up of two yellow stars, both of 4th magnitude. Zeta (ζ) is an interesting triple system, since A is a spectroscopic eclipsing binary of 1.47 days' period.

TELESCOPIC OBJECTS IN FORNAX
Double Stars

Name	RA	Dec.	Separation (arcseconds)	Mags.		Year
ω (Omega)	02h 33.8m	−28° 14′	10.8	5.0	7.7	1952
α (Alpha)	03h 12.1m	−28° 59′	1.9 (1963)	4.0	7.0	1959
B52	03h 33.9m	−31° 05′	0.2 (1965)	6.8	7.1	1960

Deep Sky Objects

Name	RA	Dec.	Type	Size	Mag.
Fornax System	02h 39.9m	−34° 32′	Gal. dE3	20′ × 13.8′	9+
NGC 1049	02h 39.7m	−34° 17′	Glob. Cl.	24″	13
NGC 1316	03h 22.7m	−37° 12′	Gal. SB0p	7.1′ × 5.5′	8.8
NGC 1360	03h 33.3m	−25° 51′	Plan. Neb	6.5′	11?
NGC 1365	03h 33.6m	−36° 08′	Gal. SBb	9.8′ × 5.5′	9.5
NGC 1398	03h 38.9m	−26° 20′	Gal. SBb	2.5′ × 2.3′	9.7

TELESCOPIC OBJECTS IN SCULPTOR
Double Stars

Name	RA	Dec.	Separation (arcseconds)	Mags.		Year
h5417	23h 44.5m	−26° 15′	8.5	6.3	9.0	1952
Δ 253	23h 54.4m	−27° 03′	6.6	6.9	7.5	1950
κ₁ (Kappa 1)	00h 09.3m	−27° 59′	1.4	6.1	6.2	1954
h3375	00h 33.7m	−35° 00′	5.3	6.6	8.4	1954
λ₁ (Lambda 1)	00h 42.7m	−38° 28′	0.7	6.7	7.0	1954
τ (Tau)	01h 36.1m	−29° 54′	1.1	6.0	7.1	1959

Deep Sky Objects

Name	RA	Dec.	Type	Size	Mag.
NGC 24	00h 09.9m	−24° 58′	Gal. Sb	5.5′ × 1.6′	11.5
NGC 55	00h 14.9m	−39° 11′	Gal. SBm	32.4′ × 6.5′	8.22
NGC 134	00h 30.4m	−33° 15′	Gal. SBb+	8.1′ × 2.6′	10.1
NGC 253	00h 47.6m	−25° 17′	Gal. Scp	25.1′ × 7.4′	7
NGC 288	00h 52.8m	−26° 35′	Glob. Cl	14′	8.1
NGC 300	00h 54.9m	−37° 41′	Gal. Sd	20.0′ × 14.8′	8.7
NGC 7793	23h 57.8m	−32° 35′	Gal. Sdm	9.1′ × 6′	9.5

TELESCOPIC OBJECTS IN PHOENIX
Double and Multiple Stars

Name	RA	Dec.	Separation (arcseconds)	Mags.		Year
β (Beta)	01h 06.1m	−46° 43′	1.4	4.0	4.2	1954
ζ (Zeta)	01h 08.4m	−55° 15′	AB 0.8	4.1	6.9	1949
			AB × C 6.4	4	6.9	1953

Deep Sky Objects

Name	RA	Dec.	Type	Size	Mag.
NGC 625	01h 35.1m	−41° 26′	Gal. SBm	3.0′ × 1.3′	12.3

Spiral galaxy NGC 253 is about half the size of our own Milky Way galaxy but is just as massive and four times brighter. It is the largest member of the Sculptor group of galaxies, some 10 million light years away. This true-color photograph, taken with the 154-inch (3.9-m) Anglo-Australian Telescope, contrasts the yellow glow from the galaxy's center with the dusty blue of the spiral arms.

Gemini

Gemini, the twins has been associated with the stars Castor and Pollux since ancient times. The Romans identified the Twins with Romulus and Remus, the brothers who traditionally founded Rome. In Greek mythology they were the sons of Leda, born of the same egg (see Cygnus), but of separate mortal and divine fathers. Poseidon made them the protectors of sailors, and they were associated with the St Elmo's fire (ball-lightning static discharges) that sometimes played among sailing ships' rigging. They are also attributed the opposing principles of war (Castor) and peace (Pollux), or at least activity and repose.

Eta Geminorum and IC 443.
Eta (η) is the star at the bottom right of this picture. IC 443 is apparently an ancient supernova remnant. It consists of an arc of cloud at top left and fainter wisps scattered across the area. The photograph was taken by California amateur Chuck Edmonds with a 16-inch (40 cm), f/5.5 Newtonian telescope. Exposure was one hour on hypered Kodak 2415 film.

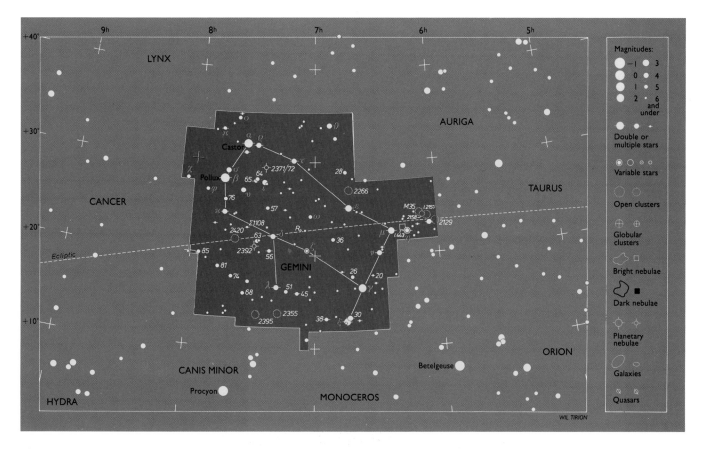

Gemini is an important constellation in the winter sky and is the third constellation of the ancient zodiac. It is east of Taurus and south of Auriga. Gemini's base is traversed by the Milky Way and contains several interesting clusters and nebulae. It is one of the few constellations to possess two 1st-magnitude stars marking the heads of the two twins, who are drawn with right and left arms entwined with their other hands held outwards from their bodies. Gemini is the radiant point for a very good meteor shower which is at its best on December 12. It is also the constellation in which the planet Pluto was discovered by Clyde Tombaugh in January 1930.

Castor and Pollux

Castor, the warrior and horseman, is the major stellar attraction in Gemini. It is a system rather than a star, because each of the three major components is itself a close pair. In the telescope, Castor resolves into two brilliant points, opening in distance since they were closest in 1968 at about 2 arcseconds separation. There is a third star composed of a close pair of red-dwarf suns, which are in a huge orbit taking them around the brighter stars in about 10,000 years. Castor AB, the brighter pair, are spectroscopic doubles. A has two stars which take 9.2128 days to complete a revolution about their center of gravity. B's two stars take 2.9283 days to revolve. These values were obtained by observing the Doppler shifts in each star's spectra – and, in fact, they can only be detected spectroscopically, as they are too close to be resolved with even the largest telescopes. The Castor family is about 45 light years from the Sun.

Pollux, the boxer, is about 4.5 degrees southeast of Castor, and shines at magnitude 1.16. It is a golden color, with a

spectrum classed as K0. This means it has a surface temperature of 4,500K, a little cooler than the Sun (5,200K). Pollux is 35 light years away, about four times the Sun's diameter and 35 times as luminous.

Multiple Stars

The Twins extend eastward from a fairly rich section of the Milky Way, and therefore contain many doubles and multiples, as well as a bright planetary nebula (NGC 2392), a supernova remnant (IC 443), and one of the best open clusters in the whole sky, M35. Eta (η) is one of the more outstanding doubles, a close 3rd- and 8th-magnitude pair whose primary star is a red-giant variable with a 233-day period and amplitude of about 1 magnitude. 20 Geminorum is an easy 20 arcsecond double of 6th and 7th magnitudes; Epsilon (ε) is of 3rd magnitude with a 9th-magnitude companion 110 arcseconds distant. 38 Geminorum has nicely contrasting colors at an easy 7 arcseconds separation; Zeta (ζ), whose primary star is a cepheid variable, has two companions at 87 and 97 arcseconds distance. Delta (δ) is a binary pair of 3rd and 8th magnitudes at 6.3 arcseconds distance. The dimmer star is a K-type dwarf and the bright star an F0, so there is a color contrast.

Deep Sky Objects

Two contrasting galactic clusters appear in one wide-field view (30 arcminutes) in western Gemini. These are the small, condensed, almost globular-looking NGC 2158, which is visible through the outside fringes of M35, an outstanding and large object. M35 (NGC 2168) can be glimpsed with the naked eye on a fine night, just at the toe of the more northern Twin, 2.5°

northwest of Eta (η) Geminorum. This glorious grouping of several hundred stars has many loops and lines of stellar points in a medium-sized telescope. The diameter is about 30 arcminutes, and the cluster lies at about 2,800 light years' distance. NGC 2158, the small outlying cluster – which looks very much like a globular – is in fact classified somewhere between open and globular by Arp and others. It is about six times further away than M35, at about 16,000 light years. This object remains unresolved in up to 16-inch (40-cm) aperture telescopes due to the faintness of the individual stars (16th magnitude and fainter). Nearby, this pair of clusters is the primarily photographic object, IC 443. It is between, and just above, a line running from Mu (μ) to Eta (η) Geminorum. Long-exposure photographs show a cirrus-like, curved cloud resembling the Veil Nebula in Cygnus. I have just managed a glimpse of this object in a 16-inch (40-cm) f/5.5 instrument with a nebular filter, which makes the sky darker behind the nebula. This appears to be a supernova remnant of considerable age, and there are smaller shards of nebulosity scattered throughout the area.

The Eskimo Nebula

The other outstanding telescopic object in Gemini is a planetary nebula (NGC 2392) called the Eskimo, or Clown Face, Nebula. It is a bright disk about 40 arcseconds in diameter near a 9th-magnitude star. Even a small telescope (under 6-inch (15-cm) aperture) will show it as a small greenish ball with slightly fuzzy edges. An 8-inch (20-cm) aperture will begin to show that the disk is surrounded by another ring or shell, which becomes conspicuous in a 16-inch (40-cm) and larger 'scope. This is the fur parka around the Eskimo's face. The central star, which is easy to see at 9th magnitude, is sometimes identified with the Eskimo's nose. Detail within the bright inner disk is complicated and made difficult to see by the presence of the central star. The distance to these concentric puffs of atmosphere blown off by the central star is variously listed as 3,000 to 10,000 light years.

Looking at stars

Much of the population today will have to travel some distance to enjoy what our fathers could see from their porch or window. I remember how, when I started doing astronomy in the early 1950s, my parents would drive me to a school at the edge of the city with my small telescope, and leave me until 11 or 12 o'clock. It was dark enough to see the constellations and for me to get a lot out of my 3-inch (7.5-cm) refractor. But since the advent of mercury vapor streetlamps, at about that time, the amateur astronomer has had to go further and further from home to attain those dark skies. Therefore we have had to make portability an important part of any consideration in astronomical equipment. I have settled upon a two-telescope strategy, since I am able to have one at home mounted and ready at any time, even with my highly light-polluted sky, and another for travelling to set up out of the car. Actually I have a third instrument, in our club's observatory, which is located in a dark sky observatory with a roll-off roof, which I can use about once a month.

The progression a beginner follows often goes something like this: good observing of many objects can be had with a good pair of binoculars, so if one is a little tentative and doesn't want to make a big investment, this is a good way to get one's feet wet. 7 × 50 or larger binoculars (remember that the first figure is the power, the second the aperture in millimetres), will be an investment which can still be used later after a telescope is acquired. There are also the "astronomical" binoculars, requiring a tripod, of 70 mm and larger aperture, which can be considered as a serious instrument, especially for variable-star observers who like to check many fields a night. The first telescope can be any size today, from a 3-inch (75 or 80-mm) refractor up to a 10-inch (25-cm) simply mounted Newtonian.

TELESCOPIC OBJECTS IN GEMINI
Double and Multiple Stars

Name	RA	Dec.	Separation (arcseconds)	Mags.		Year
η (Eta)	06h 14.9m	+22° 30'	1.4	3.3var	8	1958
20	06h 32.3m	+17° 47'	20.0	6.3	6.9	1956
ε (Epsilon)	06h 43.9m	+25° 08'	110.3	3.0	9.0	1925
38	06h 54.6m	+13° 11'	7	4.7	7.7	1976
ζ (Zeta)	07h 04.1m	+20° 34'	AB 87.0	3.8	10.5	1924
			AC 96.5	3.8	8.0	1925
λ (Lambda)	07h 18.1m	+16° 32'	9.6	3.6	10.7	1953
δ (Delta)	07h 20.1m	+21° 59'	6.3	3.5	8.2	1954
Σ 1108	07h 32.8m	+22° 53'	11.5	6.5	8.3	1934
α (Alpha) (Castor)	07h 34.6m	+31° 53'	AB 1.8	1.9	2.9	1964
			AC 72.5	1.9	8.8	1955

Deep Sky Objects

Name	RA	Dec.	Type	Size	Mag.
NGC 2158	06h 07.5m	+24° 06'	Open Cl.	5'	8.6
M35 (NGC 2168)	06h 08.9m	+24° 20'	Open Cl.	28'	5.1
IC 443	06h 16.9h	+22° 47'	SNRem.	50' × 40'	....
NGC 2371-2	07h 25.6m	+29° 29'	Plan. Neb.	>55"	13
NGC 2392	07h 29.2h	+20° 55'	Plan. Neb.	44"	9.9

NGC 2174 and M35. This tricolor photograph by the Reverend Ronald Royer shows the western end of Gemini. The nebula right of center is NGC 2174 in Orion. Directly north of it is the open cluster M35 (NGC 2168). The two bright stars in the upper half of the picture are Mu (μ) (left) and Eta (η) Geminorum. The nebulosity between them is IC 443.

GRUS/PISCIS AUSTRINUS

Grus is a medium-sized constellation in the southern sky, easily located south of 1st-magnitude Fomalhaut, which is the Alpha (α) of Piscis Austrinus, also included here for convenience. Both are fall figures for the northern hemisphere, being south of Aquarius and Capricornus. First find Fomalhaut, at the mouth of the southern fish, a bright white star in the south which culminates at 10pm on September 25. Directly south, if you are at a low enough latitude, will be the bright stars Alpha (α) and Beta (β) Gruis. From the Orange County Astronomers' observatory at + 33° 40' these stars skim the low hill to the south which protrudes about 4°above the horizon.

Grus

Grus and Piscis Austrinus occupy a somewhat star-poor section of the sky, but both contain a few doubles and there are many galaxies scattered about. The galaxies tend to cluster, and there is a good collection of them in Grus which are easily seen: NGC 7582, 7590, 7599. All are located at about −42°, so they can only be seen to best advantage by southern observers. Pi 1 (π₁) and Pi 2 (π₂) is a binocular double star, with an orange irregular variable of magnitude 6.6 and a brighter F0 star about 4 arcminutes apart. Each has a small, faint companion which a 6-inch (15-cm) aperture telescope should show. Δ246 is a fine pair of yellowish stars good for small apertures. Δ249 is a double of blue–white stars of spectral class A5.

Several galaxies which are easy for smaller telescopes dot the region. NGC 7213 is found just 16 arcminutes southeast of Alpha (α) Gruis and is a round glow, brighter at the center. We are seeing the nuclear region of a face-on spiral galaxy of low surface brightness, so the arms are too faint for most amateur-sized telescopes. IC 5201 is also a faint object, but much closer to us, and is a barred spiral 8 × 4 arcminutes in size. NGC 7410 is also seen edge-on, showing a cigar-shape and being fairly bright. NGC 7582, 7590 and 7599, mentioned above, are at the center of a small cluster of galaxies which also includes NGC 7552, about 30 arcminutes west and south of the three.

Piscis Austrinus

Piscis Austrinus, the Southern Fish, is a small group just north of Grus and south of Aquarius. The mouth of the fish is the bright star Fomalhaut (pronounced foe-mal-ought). This is the destination of the stream of water being poured by Aquarius as shown on old star charts. It has a few doubles and another grouping of galaxies which can all be seen in a wide-field telescope eyepiece.

Fomalhaut is of spectral class A, about 23 light years distant, and about 14 times more luminous than the Sun. Another star in the constellation is perhaps more interesting, Lacaille 9352. Located at 23h 06m RA, −35°52' Dec. at a distance of 11.7 light years, it displays a relatively fast proper motion across the sky. The star travels an apparent distance equal to the width of the Moon in only 260 years. This is equivalent to 6.9 arcseconds per year, making it the fourth fastest proper motion in the sky. You can see the movement relative to other stars nearby in a year or so. If you can photograph the star with a telescope with a focal length of 80 inches (2 metres) or more it will be easy to see the motion in a year between photos. This 8th-magnitude star is a relatively nearby 11.9 light years distant. It is easily found just over 1° south of the star Pi (π) Piscis Austrinus.

There are several galaxies in Piscis Austrinus that are worth finding. Three are grouped together in a trio: NGC 7172, 7173,

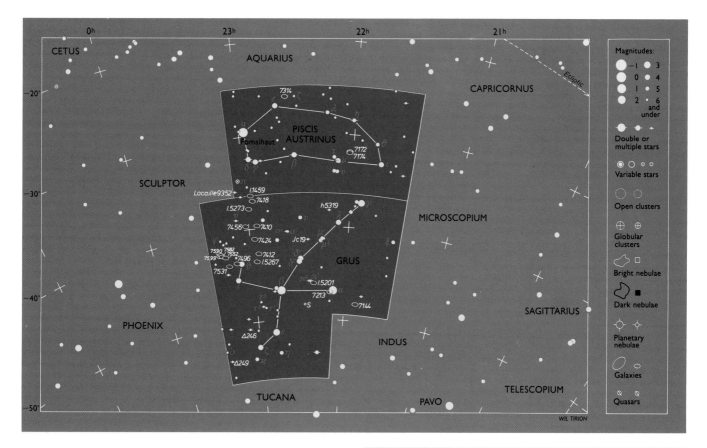

and 7176. NGC 7314 is an 11th-magnitude spiral galaxy seen in three-quarters view, with no easily discerned nucleus. As usual, aperture is the key to making galaxies more interesting: the larger the better!

The Main Sequence

Once the fires of nuclear fusion have been ignited at the cores of stars, they have their temperatures and luminosities prescribed by their masses, and these define the "main sequence" which shows the relationship between brightness and spectral class. Large white stars like Fomalhaut, which is 13 times as luminous as the Sun, are in spectral class O and sit at the top of the sequence. Below them come B, A, F, G, K and M stars in decreasing order of temperature. B stars are bluish, A stars are blue-white, F are white, G are yellow-white, like our Sun, K stars are orange, and red stars like Betelgeuse in Orion are the coolest. Stars maintain their colors as they burn in position on the main sequence for millions of years until, as their nuclear fuel is used up, they begin the series of changes that will eventually lead to their demise.

A Hertzsprung-Russell (HR) diagram is any graph on which a parameter measuring stellar brightness is plotted against a parameter related to a star's surface temperature. Commonly the plot would be of absolute magnitude against spectral class, though alternative plots may be of apparent magnitude or luminosity against color index or surface temperature. A plot of stars on an HR diagram shows that the majority lie on the main sequence.

TELESCOPIC OBJECTS IN GRUS
Double and Multiple Stars

Name	RA	Dec.	Separation (arcseconds)	Mags.		Year
h5319	22h 12.0m	−38° 18′	2.1	7.6	7.7	1955
π₁ (Pi 1)·	22h 22.7m	−45° 57′	2.7	6.6	10.8	1956
π₂ (Pi 2)	22h 23.1m	−45° 56′	4.6	5.8	11.3	1953
Jc 19	22h 24.7m	−41° 26′	24.8	6.7	8.4	1952
υ (Upsilon)	23h 06.9m	−38° 54′	1.1	5.7	8.0	1948
θ (Theta)	23h 06.9m	−43° 31′	AB 1.1	4.5	7.0	1959
			AC 160	4.5	8.1	1959
Δ 246	23h 07.2m	−50° 41′	8.6	6.1	6.8	1952
Δ 249	23h 23.9m	−53° 49′	26.5	6.5	7.3	1951

Deep Sky Objects

Name	RA	Dec.	Type	Size	Mag.
NGC 7213	22h 09.3m	−47° 10′	Gal. Sa	1.9′ × 1.8′	10.4
IC 5201	22h 21.4m	−46° 04′	Gal. SBc	8.5′ × 4.3′	11.3
NGC 7410	22h 55.0m	−39° 40′	Gal. SBa	5.5′ × 2.0′	10.4
NGC 7424	22h 57.3m	−41° 04′	Gal. SBc	7.6′ × 6.8′	11b
NGC 7582	23h 18.4m	−42° 22′	Gal. SBb−	4.6′ × 2.2′	10.6
NGC 7590	23h 18.9m	−42° 14′	Gal. Sb+	2.7′ × 1.1′	11.6
NGC 7599	23h 19.3m	−42° 15′	Gal. Sc	4.4′ × 1.5′	11.4

TELESCOPIC OBJECTS IN PISCIS AUSTRINUS
Double Stars

Name	RA	Dec.	Separation (arcseconds)	Mags.		Year
η (Eta)	22h 00.8m	−28° 27′	1.7	5.8	6.8	1955
β (Beta)	22h 31.5m	−32° 21′	30.3	4.4	7.9	1952
γ (Gamma)	22h 52.5m	−32° 53′	4.2	4.5	8.0	1957

Deep Sky Objects

Name	RA	Dec.	Type	Size	Mag.
NGC 7172	22h 02.0m	−31° 52′	Gal. S	2.2′ × 1.3′	11.9
NGC 7314	22h 35.8m	−26° 03′	Gal. Sc	4.6′ × 2.3′	10.9

HERCULES

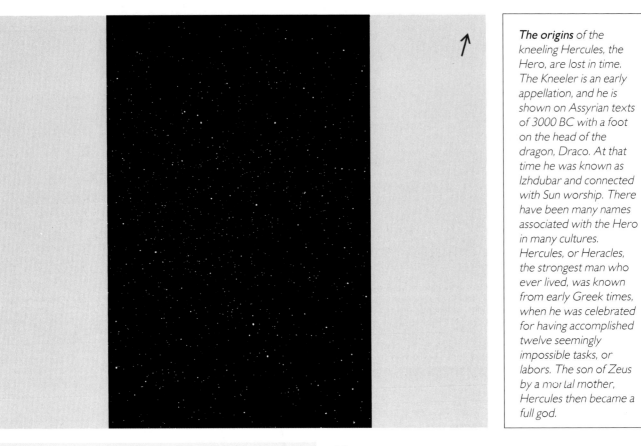

TELESCOPIC OBJECTS IN HERCULES
Double and Multiple Stars

Name	RA	Dec.		Separation (arcseconds)	Mags.		Year
κ (Kappa)	16h 08.1m	+17° 03'		28.4	5.3	6.5	1958
γ (Gamma)	16h 21.9m	+19° 09'		41.6	3.8	9.8	1938
ζ (Zeta)	16h 41.3m	+31° 36'		1.4	2.9	5.5	1961
α (Alpha)	17h 14.6m	+14° 23'		4.7	3.5	5.4	1968
δ (Delta)	17h 15.0m	+24° 50'		8.9	3.1	8.2	1958
ρ (Rho)	17h 23.7m	+37° 09'		4.1	4.6	5.6	1958
μ (Mu)	17h 46.5m	+27° 43'	AB	33.8	3.4	10.1	1970
			BC	1.8		10.6	1990
95	18h 01.5m	+21° 36'		6.3	5.0	5.1	1974
100	18h 07.8m	+26° 06'		14.2	5.9	6.0	1955

Deep Sky Objects

Name	RA	Dec.	Type	Size	Mag.
IC 4593	16h 12.2m	+12° 04'	Plan. Neb.	12/120"	10.9
M13 (NGC 6205)	16h 41.7m	+36° 28'	Glob. Cl.	16.6'	5.9
NGC 6210	16h 44.5m	+23° 49'	Plan. Neb.	>14"	9.3pg
NGC 6229	16h 47.0m	+47° 32'	Glob. Cl.	4.5'	9.4
M92 (NGC 6341)	17h 17.1m	+43° 18'	Glob. Cl.	11.2'	6.5

*H*ercules is an important spring and summer constellation. It is located between Draco and Ophiuchus to the south, and Lyra and Corona Borealis to the east and west, respectively. The kneeling figure is relatively easy to trace, but most people probably see him as a butterfly, as I do. This seems somehow easier to imagine when the figure is rising, or at least east of the meridian. Later in the summer, he seems to go upside down when dropping in the west. Hercules has many fine telescopic objects, including probably the best northern globular cluster (M13), and a couple of good planetaries (IC 4593 and NGC 6210).

Deep Sky Objects
The globular cluster M13 (NGC 6205) in Hercules is one of the finest in the sky, ranking behind Omega Centauri and 47 Tucanae (both southern objects) as most deep sky observers' favorite cluster. For northern observers, M13 has the advantage of passing almost directly overhead, and therefore being seen at its best. It can be seen by the naked eye quite easily from a dark observing site, and almost any optical aid will show a fuzzy ball making a flat triangle with two 7th-magnitude stars. The cluster begins to resolve with as small an instrument as a 4-inch (10-cm) aperture, and is truly magnificent in a 10-inch (25-cm) or larger. The ragged edges contrast with a smooth transition to a compressed, nuclear spot. Three famous dark "lanes" also become visible, and are little more than areas where there happen to be less stars. They form a "Y"-shaped pattern, meeting south-east of the core. The brain has a tendency to make them appear linear in shape, and, once they are recognized, it is hard to forget them!

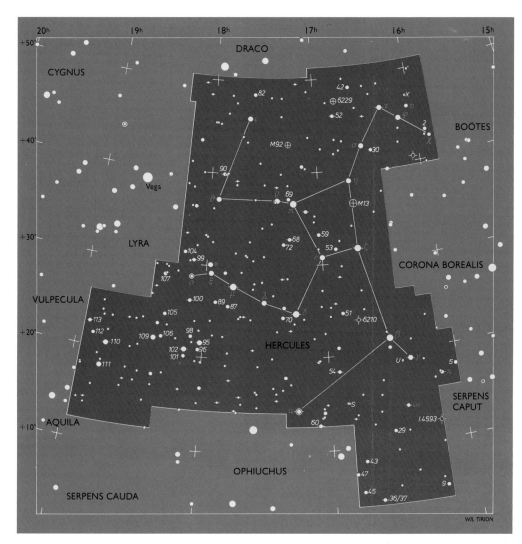

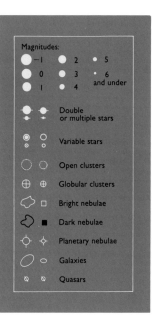

The cluster is about 24,000 light years distant, so we are seeing only the brighter stars at apparent magnitudes in the range 10–15. Remember that at the distance of M13, the Sun would appear at magnitude 19.3. The evolution of globular clusters is unexplained.

Another excellent globular cluster in Hercules is M92 (NGC 6341). It is a little more concentrated in the center than M13, smaller, and a bit less rich, yet it is well worth finding. The use of higher-power eyepieces will bring out fainter stars owing to the sky-darkening effect of the magnification. As with any object with fine structure, a night of good atmospheric steadiness and seeing conditions will allow fainter stars to be seen. NGC 6210 is a bright but small planetary nebula some 16 arcseconds by 20 arcseconds in size, a bright blue color, with a 12th-magnitude central star. Hercules contains a wonderful rich cluster of galaxies which are too faint for visual observation in anything smaller than a 16-inch (40-cm) 'scope. However, the proliferation of 20-inch (50-cm) and larger telescopes will easily allow amateurs to observe these 17th-magnitude and fainter galaxies. A famous photograph taken with the Palomar 200-inch (5-metre) telescope shows dozens of galaxies of all types in a 1° circle centered on RA 16h 05m and Dec. + 17° 45°.

M13. Photographs don't really do globular clusters any justice, since their inner areas almost inevitably "burn out" or appear overexposed. The eye easily sees the brighter core as individual stars, and to accompany the text I have chosen a photograph of M13, which approximates the visual experience with a medium to large telescope.

HOROLOGIUM/RETICULUM

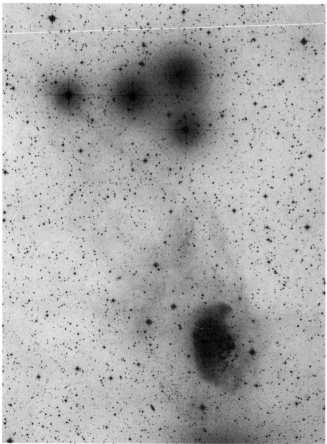

Horologium and Reticulum are small and inconspicuous southern-hemisphere constellations. The Reticle, or Net, supposedly commemorates the eyepiece cross hair system Lacaille used in his southern-sky observations from Cape Town in the 1740s. Horologium can be found in the southern spring and summer sky, a faint line of stars running from 4th-magnitude Alpha (α) Horologii southwest almost to Achernar in Eridanus, which it runs parallel to. Reticulum is a southern circumpolar grouping which lies almost at the half-way point of a line between Canopus and Achernar, near the Large Magellanic Cloud. It is marked by a wide rhombus of fairly bright stars (3rd and 4th magnitudes).

Horologium

Horologium lies in the star-poor region of sky outside the Milky Way and contains only a few objects for the telescope user. Δ7 is a nice double, with the color contrast coming with A and K spectral classes, and an easily resolved 36 arcseconds apart. Δ10 is another color-contrasting pair. There is one interesting globu-

NGC 1313 (bottom right) is seen as a relatively ordinary barred spiral galaxy in short-exposure photographs, but in this high-contrast negative print of a long-exposure picture, the normal parts of the galaxy are lost in the burnt-out image. The picture was made to bring out the remarkable "tail" of faint extensions that stretches almost half-way up the picture. The actual limits of NGC 1313 are hard to determine, and the nature of the galaxy's faint extensions is unknown. The photograph was taken with the 48-inch (1.2-m) UK Schmidt Telescope in Australia.

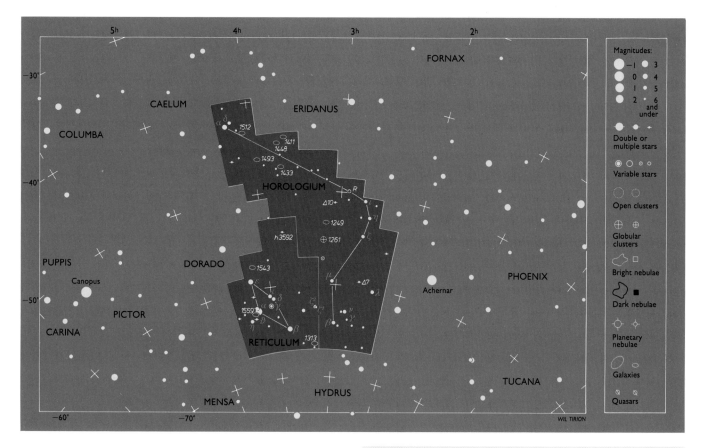

lar cluster in Horologium, NGC 1261, which is a small globe of faint stars in a 12-inch (30-cm) telescope. It is quite distant at about 70,000 light years. NGC 1433, not too far away, is a good example of a low-surface-brightness barred spiral, about 7 arcminutes in diameter, with a small bright nucleus. One more galaxy is worth finding, NGC 1448, a nearly edge-on spiral which is 8 arcminutes long and only 1 arcminute wide. These galaxies are of 10th and 11th magnitude.

Reticulum

Reticulum boasts few double stars with only Theta (θ) standing out, although Zeta (ζ) is composed of two bright yellow stars slightly over 5 arcminutes apart. They make a good test for visual acuity, being at the resolution limit of most unaided eyes, but are a little faint.

Supernova in NGC 1313

There is another large – but faint – barred spiral in Reticulum, NGC 1313. It is 8.5 by 6.5 arcminutes in extent, with hints of arms at the end of a fuzzy, linear nucleus. A 10th-magnitude supernova erupted here in 1962, proving the galaxy's relative nearness because supernovae can be used as a rough distance indicator. Supernovae all have approximately similar absolute magnitudes within the classes I or II, so their brightness can be used to estimate their distance, and thus the distance of the galaxies which contain them.

NGC 1559 is a high-surface-brightness (and somewhat edge-on) barred spiral, which is smoothly brighter toward the middle.

TELESCOPIC OBJECTS IN HOROLOGIUM
Double Stars

Name	RA	Dec.	Separation (arcseconds)	Mags.		Year
Δ 7	02h 39.7m	−59° 34′	36.6	7.2	7.5	1953
Δ 10	03h 04.6m	−51° 19′	38.2	7.5	8.8	1916

Deep Sky Objects

Name	RA	Dec.	Type	Size	Mag.
NGC 1261	03h 12.3m	−55° 13′	Glob. Cl	6.9′	8.4
NGC 1433	03h 42.0m	−47° 13′	Gal. SBa	6.8′ × 6.0′	10
NGC 1448	03h 44.5m	−44° 39′	Gal. Sc	8.1′ × 1.8′	11.3

TELESCOPIC OBJECTS IN RETICULUM
Double Stars

Name	RA	Dec.	Separation (arcseconds)	Mags.		Year
ζ (Zeta)	03h 18.2m	−62° 30′	310	5.2	5.5	1952
h3592	03h 44.6m	−54° 16′	5.2	6.4	9.0	1951
θ (Theta)	04h 17.7m	−63° 15′	4.1	6.2	8.2	1943

Deep Sky Objects

Name	RA	Dec.	Type	Size	Mag.
NGC 1313	03h 18.3m	−66° 30′	Gal. SBd	8.5′ × 6.6′	9.4
NGC 1559	04h 17.6m	−62° 47′	Gal. SBc	3.3′ × 2.1′	10.45

HYDRA

M83 (NGC 5236) is a face-on spiral galaxy that has roughly the same mass and brightness as the Milky Way. Although it appears flat, radio maps have shown that its gas extends beyond the visible spiral arms, with one side curling slightly towards us and the other curling away. M83 is also known for its frequent supernovae, which occur every 10–15 years. The picture has been computer-colored from original black-and-white photographs by Dr Jean Lorre.

Hydra is the largest constellation in the sky and extends for nearly 95°, or 6 hours of RA. The Snake's head, which marks the start of the constellation, is located 18° east of Procyon (about a fist's width at arm's length), and zig-zags eastward and south to the tail, just south of Libra. It is therefore a spring constellation which starts in the winter and ends in summer. When Corvus is on the meridian, the whole of Hydra stretches from the western to almost the eastern horizon. There are many double and multiple stars, as might be expected, and quite a lot of deep sky objects. Many of Hydra's stars are fairly bright, but they are so scattered that a star map or atlas is needed to trace the figure.

Alpha (α) Hydrae is a conspicuous object occupying a relatively empty area following the brilliance of the winter Milky Way. Its name, Alphard, meaning "the Solitary One", is quite appropriate. It is almost exactly 2nd magnitude (1.97), and seems redder than its K3 spectral type would indicate. Known also as Cor Hydrae, the Hydra's heart, it is about 110 light years distant.

Deep Sky Objects

Some of the many doubles and multiples are listed below but none are showpiece objects. There are, however, several deep sky wonders which should be described, starting at the western head of Hydra and progressing eastward down the body of the snake. M48 is a fine open cluster situated on the outskirts of the Galaxy, at the western border of the constellation. It makes an equilateral triangle with Procyon and the small asterism at the head of Hydra. This group of about 50 stars can be seen as a tiny spot with the naked eye, and presents a lovely field in a low-power eyepiece. There are several yellowish stars seen together with mostly white ones, making a beautiful impression. The

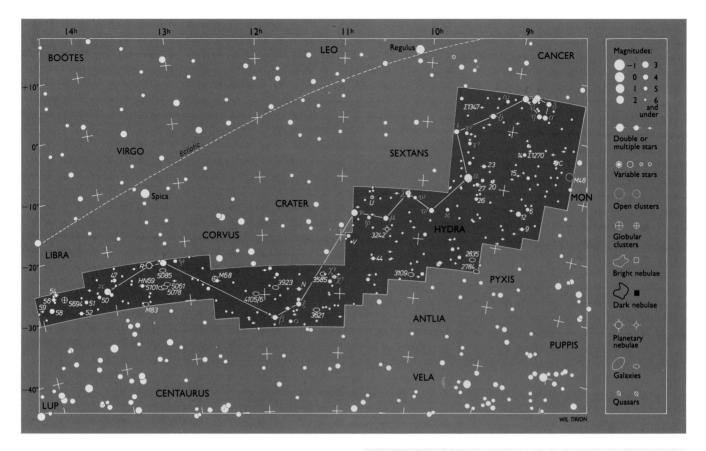

cluster is about 1,500 light years distance, so most of the brighter stars must be quite luminous to appear so bright to us.

NGC 3109 is a large irregular galaxy which must be relatively nearby, as its giant stars are well-resolved in photographs. It appears as an 11-arcminute-long haze in a 10-inch (25-cm) telescope. Also in Hydra is one of the sky's brightest planetary nebulae, NGC 3242, known as the Ghost of Jupiter Nebula. It is found less than 2° south of Mu (μ) and contains an easily seen central star. An instrument with a 10-inch (25-cm) or larger aperture will show some detail in the eye-like shells which surround the star. This planetary exhibits the common blue–green color caused by ionized oxygen, but in a color photograph it shows pink tinges as well. The nebula is at least 2,000 light years away, at which distance the outer round shell is about 0.6 light year in diameter. NGC 4105 and 4106 are intereacting galaxies which are tidally distorted. M68 (NGC 4590) is a globular cluster which resolves in a good 6-inch (15-cm) telescope. There are many faint stars of about the same brightness in swirling patterns in this rich cluster.

M83 (NGC 5236) is a fine example of a nearby face-on spiral galaxy, which is sometimes classified as a barred spiral. It is one of the few in which the arms and the bar can be seen in amateur-sized telescopes. A 12-inch (30-cm) aperture will show a bright nucleus with a roundish glow, upon which two faint arms are superimposed. A third arm has more diffuse structure, but can be detected. There are several stars seen against the galaxy, and the observer should check for any that "don't belong", as four supernovae have appeared in this galaxy over the past 60 years. M83 is about 20 million light years away, according to the 1988 Royal Canadian Astronomical Society *Observer's Handbook*.

TELESCOPIC OBJECTS IN HYDRA
Double and Multiple Stars

Name	RA	Dec.	Separation (arcseconds)	Mags.		Year
Σ 1270	08h 45.3m	−02° 36′	4.7	6.4	7.4	1955
ε (Epsilon)	08h 46.8m	+06° 25′	0.3	3.8	4.7	1968
			AB×C 2.8	3.8	6.8	1976
			AB×D 19.2	3.8	12.4	1938
			AB×E 336	3.8	10.0	1921
			AB×F 424	3.8	10.1	1921
15	08h 51.6m	−07° 11′	AB 0.9	5.6	8.6	1958
			AC 45.7	5.6	9.6	1924
			AD 51.9	5.6	10.7	1924
Σ 1347	09h 23.3m	+03° 30′	21.2	7.3	8.6	1937
N	11h 32.3m	−29° 16′	9.1	6	6	1952
β (Beta)	11h 52.9m	−33° 54′	0.9	4.7	5.5	1959
HN 69 (S651)	13h 36.8m	−26° 30′	10.1	5.9	6.8	1953
54	14h 46.0m	−25° 27′	8.6	5.1	7.1	1954
59	14h 58.7m	−27° 39′	0.8	6.3	6.6	1953

Deep Sky Objects

Name	RA	Dec.	Type	Size	Mag.
M48 (NGC 2548)	08h 13.8m	−05° 48′	Open Cl.	54′	5.8
NGC 2835	09h 17.9m	−22° 21′	Gal. Sp.	6.3′ × 4.4′	11.1
NGC 3109	10h 03.1m	−26° 09′	Gal. Irr	14.5′ × 3.5′	10.36
NGC 3242	10h 24.8m	−18° 38′	Plan. Neb	16″	8.6
NGC 4105	12h 06.7m	−29° 46′	Gal. E2	2.4′ × 1.9′	12
NGC 4106	12h 06.8m	−29° 46′	Gal. E0	1.9′ × 1.5′	11.3
M68 (NGC 4590)	12h 39.5m	−26° 45′	Glob. Cl	12′	8.2
M83 (NGC 5236)	13h 37.0m	−29° 52′	Gal. SBd	11.2′ × 10.2′	8.2
NGC 5694	14h 39.6m	−26° 32′	Glob. Cl	3.6′	10.2

HYDRUS/TUCANA

Both Hydrus, the Little Snake and Tucana, the Toucan, were introduced by Johann Bayer in his atlas of 1603. The Water Snake and the Toucan were newly found creatures from the interior of South America at the time, so Bayer celebrated their discovery with constellation names. The Toucan was alternately named the American Goose, but this was eventually discarded permanently by the 1880s. The SMC is also known as the Lesser Cloud, or by its Latin equivalent, Nubecula Minor, and is sometimes accorded separate constellation stature along with the LMC, Nubecula Major.

*T*hese medium-sized southern constellations are grouped together for convenience. Hydrus is chiefly recognized by the large triangle made by the stars Alpha (α), Beta (β) and Gamma (γ), all 3rd-magnitude stars. Alpha is only 3.5° south of brilliant Achernar in Eridanus, and is actually a distant binary companion. The constellation lies south of Eridanus and ends near the southern celestial pole. Tucana is also a small south circumpolar constellation, which is noted for containing the Small Magellanic Cloud (SMC), companion to the Large Magellanic Cloud (LMC), both of which are the nearest external galaxies to our own Milky Way. There is also the second largest and brightest globular cluster in the sky here, 47 Tucanae (NGC 104). Both of these constellations are invisible to northern viewers, but for southern hemisphere observers the SMC culminates at 10 pm about 1 November.

Hydrus

In Hydrus, the only deep sky object of interest is a small diffuse nebula, NGC 602. This object is a small but fairly bright cloud which is irregularly divided by dust. Most authors feel it is a nebula associated with the Small Magellanic Cloud galaxy. One double stands out because it has a colour contrast, h3568. The brighter star is yellow, with a fainter blue–white companion.

Tucana

Tucana has several excellent doubles. Delta (δ) Tucanae is a bright white star and has a small 9th-magnitude companion, an easy 7 arcseconds distant. Beta (β) is composed of two bright stars, and has an interesting field. There is also another bright star in the area, the 5th-magnitude CPD 52, 10 arcminutes to the

southeast. This star, also known as Beta 3 (β₃), is a very close double, as is Beta 2 (β₂). Therefore this system (since they all share the same proper motion) is probably a multiple one. Kappa (κ) is another fine double, stars of 5th and 7th magnitude at 5.4 arcseconds. In that field is Innes 27, a 1-arcsecond double of 8th-magnitude components. This 81-year-period binary shares the same proper motion as Kappa, and may be in orbit around their center of gravity.

The cluster 47 Tucanae (NGC 104) is undoubtedly the second best globular cluster in the heavens after Omega Centauri. With any aperture over 4 inches (10cm), it is a bright ball of stars, strongly concentrated in the middle. I first observed it in a 10.1-inch (25-cm) at Omerama in New Zealand in 1986, and it was a wonderful experience. The cluster is earily visible to the naked eye just next to the SMC (it is in the foreground, only about one-tenth of the distance to that galaxy) and looks like a slightly fuzzy star. Another globular which appears on the edge of the SMC is NGC 362, a "normal" globular cluster of about 9th magnitude (integrated) with stars from 13 fainter.

The Small Magellanic Cloud (SMC) is an irregular companion to the Large Magellanic Cloud (LMC) (see Dorado). These are both our Milky Way Galaxy's companions in space, the LMC about 180,000 light years away, and the SMC a bit beyond that at 195,000 light years. The small cloud appears as a fuzzy elongated patch between Achernar and the south celestial pole. The photograph was taken by Massachusetts amateur Dennis di Cicco with a Schmidt camera, a 10-minute exposure, and Fuji 400D film. The bright object below the SMC is the giant globular star cluster 47 Tucanae (NGC 104).

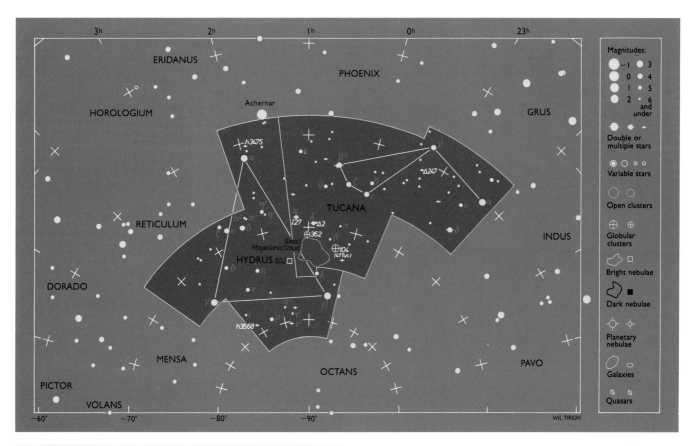

Magnitudes:

Symbol	Mag
●	−1
●	0
●	1
●	2
•	3
•	4
·	5
·	6 and under

Double or multiple stars

Variable stars

Open clusters

Globular clusters

Bright nebulae

Dark nebulae

Planetary nebulae

Galaxies

Quasars

WIL TIRION

TELESCOPIC OBJECTS IN HYDRUS
Double Stars

Name	RA	Dec.	Separation (arcseconds)	Mags.		Year
h3475	01h 55.3m	−60° 19′	2.4	7.1	7.3	1964
h3568	03h 07.5m	−78° 59′	15.2	5.6	9.3	1939

Deep Sky Objects

Name	RA	Dec.	Type	Size	Mag.
NGC 602	01h 29.6m	−73° 33′	Diff. Neb.	1.5′ × 0.7′	9?

TELESCOPIC OBJECTS IN TUCANA
Double and Multiple Stars

Name	RA	Dec.	Separation (arcseconds)		Mags.		Year
δ (Delta)	22h 27.3m	−64° 58′		6.9	4.5	9.0	1928
Δ 247	23h 18.0m	−61° 00′		46.6	6.7	7.8	1959
β₁ (Beta 1)(A)	00h 31.5m	−61° 58′	AB	2.4	4.4	13.5	1932
β₂ (Beta 2)(C)			AC	27.1	4.4	4.8	1952
Δ 2	00h 52.4m	−69° 30′		20.7	6.5	7.9	1952
κ (Kappa)	01h 15.8m	−68° 53′	AB	5.4	5.1	7.3	1954
			A×CD	319.3	5.1	7.8	1898
I 27			CD	1.0	7.8	8.2	1926

Deep Sky Objects

Name	RA	Dec.	Type	Size	Mag.
47 (NGC 104)	00h 24.1m	−72° 05′	Glob. Cl.	30.9′	4.0
SMC (NGC 292)	00h 52.7m	−72° 50′	Gal. Irr.	280′ × 160′	2.3
NGC 362	01h 03.2m	−70° 51′	Glob. Cl.	12.9′	9.0

INDUS/PAVO/TELESCOPIUM

Indus, the Indian, was raised to the sky by Johann Bayer in his 1603 star atlas, the famous Uranometria. *The figure was no doubt inspired by the native North and South Americans brought back to Europe by explorers to be shown off at around this time.*
Pavo, the Peacock, was also originated by Bayer and introduced in the Uranometria; *in Greek mythology it was to her favourite bird, the peacock, that Hera gave the hundred eyes of her servant, the giant Argus, after his murder by Hermes.*
Telescopium, the Telescope, was introduced by Nicolas Louis de Lacaille in 1752.

Pavo 5 cluster. This false-color optical picture of the Pavo 5 cluster of galaxies has been computer-enhanced to bring out the faint and tenuous halos of gas that surround the galaxies and link them together. The galaxies are the contoured, predominantly pink objects; their halos are portrayed in blue.

The southern circumpolar constellations, Indus, Pavo and Telescopium, are grouped together for convenience. They have no conspicuous figures, although Pavo has several fairly bright stars. They can all be considered as southern spring constellations, as they culminate in early September at 10 pm. Pavo is the only one of the three that has a star pattern that can be imagined fairly easily — as a bird, which appears to stand on the ground at culmination. The beak is Eta (η), the eye is Pi (π) or Nu (ν), the chest is Kappa (κ), the feet are Zeta (ζ) and Epsilon (ε) and the tail feathers Beta (β) and Gamma (γ) and are crowned by Alpha (α), a 2nd-magnitude white star. These constellations are quite distant from the plane of the Milky Way, so we might expect double stars and galaxies to predominate among the telescopic objects.

Indus

In Indus, only the double star Theta (θ) is notable, although Hd 296 is listed as a test object; it is a binary with a 29-year period.

Pavo

Pavo has an interesting object, NGC 6744, a large (15 × 10 arcminute) barred spiral galaxy, which must be fairly close by to appear so large. It is, however, a low-surface-brightness object and therefore only the nuclear area is seen in common telescopes. In apertures from 10-inch up (25-cm) it becomes more interesting because it has many HII regions and OB star associations in its arms, and these can be seen with this aperture and larger scopes. The extent of the graceful arms may be traced by these small groupings for about 180° in each arm, especially to the north of the nucleus. There is one excellent

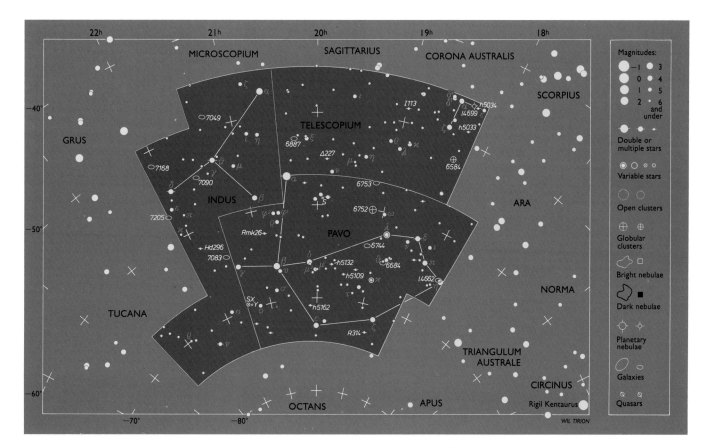

globular cluster in Pavo, NGC 6752, which has been described as "one of the gems of the sky". It is a large (15-arcminutes) condensed globular cluster, with stars from 11th-magnitude which a 3-inch (7.5-cm) aperture telescope will show under good conditions. Look for a double star of magnitudes 7.7 and 9.3 separated by 3 arcseconds within the outer stars of the cluster.

Telescopium

Telescopium has many small and rather faint galaxies, a loosely condensed globular cluster (NGC 6584), and a small planetary nebula (IC 4699). Dunlop (Δ) 227 is an excellent double star for small apertures, with an orange and white star 23 arcseconds away. Telescopium's alpha (α), delta (δ), epsilon (ε), zeta (ζ) asterism may be seen at top left in the constellation photograph of Ara on page 22.

TELESCOPIC OBJECTS IN INDUS
Double Stars

Name	RA	Dec.	Separation (arcseconds)	Mags.		Year
θ (Theta)	21h 19.9m	−53° 27′	6.0	4.5	7.0	1957
Hd 296	21h 55.2m	−61° 53′	0.3	6.6	6.7	1945

Deep Sky Objects

Name	RA	Dec.	Type	Size	Mag.
IC 4699	18h 18.5m	−45° 59′	Plan. Neb.	<10″	11.9 pg
NGC 7090	21h 36.5m	−54° 33′	Gal. SBc	7.1′ × 1.4′	11.1
NGC 7205	22h 08.5m	−57° 25′	Gal. Sb+	4.3′ × 2.2′	11.38

TELESCOPIC OBJECTS IN PAVO
Double and Multiple Stars

Name	RA	Dec.	Separation (arcseconds)	Mags.		Year
ξ (Xi)	18h 23.2m	−61° 30′	3.3	4.4	8.6	1955
R 314	18h 49.7m	−73° 00′	1.9	6.3	8.3	1947
h5109	19h 29.8m	−67° 18′	AB 24.7	7.7	9.5	1940
			AC 36.4	7.7	10.0	1940
h5132	19h 44.0m	−66° 18′	21.5	7.7	10.0	1916
h5162	20h 07.9m	−70° 49′	6.7	8.0	10.5	1917
Rmk 26	20h 51.6m	−62° 26′	2.3	6.5	6.5	1959

Deep Sky Objects

Name	RA	Dec.	Type	Size	Mag.
IC 4662	17h 47.1m	−64° 38′	Gal. Irr.+	2.2′ × 1.4′	11.43
NGC 6744	19h 09.8m	−63° 51′	Gal. SBb+	15.5′ × 10.2′	9.03
NGC 6752	19h 10.9m	−59° 59′	Glob. Cl.	20.4′	5.4
NGC 6753	19h 11.4m	−57° 03′	Gal. Sb	2.5′ × 2.2′	12

TELESCOPIC OBJECTS IN TELESCOPIUM
Double and Multiple Stars

Name	RA	Dec.	Separation (arcseconds)	Mags.		Year
h5033	18h 15.4m	−48° 51′	AB 17.3	6.8	10.8	1913
			AC 18.2	6.8	12.2	1913
			AD 27.9	6.8	10.7	1913
h5034	18h 16.2m	−46° 02′	2.4	7.5	8.8	1959
I 113	18h 58.9m	−48° 30′	3.0	6.7	10.5	1948
Δ 227	19h 52.6m	−54° 58′	22.9	6.1	6.8	1952

Deep Sky Objects

Name	RA	Dec.	Type	Size	Mag.
NGC 6584	18h 18.6m	−52° 13′	Glob. Cl.	7.9′	9.2
NGC 6887	20h 17.2m	−52° 47′	Gal. Sb+	4.1′ × 1.7′	12.46

LACERTA

Lacerta is a small northern constellation located between Cygnus and Andromeda. Its upper half is immersed in the fairly rich Milky Way, and the lower half has many rather faint stars. The only recognizable figure here is the zig-zag line of stars forming a "W" on its side, made up of 4th-magnitude stars. You can find it by looking almost halfway between Deneb in Cygnus and the "W" figure of Cassiopeia. This means that Lacerta is a late summer/early fall figure. It culminates almost exactly overhead at 10 pm on October 1.

Lacerta contains a number of quite nice doubles and a couple of triple stars, as might be expected of a constellation near to the Milky Way. They are detailed in the table below. It has several open or galactic clusters, most of them small and not very rich in stars.

Deep Sky Objects

NGC 7209 is a fairly concentrated galactic cluster and is made up of several dozen stars from 8th- to 11th-magnitude. NGC 7243 is another galactic cluster of about 40 stars, which includes the triple Struve (Σ) 2890 consisting of a pair of magnitude 8.5 stars separated by 9.4 arcseconds, and another of magnitude 9.5 some 73 arcseconds away. There is a small but fairly bright planetary nebula, IC 5217, which is elliptical and must be found either with a high-power eyepiece or by the use of a small, low-dispersion prism held up to the eyepiece. The nebula shows a single Oxygen II image (green), while normal stars show a continuum streak. A deep sky filter will also detect a planetary. It dims the stars considerably while allowing the nebular light through. If you move the filter in and out above the eyepiece then the stars will change brightness considerably, while the planetary will stay about the same. This assumes the filter is made to allow the OII emission through. Some "light pollution" filters will remove it, and with this type of filter planetaries will generally dim more than the stars. IC 5217 is only about 6 × 8 arcseconds in size, and appears greenish.

BL Lacertae

Another interesting object in Lacerta is a challenge to owners of even large amateur 'scopes: the variable galaxy BL Lacertae. It changes brightness in fairly small time periods from 14th to about 17th magnitude. The fact that a whole galaxy (actually we are probably only seeing the nucleus) can change brightness in such short periods means that the region of activity must be fairly small. Yet the galaxy is very far away, so whatever is happening must be extremely energetic. Each such quasi-stellar object (QSO for short) is probably "powered" by a huge black hole with an accretion disk surrounding it. The hole is literally eating its host galaxy, and the variations in brightness which are observed (it is a radio source too) are the emissions produced when matter (whole stars, probably) is destroyed as it is sucked into the maw of the enormous gravitational field near the singularity at the core of the black hole. A finder chart for BL is given for the adventurous.

BL Lacertae finder chart. The quasi-stellar object varies from about 14th magnitude to about 17th on an irregular time scale.

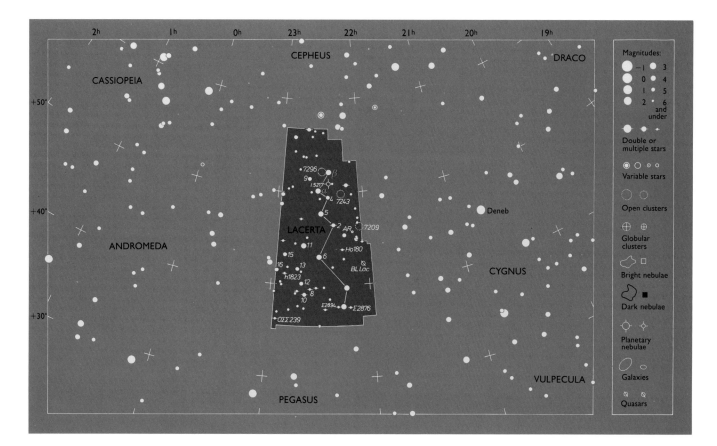

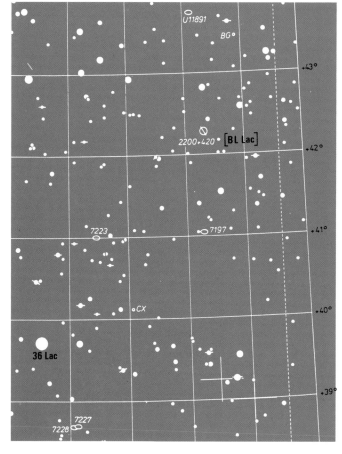

TELESCOPIC OBJECTS IN LACERTA
Double and Multiple Stars

Name	RA	Dec.	Separation (arcseconds)	Mags.		Year
Σ 2876	22h 12.0m	+37° 39'	11.8	7.8	9.3	1931
Ho 180	22h 15.7m	+43° 54'	0.7	8.2	8.2	1959
Σ 2894	22h 18.9m	+37° 46'	AB 15.6	6.1	8.3	1955
			AC 43.7	6.1	13.0	1905
			AD 221.7	6.1	9.4	1918
			BD 206.6	8.3	9.4	1918
8	22h 35.9m	+39° 38'	AB 22.4	5.7	6.5	1969
			AC 48.8	5.7	10.5	1956
			AD 81.8	5.7	9.3	1968
			AE 336.6	5.7	7.8	1968
10	22h 39.3m	+39° 03'	62.3	4.9	8.4	1974
h1823	22h 51.8m	+41° 19'	AB 19.2	7.1	12.8	1921
			AC 82.1	7.1	8.8	1923
			AE 118.3	7.1	9.2	1921
OΣΣ 239	22h 55.7m	+36° 21'	51.0	5.6	9.5	1923

Deep Sky Objects

Name	RA	Dec.	Type	Size	Mag.
BL	22h 02.7m	+42° 16' 40"	QSO	<1'	14.7
NGC 7209	22h 05.2m	+46° 30'	Gal. Cl.	25'	6.7
NGC 7243	22h 15.3m	+49° 53'	Gal. Cl.	21'	6.4
IC 5217	22h 23.9m	+50° 58'	Plan. Neb.	6" × 8"	12.6pg

*T*he large and important zodiacal constellation of Leo and the smaller Leo Minor and Sextans are all grouped together here for photographic convenience. Leo is composed of two easily found figures, the famous "sickle" or backwards question-mark, with 1st-magnitude Regulus (Alpha (α) Leonis) at the bottom, and a triangle or trapezoid (if you include iota (ι)), with 2nd-magnitude Denebola (Beta (β) Leonis) at the eastern end. Regulus is located almost on the ecliptic, and therefore solar system objects regularly pass close to it. My first ever published photo was of Jupiter "passing" Regulus. I shot film on three different nights, sandwiched the negatives in register, and printed a photo showing three Jupiters against the starfield with Regulus prominent. Eventually all the solar system objects including the Sun and Moon will pass nearby or occult (pass in front of) Regulus.

This constellation is a spring group, culminating at 10 pm on April 1. Leo Minor is a small grouping of faint stars above the sickle, while Sextans is directly below Regulus and has only a few naked-eye stars. This whole area lies on the western edge of the Ursa Major–Coma–Virgo cloud of galaxies, and there are dozens of galaxies worth finding in the three star groups. There are few clusters and planetaries. Double stars are present, with the beautiful Gamma (γ) Leonis leading their number.

Double Stars

Gamma (γ) is also known as Algeiba, the Lion's Mane. The sickle figure represents the neck and head of the lion, with Regulus or "Cor Leonis" the heart of Leo. Algeiba consists of two orange-yellow stars of 2nd and 3rd magnitudes, adding together to almost exactly 2nd magnitude. Currently the distance apart is about 4.4 arcseconds, almost as wide as this binary gets. It has a period of about 618 years and is still widening. Because of their orange color, these stars are observable against clear blue sky in the daytime. The easiest way to do this is to observe in the winter months, when Leo is coming up in the east as dawn proceeds. Find the pair when it's still dark and, assuming you have a motor-driven mount, follow it as it gets light. With a medium-power eyepiece, you should be able to see it after sunrise. If you do this in December, Gamma will be right on the meridian as the Sun rises. Another way to find objects in daylight involves offsetting with your setting circles from an easily visible object such as Venus, the Moon or the Sun. Here you find the coordinates of the bright object in the American Ephemeris or other source, set the 'scope on that object and set your circles for those numbers. **Be very careful when observing the Sun: never look at it directly through telescopes! Even using setting circles, keep the end cap in position to avoid damage to the optics.** To observe Algeiba, move the 'scope to the RA and Dec. values given in the table. When the circles indicate those coordinates, the star should be in your low-power field. Iota (ι) Leonis, as well as 54 and 90 Leonis, are interesting double stars in Leo.

Deep Sky Objects in Leo

These constellations have many galaxies which are outstanding examples of their various types. Starting with Leo, I will describe objects from west to east, in ascending Right Ascension, then consider Leo Minor and Sextans separately. NGC 2903 is a large, bright galaxy, so much so that one wonders how Messier missed it. It is easily found just off the "tip" of the sickle. Move the telescope about 2.5° west of Epsilon (ε), and you come upon 4th-magnitude Lambda (λ). Lock the RA axis and move south in

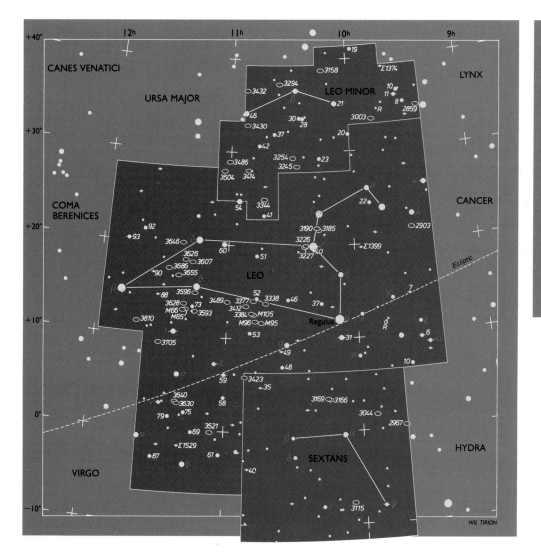

declination about 1.5° and you'll see the galaxy making a pretty right-angled triangle with two 7th-magnitude stars. The larger the telescope, the larger the galaxy will appear. 'Scopes up to 8 inches (20cm) will show an elliptical fuzz of light which is brighter in the center. Larger telescopes start to hint at more detail, with a brighter nucleus and faint mottlings indicating dust lanes between the spiral arms. Two more galaxies which are easy to find are NGC 3226 and NGC 3227.

Messier objects M95 and M96 (NGC 3351 and 3368 respectively) form a loose pair in the midst of the Lion's body. M95 is a barred spiral which looks like the Greek letter theta (θ) in photographs. The bar is visually faint, only being suspected in a 16-inch (40-cm) aperture telescope. M96 is a larger, brighter object, a nice threequarter-view spiral with a dust lane separating one of the arms from the nucleus. Nearby is M105 (NGC 3379), a fairly bright elliptical which is a fuzz ball, brighter towards the center. It is in a group which includes NGC 3384. One of the better spiral galaxies with Sb classification in the Hubble system is NGC 3521. It is an 8.9-magnitude spiral which we are seeing only about 20° from edge-on. In the telescope we see the nucleus appearing offset, with the closer spiral arms showing as a haze with the nucleus brighter and east (following).

The galaxy showpiece objects in Leo are M65 and M66, which form a trio with NGC 3628. M65 and M66 are both spiral galaxies, with M65 being similar in type to NGC 3521, i.e. an early spiral type with many dusty arms. Photographs show a strong band of dust around the edge of the visible portion, and dust lanes in the disk itself. M66 has arms that are among the most easily seen of all galaxies: two prominent arms are faintly seen in a 10-inch (25-cm) and very easily seen in a 16-inch (40-cm). Both of these bright galaxies can be seen in a low-power field. Just one field north lies NGC 3628, an edge-on spiral with an almost central dust lane which is obvious in a 12-inch (30-cm) aperture telescope. These galaxies are at about 37 million light years distance, somewhat closer than the bulk of the Coma-Virgo cluster.

Leo Minor

Leo Minor contains many small and faint galaxies within its borders. There are several edge-on examples here, notably NGC 3003, which is 5 arcminutes long, and NGC 3432, another object which is edge-on, covering 6 × 1 arcminutes in extent. There are also two face-on spirals, which are large but of low surface brightness. NGC 3344 and NGC 3486. There is also a small cluster of galaxies here, centered around NGC 3158.

Sextans

Sextans contains many small galaxies as well, with only one being of interest, NGC 3115. This is a transitional object between the elliptical and spiral form, seen edge-on. In the telescope we see a cigar-shaped object with rounded ends, unlike its photograph which shows sharp ends. It is much brighter down the middle with no apparent dust. Sextans may be seen photographically in the constellation shot for Hydra.

TELESCOPIC OBJECTS IN LEO
Double and Multiple Stars

Name	RA	Dec.	Separation (arcseconds)	Mags.		Year
7	09h 35.9m	+14° 23′	41.2	6.2	10.0	1946
Σ 1399	09h 57.0m	+19° 46′	30.3	7.7	9.6	1958
α (Alpha) (Regulus)	10h 08.4m	+11° 58′	176.9	1.4	7.7	1924
γ (Gamma) (Algeiba)	10h 20.0m	+19° 51′	4.4	2.2	3.5	1976
49 (TX)	10h 35.0m	+08° 39′	2.4	5.8	8.5	1971
54	10h 55.6m	+24° 49′	6.5	4.5	6.3	1958
Σ 1529	11h 19.4m	−01° 39′	9.6	7.0	8.0	1955
ι (Iota)	11h 23.9m	+10° 32′	1.0 (1962)	4.0	6.7	1962
τ (Tau)	11h 27.9m	+02° 51′	91.1	5.1	8.0	1932
88	11h 31.7m	+14° 22′	15.4	6.4	8.4	1958
90	11h 34.7m	+16° 48′	AB 3.3	6.0	7.3	1958
			AC 63.1		8.7	1938
			BC 64.6	8.7	9	1938
93	11h 48.0m	+20° 13′	74.3	4.5	9.6	1925

Deep Sky Objects

Name	RA	Dec.	Type	Size	Mag.
NGC 2903	09h 32.2m	+21° 30′	Gal. Sb I	12.6′ × 6.6′	8.9
NGC 3185	10h 17.6m	+21° 41′	Gal. SBb	2.3′ × 1.6′	12.2
NGC 3226	10h 23.4m	+19° 54′	Gal. E2	2.8′ × 2.5′	11.4
NGC 3227	10h 23.5m	+19° 52′	Gal. Sb	5.6′ × 4.0′	10.8
M95 (NGC 3351)	10h 44.0m	+11° 42′	Gal. SBb	7.4′ × 5.1′	9.7
M96 (NGC 3368)	10h 46.8m	+11° 49′	Gal. Sbp	7.1′ × 5.1′	9.2
M105 (NGC 3379)	10h 47.8m	+12° 35′	Gal. E1	4.5′ × 4.0′	9.3
NGC 3521	11h 05.8m	−00° 02′	Gal. Sb+	9.5′ × 5.0′	8.9
M65 (NGC 3623)	11h 18.9m	+13° 05′	Gal. Sb	10.0′ × 3.3′	9.3
M66 (NGC 3627)	11h 20.2m	+12° 59′	Gal. Sb	8.7′ × 4.4′	9.0
NGC 3628	11h 20.3m	+13° 63′	Gal. Sb	14.8′ × 3.6′	9.5

TELESCOPIC OBJECTS IN LEO MINOR
Double Stars

Name	RA	Dec.	Separation (arcseconds)	Mags.		Year
Σ 1374	09h 41.4m	+38° 57′	2.9	7.3	8.6	1976

Deep Sky Objects

Name	RA	Dec.	Type	Size	Mag.
NGC 2859	09h 24.3m	+34° 31′	Gal. SBa	4.8′ × 4.2′	10.7
NGC 3003	09h 48.6m	+33° 25′	Gal. SBc	5.9′ × 1.7′	11.7
NGC 3158	10h 13.8m	+38° 46′	Gal. E2	2.3′ × 2.1′	11.8
NGC 3344	10h 43.5m	+24° 55′	Gal. Sc	6.9′ × 6.5′	10.0
NGC 3432	10h 52.5m	+36° 37′	Gal. SBm	6.2′ × 1.4′	11.3
NGC 3486	11h 00.4m	+28° 58′	Gal. Sc	6.9′ × 5.4′	10.3

TELESCOPIC OBJECTS IN SEXTANS
Double Stars

Name	RA	Dec.	Separation (arcseconds)	Mags.		Year
35	10h 43.3m	+04° 45′	6.8	6.3	7.4	1958
40	10h 49.3m	−04° 01′	2.2	7.0	7.8	1958

Deep Sky Objects

Name	RA	Dec.	Type	Size	Mag.
NGC 3044	09h 53.7m	+01° 35′	Gal. Sc	4.8′ × 0.9′	12.0
NGC 3115	10h 05.2m	−07° 43′	Gal. E6/S0	8.3′ × 3.2′	9.2

Wolf 359

The star Wolf 359 should be mentioned in any discussion of the constellation of Leo. Wolf 359 is the third nearest star to us, at a distance of 7.75 light years. This is a faint, low-luminosity red-dwarf star, with a visual magnitude of 13.5. It is located 1.4° northwest of 5th-magnitude 59 Leonis. (The star is plotted on the *Uranometria* 2000, chart 190). This neighbor of the solar system has the rapid proper motion of 4.71 arcseconds per year in position angle 235°. It is a cool, red star having a diameter similar to that of Jupiter (86,000 miles, or 142,800 kilometres). At the standard distance of 10 parsecs (32.6 light years), it would appear at 16.65 magnitude.

Galaxies M65, M66 and NGC 3628 can all be seen in this true-color photograph. M65 (NGC 3623) is at bottom left and M66 (NGC 3627) is at bottom right. Their bright central regions and fainter spiral arms can just be made out. NGC 3628, at top left, is also a spiral galaxy, but we see it edge-on, with a central dust lane. The three galaxies are all about 37 million light years away. A supernova was discovered in M66 in January 1989.

LIBRA

Libra is the seventh zodiacal constellation and is an early summer group. Its place is between Virgo and Scorpius, and there are two prominent stars (Alpha (α) and Beta (β)) which along with the next two in brightness (Gamma (γ) and Sigma (σ)) make a skewed trapezoidal figure. This area of sky is sparsely decorated with stars, and there are few bright deep sky objects, although Libra boasts quite a number of fine double-star systems. There is one medium-quality globular cluster and a small planetary nebula. Many galaxies dot Libra but are all fairly faint for the average-sized telescope.

Multiple Stars

The double-star line-up is led by Alpha (α), known as Zubenelgenubi, the southern claw.(To the ancient Greeks and in Arabic times, Libra was part of Scorpius' claws.) Here are two stars at the limit that the human eye can resolve (231 arcseconds). The fainter star is of 5th magnitude, which makes it difficult for the naked eye to split. In binoculars or a telescope, this is a splendid object. The two stars are white, but the fainter of the two (8 Librae) looks yellow at times. The bright star is a spectroscopic double with a 20-day period of revolution. Beta (β), Zubeneschamali, the northern claw, is of an unusual color. It has been called the only green naked-eye star. It is up to the reader to decide what color Zubeneschamali is after observing it a few times. Mu (μ) is a fine double, fairly close at 1.8 arcseconds

NGC 5792 is a spiral galaxy of 12.9 magnitude. This photograph from the UK Schmidt telescope survey shows a bright nucleus and faint spiral arms.

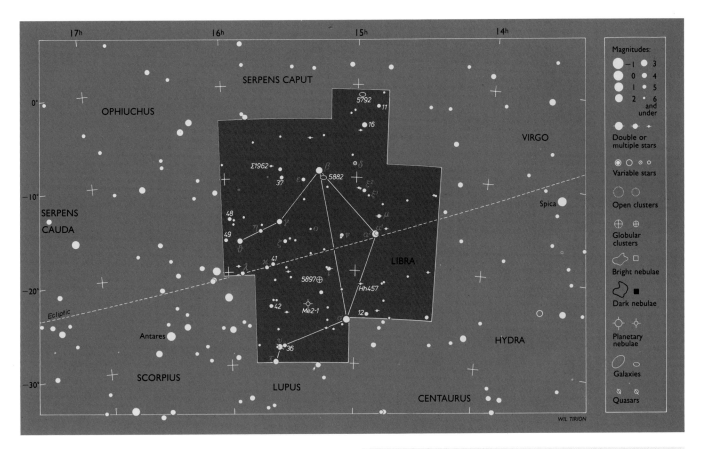

separation, but with bright components of 5th and 6th magnitudes. Both are yellow in color. **Σ** 1962 is a beautiful, equal-magnitude pair of white stars, both of which are white dwarfs. Iota (ι) is an interesting multiple system. The bright component A is a close binary itself, which is almost impossible to split (0.1 arcseconds). B is also a close double (1.9 arcseconds), with 9.4 and 11.1 magnitude components. The star Delta (δ) Librae is a good example of an Algol-type eclipsing binary star. Its range is 4.8 to 5.9. Here are two stars revolving, with the brighter being eclipsed every 2.327 days by the fainter.

Deep Sky Objects

NGC 5792 is an edge-on galaxy located in the western end of the constellation 3° north of 16 Librae. It is 12.3 magnitude, so at least an 8-inch (20-cm) 'scope is needed to see it well. NGC 5897 is a loosely organized globular cluster of faint stars with some central condensation. Resolution of the brighter stars is possible with a 6-inch (15-cm) telescope, but the majority are much fainter, since the cluster has a listed distance of 45,000 light years. A small, rather dim planetary nebula is present, called Me 2-1 or VV 72. This tiny, egg-shaped planetary nebula is only 6 or 7 arcseconds across, but has the unmistakable blue-green color of most objects of this type. It follows a 10th-magnitude star by about 60 arcseconds, according to Hartung. The unusual nomenclature Me 2-1 of the planetary derives from its discoverer Paul Merrill who observed its strong emission spectrum in the 1940s, and the alternative VV 72 designation stands for Boris Vorontsov-Velyaminov, a soviet astronomer who studied the object.

TELESCOPIC OBJECTS IN LIBRA

Double Stars

Name	RA	Dec.	Separation (arcseconds)	Mags.		Year
μ (Mu)	14h 49.3m	−14° 09'	1.8	5.8	6.7	1958
α (Alpha)	14h 50.9m	−16° 02'	231.0	2.8	5.2	1913
Hh 457	14h 57.5m	−21° 25'	23.0	5.7	8.0	1976
ι (Iota)	15h 12.2m	−19° 47'	AB 57.8	5.1	9.4	1919
			BC 1.9	9.4	11.1	1943
Σ 1962	15h 38.7m	−08° 47'	11.9	6.5	6.6	1958

Deep Sky Objects

Name	RA	Dec.	Type	Size	Mag.
NGC 5792	14h 58.4m	−01° 05'	Gal. Sbp	7.2' × 2.1'	12.3
NGC 5897	15h 17.4m	−21° 01'	Glob. Cl.	12.6'	8.55
Me 2-1	15h 22.3m	−23° 38'	Plan. Neb.	7"	12

LUPUS/NORMA

Lupus, the Wolf, has a somewhat confused history and is apparently a misnomer applied after a medieval mistake in translation. The Arabs had it as a leopard or panther, and before that the Greeks just called it a wild animal, of no particular species. It has been associated with the Centaur, who is grasping the animal and bringing it to the Altar (Ara) as a sacrifice. The Greek astronomer Eratosthenes wrote of a wineskin from which the Centaur is about to drink.

Norma, the Level, is another of Nicolas Louis de Lacaille's groups, introduced in 1752, which include surveying and astronomical instruments.

Lupus is a prominent constellation positioned between Centaurus and Scorpius. A fairly rich portion of the Milky Way runs southwestward through Lupus, and as a result there are a good number of multiple stars as well as galactic objects to be seen. Norma is included for convenience and is a small southern group. The stars in Lupus are bright, but tracing a wolf out of them requires a great deal of imagination. There are two more or less parallel lines of stars which start with Chi (χ) to the right and Theta (θ) to the left. The lines end up with Sigma (σ) on the right and Zeta (ζ) at the south end of the eastern line. At the heart of the group is an ovoid of 3rd-magnitude stars, including Alpha (α), Beta (β), Gamma (γ), Delta (δ), Epsilon (ε) and Pi (π). Much of the constellation can be seen from northern temperate latitudes, since the northern border is at about − 30°, just 4° below Antares. The southern end, however is at −55°, below the horizon for observers north of +40°. This is a later-spring/ early-summer group for northern observers, and a late-fall constellation for southern-hemisphere skygazers. Its center culminates at 10 pm about June 15. Norma follows Lupus and lies west of, and below, the tail of Scorpius.

Multiple Stars

Many of the bright stars in this area are members of a group which are moving in the same direction and called the Scorpius– Centaurus stellar association. These are predominantly young blue O or A spectral type stars, except for Antares, its brightest member. Their motion is taking them all toward Beta (β) Columbae in the winter sky. The center of the association is near Alpha (α) Lupi, and is about 550 light years away from the Sun.

Pi (π) leads the double star array in Lupus. It has two compo-

nents of 5th magnitude which are widening according to Hartung. Kappa (κ) is a widely separated pair, both of which are yellow. These bright stars make a fine sight in any size of telescope. Mu (μ) is an interesting triple star, two close ones at 1.2 arcseconds separation and a third star of 7th magnitude 23.7 arcseconds away. Herschel (h) 4788 is a double of yellow stars, separated by 2.2 arcseconds: the pair seems to be closing from Herschel's measure of 3.1 arcseconds in 1836. Xi (ξ) is another almost-equal-brightness pair, both yellow, and excellent for observers with small-aperture telescopes.

Deep Sky Objects

Starting at the western end of the Lupus and progressing eastward, the deep sky objects of interest in amateur telescopes are as follows. IC 4406, a 20-arcsecond diameter disk, is a planetary nebula of 11th magnitude. There is apparently a larger, much fainter, extension of gas listed as 100 arcseconds in diameter in some sources. NGC 5824 is a globular cluster, fairly small but quite bright and strongly condensed. The outer, fainter stars may be obscured owing to dust in the Galaxy. It starts to resolve into stars with a 12-inch (30-cm) aperture telescope. NGC 5822 is a widely scattered open cluster, an excellent object for astronomical binoculars. NGC 5873 is a tiny blue planetary nebula only 3 arcseconds in diameter, which lies in a charming figure of faint stars. NGC 5882 is a bright planetary nebula about 7 arcseconds across, and of 10.5 magnitude. NGC 5927 is a globular cluster, which is dimmed some 4 magnitudes by interstellar absorption. It can be resolved with a 6-inch (15-cm) aperture and is about 12 arcminutes in diameter. NGC 5986 is a small, distant globular, about 10 arcminutes in diameter, with

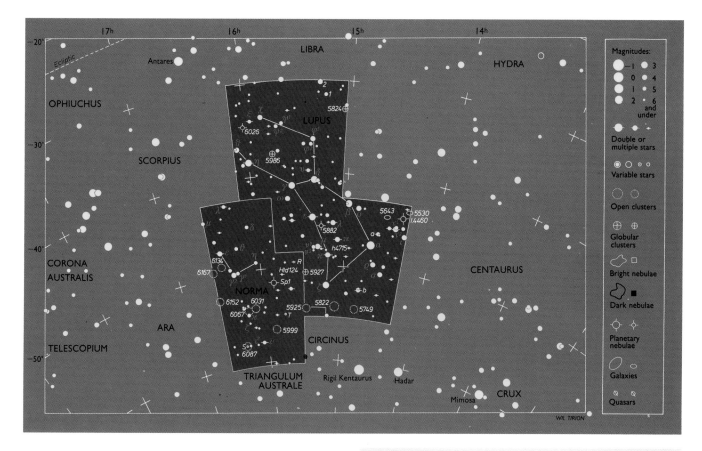

stars from 13th magnitude and fainter. NGC 6026 is a planetary nebula which looks like a galaxy and was classified as one until 1955, when Gérard de Vaucouleurs corrected the mistake. It is about 45 arcseconds in diameter, faint, and with a ring shape visible in photographs.

Norma

Epsilon (ε) Normae is one of the few doubles of note in Norma. Note the colors, which are only slightly different but which look yellow and blue by contrast.

Norma is in the heart of the southern Milky Way and contains rich binocular and telescope fields. There are several object of note, including NGC 5999, an open cluster, with lines and curves of stars and a curious circlet in the center. NGC 6067 is another fine open cluster of about 100 stars in a 13 arcminute diameter group. The planetary Sp1 is faint but worth finding with larger amateur 'scopes.

TELESCOPIC OBJECTS IN LUPUS
Double and Multiple Stars

Name	RA	Dec.	Separation (arcseconds)	Mags.		Year
a (h4690)	14h 37.3m	−46° 08′	19.3	6.2	9.2	1933
h4715	14h 56.5m	−47° 53′	2.4	6.0	6.8	1952
π (Pi)	15h 05.1m	−47° 03′	1.4	4.6	4.7	1956
κ (Kappa)	15h 11.9m	−48° 44′	26.8	3.9	5.8	1951
μ (Mu)	15h 18.5m	−47° 53′	AB 1.2	5.1	5.2	1955
			AC 23.7	5.1	7.2	1955
d (h4788)	15h 35.9m	−44° 58′	2.2	4.7	6.7	1955

TELESCOPIC OBJECTS IN LUPUS continued
Double and Multiple Stars

Name	RA	Dec.	Separation (arcseconds)	Mags.		Year
ξ (Xi)	15h 56.9m	−33° 58′	10.4	5.3	5.8	1951
(η (Eta)	16h 00.1m	−38° 24′	15.0	3.6	7.8	1934

Deep Sky Objects

Name	RA	Dec.	Type	Size	Mag.
IC 4406	14h 22.4m	−44° 09′	Plan. Neb.	>28″	10.6pg
NGC 5824	15h 04.0m	−33° 04′	Glob. Cl.	6.2′	9.0
NGC 5822	15h 05.2m	−54° 21′	Open Cl.	40′	6.5
NGC 5873	15h 12.7m	−38° 06′	Plan. Neb.	3″	13.5
NGC 5882	15h 16.8m	−45° 39′	Plan. Neb.	7″	10.5pg
NGC 5927	15h 28.0m	−50° 04′	Glob. Cl.	12.0′	8.3
NGC 5986	15h 46.1m	−37° 47′	Glob. Cl.	9.8′	7.1
NGC 6026	16h 01.4m	−34° 32′	Plan. Neb.	45″	12.5

TELESCOPIC OBJECTS IN NORMA
Double and Multiple Stars

Name	RA	Dec.	Separation (arcseconds)	Mags.		Year
Hld 124	15h 45.0m	−50° 47′	2.5	6.8	8.4	1953
ι (Iota ι)	16h 03.5m	−57° 47′	AB 0.6 (1969)	5.3	5.5	1969
			AB×C 10.8	5.3	8.1	1946
ε (Epsilon)	16h 27.2m	−47° 33′	22.8	4.8	7.5	1951

Deep Sky Objects

Name	RA	Dec.	Type	Size	Mag.
Sp 1	15h 51.7m	−51° 31′	Plan. Neb.	76″	13.6pg
NGC 5999	15h 52.2m	−56° 28′	Open Cl.	5′	9.0
NGC 6067	16h 13.2m	−54° 13′	Open Cl.	13′	5.6
NGC 6134	16h 27.7m	−49° 09′	Open Cl.	7′	7.2

LYNX

Lynx, the Lynx, is of recent origin, dating from a map by Johannes Hevelius in 1690. He used 19 stars to make up this figure. Hevelius was quick to note that you had to be iynx-eyed to see its faint stars! Lynx may have some connection with Ursa Major, perhaps once having been thought of as the Bear's prey.

NGC 2683 is a spiral galaxy which we see almost edge-on, with the result that its beautiful spiral structure is very difficult to discern. The red-colored region in this true-color CCD image shows where dust on the nearer side of the galaxy has obscured and reddened the light from the more distant side. The photograph was taken by Dr Rudolph Schild, at the Smithsonian Astrophysical Observatory.

Lynx is a medium-sized constellation which occupies a part of the sky in which there are few bright stars. It is a northern constellation, located between Ursa Major and Gemini and Cancer. The only pattern of stars which can be made out is a ragged line, a couple of degrees in length towards the southern end of the group. This is found by looking south of the two prominent triangles marking the forepaws of the Great Bear (Ursa Major). It is a winter constellation, culminating at 10 pm on February 10. The constellation is not rich in telescopic objects, although the eastern end is populated by a number of galaxies of the Coma–Virgo cloud.

Multiple Stars

There are a number of good doubles in Lynx, and an equatorial mount with setting circles will make finding them a lot more convenient, as there are so few naked-eye stars to use as markers. 12 Lynxis is a nice triple, with 5th-, 6th- and 7th-magnitude stars arranged in a very oblique triangle. Another triple is Σ 1032, which has 7th- and 11th-magnitude stars at 2.6 arcseconds separation, and 10th-magnitude star at 32.7 arcseconds' distance. A challenge for resolving power and seeing (steadiness) conditions is Σ 1211, a close binary of 8th- and 9th-magnitude components separated by 0.4 arcseconds, and a 12th-magnitude atar at 27.1 arcseconds. There is another 9th-magnitude star at 100 arcseconds distance, making this a quadruple system. 38 Lynxis is another triple system, with 3.9 and 6.6 magnitude stars at 2.7 arcseconds with a third star of 10.8 at 87.7 arcseconds. These stars are approximately in line and form a very oblique triangle.

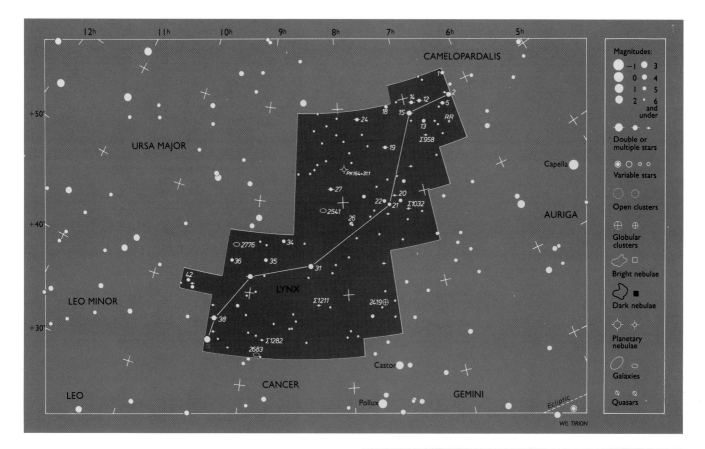

Deep Sky Objects

Lynx contains a globular cluster which is the most distant of all globulars. NGC 2419 has been called the "Intergalactic Wanderer", as it is so far away from the Galaxy that its connection with our system is tenuous at best. This cluster is about 210,000 light years from the center of the Galaxy – further than the Large Magellanic Cloud! Its independence is strengthened by the fact that there is no other globular cluster within about 60°. Although the brightest stars are fainter than 17th magnitude, the whole cluster can be seen because their total brightness comes up to about 11.5. This is a bright cluster, with a total luminosity 175,000 times the Sun's output. The diameter of the cluster is around 400 light years, making this quite a large object indeed.

There is also a large, but faint, planetary nebula which makes an interesting object in a large telescope with a deep sky filter, PK 164 + 31.1. It is 300 arcseconds in diameter, annular in photographs, with a 17th-magnitude central star. NGC 2683 is by far the best galaxy in Lynx, among many faint ones. Its size is 9.3 × 1.3 arcminutes, meaning we are seeing it almost edge-on, and at magnitude 9.7 in brightness, one of the brighter galaxies of the Coma–Virgo cloud. The *New General Catalog* description is "very bright, very large, very much extended, gradually much brighter middle". The author observed NGC 2419 in the 22-inch Cassegrain at Anza Observatory, and it appeared as a dim round spot, not much brighter toward the center. At 176×, no individual stars were seen. The cluster makes an interesting contrast with a 7th-magnitude field star nearby.

TELESCOPIC OBJECTS IN LYNX
Double and Multiple Stars

Name	RA	Dec.	Separation (arcseconds)		Mags.		Year
12	06h 46.2m	+59° 27′	AB	1.8	5.4	6.0	1959
			AC	8.7	7.3		1959
			AD	170.0	10.6		1910
Σ 958	06h 48.2m	+55° 42′	AB	4.8	6.3	6.3	1956
			BC	164.3	6.3	11.2	1910
Σ 1032	07h 13.9m	+48° 30′	AB	2.6	7.7	11.0	1935
			AC	32.7	7.7	9.8	1908
20	07h 22.3m	+50° 09′		15.0	7.3	7.4	1950
Σ 1211	08h 18.3m	+39° 00′	AB	0.4	8.5	9	1967
			AC	27.1	8.5	12.5	1900
			AD	100	8.5	9.5	1925
Σ 1282	08h 50.7m	+35° 04′		3.6	7.5	7.5	1956
38	09h 18.8m	+36° 48′	AB	2.7	3.9	6.6	1968
			AC	87.7	3.9	10.8	1909

Deep Sky Objects

Name	RA	Dec.	Type	Size	Mag.
NGC 2419	07h 38.1m	+38° 53′	Glob. Cl.	4.1′	11.5
*PK 164 + 31.1	07h 57.8m	+53° 25′	Plan. Neb.	360″ × 300″	14pg
NGC 2683	08h 52.7m	+33° 25′	Gal.	9.3′ × 1.3′	9.7

* NGC 2474 & 2475: The planetary nebula is misidentified as 2474/75 in several catalogs. 2474/75 are two faint galaxies ±30′ to the south.

LYRA

Lyra, the Lyre, *as befits its prominence, is a very old grouping, named long before the ancient Greeks, who knew it well. It appears originally to have been shown as a bird of prey of some kind, sometimes diving on its hapless victim. Later, with the invention of musical instruments, the appellation of the Lyre or Harp came along. The creation of the harp is credited to the inventiveness of one of the Argonauts, who used a tortoise shell to fashion a lyre. It was subsequently transferred to the heavens as Apollo was particularly pleased by its music. Orpheus mastered it and used it to charm the keepers of the underworld.*

Lyra is one of the few constellations which actually looks something like the object it is supposed to represent. This charming group of fairly bright stars is headed by the brilliant Vega, the fifth brightest star in the sky. Its parallelogram shape is the harbinger of northern spring, as it rises in the northeast during late winter for observers north of the equator. Vega is one of the stars of the so-called summer triangle, along with Deneb and Altair. Lyra culminates virtually overhead for temperate zone observers at 10 pm on August 2. Lyra has something for everyone. The highlights of Lyra are the eclipsing binary Beta (β) Lyrae; Alpha (α) Lyrae, Vega; Epsilon (ε) Lyrae, a double double star which is a test for visual resolving power; and the famous Ring Nebula, M57.

Beta Lyrae

Beta (β) Lyrae is a fascinating enigma to astronomers. It is an eclipsing binary with many peculiar properties. In addition to the two major objects, there are streams of gas in the system. The primary is a luminous blue star of massive proportions, with another star, which has not yet been observed directly, circling closely – almost in contact with the primary. As a result they are both egg-shaped and mass in the form of hot gas is being transferred from the primary to the secondary. One theory suggests that the secondary body is a black hole into which the atmosphere of the bright star is streaming. The stars are so close that they are expending angular momentum at a rate which is slowing their rotational period by 9.4 seconds a year. It has been found that the secondary object has about 3 times the mass of the luminous body! The fact that the secondary object has not been detected spectroscopically might indicate that it is indeed a

black hole. The star has been closely monitored in order to try to understand its bizarre behavior better. Currently the period of the eclipses is 12.93681 days, and the change in brightness from 3.4 to 4.3 magnitude.

Vega

Vega, the Harp Star, is a brilliant blue white gem seen in almost any telescope. Astrophysically speaking, it is similar to Sirius and about 3 times larger than our Sun, and 58 times more luminous (due to its being about twice as hot). The star is some 27 light years distant from the Sun. About 10,000 BC, Vega was the north pole star, passing about 4.5° from the celestial pole (see Draco). Some authorities believe that the early civilizations just emerging at that time (Egypt and Mesopotamia) were interested in Vega and built some temples in alignment with its position. It will again be the pole star in AD 14,500, the position of the pole having made one precessional rotation. Vega was the first star to have its picture taken, by William Cranch Bond and the photographer Whipple, on July 16, 1850, with the Harvard College 15-inch (36-cm) refractor.

The "Double-doubles"

Two other objects in Lyra appear on almost everyone's favorite telescopic objects list. One is the "double-double" Epsilon (ε_1, ε_2). Here we see two stars separated by 207 arcseconds, both of the 5th magnitude. I have always been able to split them with the naked eye assisted by correctional glasses. Even the slightest optical aid easily separates the two stars, which are 1.5° northeast of Vega. A good 3-inch (75-mm) telescope with an eyepiece of × 100 will show that each of the wide components is a fairly

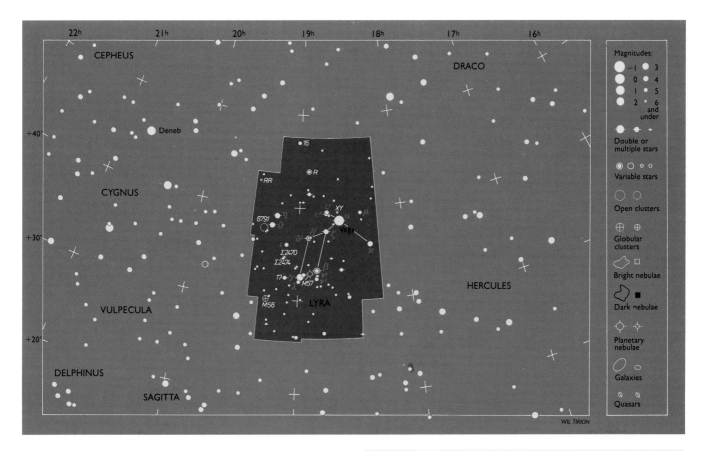

close double itself. The four components are almost of equal magnitude. The slightly brighter pair is closer at 2.3 arcseconds separation and the other pair are separated by 2.9 arcseconds. Their axes of separation are almost at right angles to each other. There is a second "double-double" in Lyra. These are much easier to see than the Epsilon (ε₁, ε₂) quartet, each pair separated by 14 arcseconds and 16 arcseconds respectively, but are rather farther apart at 11 arcminutes. Σ 2470-4 are located directly south of Iota (ι) or 18 Lyrae and are worth looking up!

The Ring Nebula

Another showpiece in Lyra is the Ring Nebula, M57 (NGC 6720). This 9th magnitude nebula looks exactly like a smoke ring in a dark sky with almost any 'scope from 3-inch (75-mm) aperture and up. The round blob of luminous gas is about one arcminute in diameter and "takes power" very well, i.e. it can be observed without loss of detail at ever greater magnifications. Since power darkens the background behind the nebula, don't use too little power with this object. Anything from 8 inches (20cm) up will allow a magnification of × 200 or more to be used without "overpowering" the limited brightness of the nebula. A deep sky filter changes the appearance of the nebula and shows the glowing gas in the center of the ring better. It gives a "filled-in" look to the whole thing. The famous central star is a very blue hot star with a surface temperature of 100,000 K. The central star is a good test of eyesight, to the extent that this star is unmistakable to one person while wholly invisible to another. In any event, the 14.2 magnitude star is difficult to observe and only high powers and larger instruments (at least 14-inch (35-cm) aperture) will show it unmistakably, and then only on a still night.

TELESCOPIC OBJECTS IN LYRA
Double and Multiple Stars

Name	RA	Dec.	Separation (arcseconds)	Mags.		Year
α (Alpha), (Vega)	18h 36.9m	+38° 47'	AB 62.8	0.0	9.5	1946
			AC 54.4	0.0	11.0	1899
			AE118.5	0.0	9.5	1921
ε₁,₂ (Epsilon)	18h 44.3m	+39° 40'	207.7	5	5	1955
ε₁			2.9	5.0	6.1	1976
ε₂			2.3	5.2	5.5	1975
ζ (Zeta)	18h 44.8m	+37° 36'	43.7	4.3	5.9	1955
β (Beta)	18h 50.1m	+33° 22'	45.7	3.4–4.3v	8.6	1955
Σ 2470	19h 08.8m	+34° 46'	13.4	6.6	8.6	1933
Σ 2474	19h 09.1m	+34° 36'	16.2	6.7	8.8	1974
η (Eta)	19h 13.8m	+39° 09'	28.1	4.4	9.1	1969
θ (Theta)	19h 16.4m	+38° 08'	AB 99.8	4.4	9.1	1924
			AC 99.9	4.4	10.9	1908

Variable Stars

Name	RA	Dec.	Type	Variation	Period
β (Beta)	18h 50.1m	+33° 22'	Beta Lyrid	3.4–4.3	12.93681 days
RR	19h 25.5m	+42° 17'	Std cluster type var.	7.1–8.0	0.5668 days

Deep Sky Objects

Name	RA	Dec.	Type	Size	Mag.
M57 (NGC 6720)	18h 53.6m	+33° 02'	Plan. Neb.	70" × 150"	9.7pg
M56 (NGC 6779)	19h 16.6m	+30° 11'	Glob. Cl.	7.1'	8.3
NGC 6791	19h 20.7m	+37° 51'	Open Cl.	16'	9.5

MICROSCOPIUM

Microscopium, the Microscope, was created by Nicolas Louis de Lacaille in 1752 when he elevated fourteen of the "names of the principle implements of the sciences and fine arts" to the heavens. Lacaille preceded John Herschel by some 83 years in observing the glorious southern heavens from Cape Town in 1751. He lost no time in giving order to the southern skies by originating the 14 groups soon thereafter in his Mémoires *and* Coelum Stelliferum.

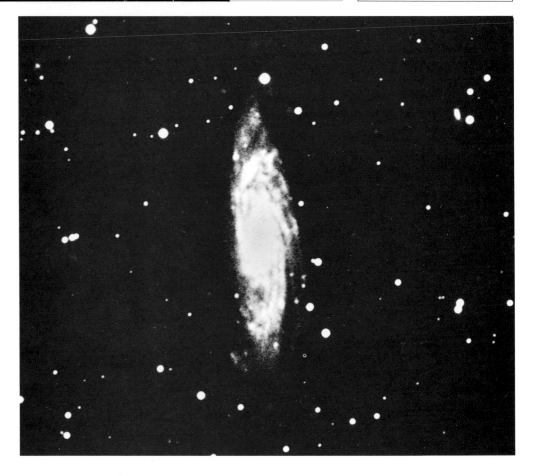

NGC 6925 is a spiral galaxy with tightly wound spiral arms. This photograph was taken from one of the plates of the telescope survey of the southern sky made by the 48-inch (1.2-m) UK Schmidt telescope located at the Siding Spring Observatory in New South Wales, Australia.

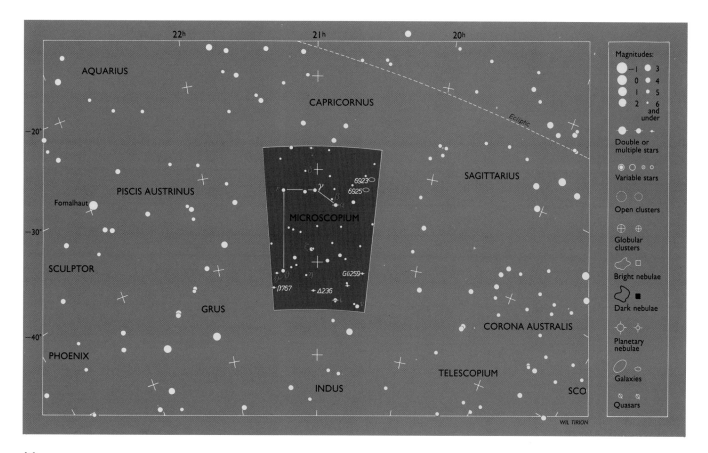

Microscopium is a small constellation lying south of Capricornus and east of the southern extension of Sagittarius. It has a number of rather faint stars and contains several good telescopic objects. It reaches the meridian at 10 pm on September 1 and is therefore a fall constellation for northern observers and an early spring one for those in the southern hemisphere. Its southwestern corner touches the northeastern corner of Telescopium, so that the two optical instruments which revolutionized our view of the Universe are neighbors in the sky.

Multiple Stars

Microscopium has a number of doubles and a triple, as well as a few galaxies, mostly small and faint. Alpha (α) is an easy double star in most telescopes, 5th and 10th magnitudes at 20.5 arcseconds separation. Dunlop (Δ) 236 is a nice wide pair with common proper motion, meaning they are probably gravitationally involved, i.e. a binary system. They are yellow, spectral classes G3 and K0, and of magnitudes 6.5 and 6.9 separated by 57.4 arcseconds. Theta 2 (θ₂) is a triple system, with a close pair separated by 0.5 arcseconds (a good test of resolving power for a 10-inch (25-cm) telescope), and a third star of 10th magnitude 78.4 arcseconds distant.

Deep Sky Objects

One of the better galaxies of the several small ones is NGC 6925, a spiral type galaxy of the 11th magnitude. Its *New General Catalog* description reads: "considerably bright, much extended, pretty suddenly brighter towards the middle". The Revised NGC description is "spiral, elongated, brighter middle, tighly wound diffuse arms." The older description is from obser-

vations by the Herschels and other 19th-century visual observations. The newer description is from an examination of the Palomar Observatory Sky Survey plates made with the 48-inch (1.2-m) Schmidt camera from 1952 to 1957.

TELESCOPIC OBJECTS IN MICROSCOPIUM

Double and Multiple Stars

Name	RA	Dec.	Separation (arcseconds)	Mags.		Year
Gls 259	20h 31.9m	−40° 54′	AB 3.8	8.2	8.3	1959
			AC 10.3	8.2	12.5	1959
α (Alpha)	20h 50.0m	−33° 47′	20.5	5.0	10.0	1933
Δ 236	21h 02.2m	−43° 00′	57.4	6.5	6.9	1951
θ₂ (Theta 2)	21h 24.4m	−41° 00′	AB 0.5	6.4	7.0	1959
			AC 78.4	6.4	10.5	1879
Burnham 767	21h 27.0m	−42° 34′	2.9	5.6	7.9	1959

Deep Sky Objects

Name	RA	Dec.	Type	Size	Mag.
NGC 6925	20h 34.3m	−31° 59′	Gal. Sb+	4.1′ × 1.6′	11.3

OPHIUCHUS

Ophiuchus, the Serpent Bearer, has been identified with several mythological figures over the ages. Since it casts its skin every year, the serpent is a symbol of renovation and hence of healing. The Greek god of medicine, Asclepius (Aesculepius to the Romans), was the son of Apollo and Coronis (see Corvus), and according to the myth, during his earthly years as a doctor was able even to bring back the dead to life. He is generally shown as a mature figure in control of the snake he is holding – which remains the symbol of western medicine.

TELESCOPIC OBJECTS IN OPHIUCHUS
Double and Multiple Stars

Name	RA	Dec.	Separation (arcseconds)	Mags.		Year
ρ (Rho)	16h 25.6m	−23° 27′	3.1	5.3	6.0	1959
λ (Lambda)	16h 30.9m	+01° 59′	I (1967)	4.2	5.2	1960
36	17h 15.3m	−26° 36′	4.4 (1962)	5.1	5.1	1976
o (Omicron)	17h 18.0m	−24° 17′	10.3	5.4	6.9	1951
ξ (Xi)	17h 21.0m	−21° 07′	3.7	4.4	8.9	1959
Σ 2173	17h 30.4m	−01° 04′	0.7 (1968)	6.0	6.1	1960
53	17h 34.6m	+09° 35′	AB 41.2	5.8	8.5	1949
			AC 94	5.8	10.8	1912
			AD 91.4	5.8	10.8	1912
61	17h 44.6m	+02° 35′	AB 20.6	6.2	6.6	1968
			AC 95.9	6.2	12.5	1912
τ (Tau)	18h 03.1m	−08° 11′	AB 1.8 (1967)	5.2	5.9	1976
			AC 100.3	5.2	9.3	1959
70	18h 05.5m	+02° 30′	2.8 (1967)	4.2	6.0	1976

Deep Sky Objects

Name	RA	Dec.	Type	Size	Mag.
IC 4604	16h 25.6m	−23° 26′	Diff./dust	60″ × 25″	—
M12 (NGC 6218)	16h 47.2m	−01° 57′	Glob. Cl.	14.5′	6.6
M10 (NGC 6254)	16h 57.1m	−04° 06′	Glob. Cl.	15.1	6.6
M62 (NGC 6266)	17h 01.2m	−30° 07′	Glob. Cl.	14.1′	6.6
M19 (NGC 6273)	17h 02.6m	−26° 16′	Glob. Cl.	13.5′	7.2
NGC 6309	17h 14.1m	−12° 55′	Plan. Neb.	14″ × 66″	10.8pg
M9 (NGC 6333)	17h 19.2m	−18° 31′	Glob. Cl.	9.3′	7.9
B 72 Barnard S Neb.	17h 23.5m	−23° 38′	Dark Neb.	30′	
NGC 6369	17h 29.3m	−23° 46′	Plan. Neb.	28″	10.4
M14 (NGC 6402)	17h 37.6m	−03° 15′	Glob. Cl.	11.7′	7.6
NGC 6572	18h 12.1m	+06° 51′	Plan. Neb.	8″	9.0pg

Ophiuchus is a large constellation with many scattered stars, none of which is brighter than 2nd magnitude. It is located north of Scorpius and south of Hercules, and culminates at 10 pm on July 5. In the sky, the serpent (Serpens) is being held by Ophiuchus, with its head (Serpens Caput) near Corona Borealis, and the tail (Serpens Cauda) on the eastern side of Ophiuchus, near Aquila. The main stars form a large, roundish figure with an almost empty center as seen by the naked eye. The Milky Way is present in the southern and eastern parts of the group, and many fine fields are therefore available for binocular and telescope users. The constellation is known for being home to 22 globular clusters, a sizable fraction of all those which are known. Not only is Ophiuchus home to globulars, but it also has several excellent planetary nebulae, a great complex of dust and glowing gas near Rho (ρ), and a couple of open clusters, as well as Barnard 72, the famous Barnard "S" nebula. Barnard's star, also famous, which exhibits the largest proper motion of any star in the sky, is a nearby red dwarf. Binoculars will show many of the globulars as fuzzy stars, and under a really dark sky, the dust and glowing gas nebulae of the Rho (ρ) Ophiuchi region.

Dust and Gas

Rho (ρ) lies north of Antares in neighboring Scorpius, and is the center of a wonderful complex of dust and gas IC 4604. This is chiefly revealed by photography, since to the eye the dust and gas looks somewhat suppressed in brightness. With 7 × 50 binoculars dust lanes can be traced from the dust-darkened area leading eastwards. The nebula around Rho is seen as a slightly brightened area superimposed on the dull grayness of the dust cloud behind, and slightly larger than the reflection nebula which

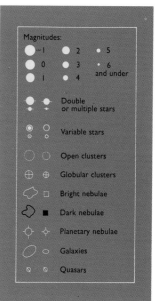

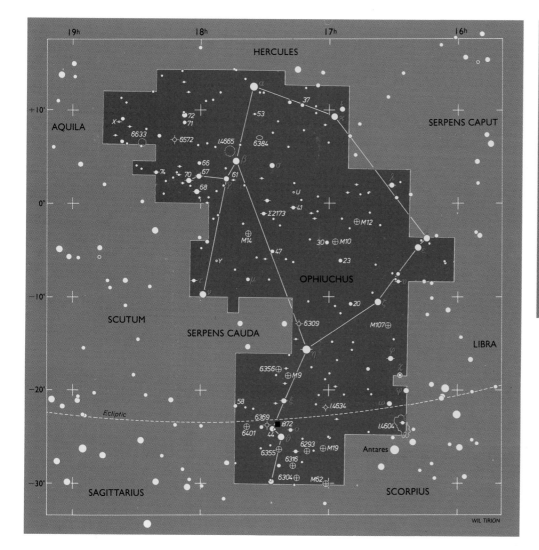

WIL TIRION

appears blue in photographs. Toward the south there is blending of the blue nebula with a red colour surrounding Antares, and this continues to spread northwards. Few modern photographs seem to be as wonderful as those E. E. Barnard took in the early 1900s from the darkness of Mt Wilson, when he used several hours of exposure with the Bruce 10-inch (25-cm) lens. One that does was taken by David Malin of the Siding Spring Observatory in Australia, using modern tri-color and contrast-enhancement techniques.

Globular Clusters

The globulars of Ophiuchus are too numerous to describe here, but some outstanding examples are M12 (NGC 6218), a 10-arcminute-diameter ball of 11th-magnitude and fainter stars; M10 (NGC 6254) is nearby and quite similar in size and brightness. I like to call these the western globulars in Ophiuchus, as opposed to the southern and eastern ones, which are connected with the Milky Way and are all somewhat obscured by our Galaxy. M19 (NGC 6273) is the westernmost of the southern globulars. It is a bright ball of faint stars with two brighter ones on either side of the nucleus, probably field stars. M9 (NGC 6333) is a heavily obscured southern globular which is on the edge of a dark lane in the Milky Way.

Planetary Nebulae

The planetary nebulae of Ophiuchus provide good examples of several types which have been described by professional astronomers. NGC 6309 for example is an elliptical blob with a blue-gray color, at 10.8 magnitude. With a 12-inch (30-cm) aperture and high power the shell seems to contain fine details which just escape definition, an effect which is common with smaller telescopes. The detail can be well seen in a 16-inch (40-cm) aperture instrument or larger. NGC 6369 is a perfect miniature of the Ring Nebula in Lyra. The doughnut can be seen with an 8-inch (20-cm) aperture, but at least a 16-inch (40-cm) is needed to have a chance to see the central star, which is 16th magnitude. NGC 6572 is probably the brightest planetary in Ophiuchus. It's located high on the Serpent Bearer's shoulder, and makes a long isosceles triangle with Beta (β) and Gamma (γ) to the northwest. It is small and looks like a 9th-magnitude blue–green star at low powers of magnification. Its small, slightly elliptical disk is not diminished by increases in magnification powers. The 12th-magnitude central star is about the same brightness, so is difficult to pick out. While in this vicinity, you might look up Barnard's Star, a 9th-magnitude red dwarf. At only 5.9 light years distance it is the second nearest after Proxima Centauri.

ORION

Orion, the Hunter, was named by the Greeks, but this obvious figure was variously known as a god, hero, warrior, and hunter by almost every culture that cared about naming stellar groupings. It was already known as Orion by 425 BC, and there are connections in ancient legend with Ares, god of war.

In the classical myth, Orion was the son of Poseidon and a mortal mother, and was the most handsome man who ever lived. Blinded by the jealous father of his intended bride, he eventually regained his sight by looking at the sunrise. Aurora, goddess of dawn and Apollo's sister, became his lover.

Orion is one of best known of the constellations. The celestial equator passes through his waist, so the figure is equally well known north and south of the Earth's Equator (although the views from the different hemispheres are upside-down relative to each other). Orion is the brightest constellation because it contains two 1st magnitude stars (Betelgeuse and Rigel), several between the 1st and 2nd, and many more between 2nd and 3rd magnitude. The stars of Orion's belt are a striking asterism of 3 stars, almost in a straight line and equally spaced. Orion is the most famous of the winter constellations and culminates at 10 pm on January 15. It is one of a handful of star groups that actually look very much like the figure they are supposed to represent.

Betelgeuse and Rigel
Orion is a treasure-trove of interesting objects and, starting with

Zeta Orionis and the Horsehead Nebula. The region shown in this photograph is part of the complex of stars and nebulae near Orion's belt and sword. The bright star at the top is Alnitak, or Zeta (ζ) Orionis, the eastern star in the belt. The nebula immediately to the left of Alnitak is NGC 2024, a cloud of hot gas bisected by a foreground lane of dust. The pink nebulosity stretching down from Alnitak is IC 434. Silhouetted against it is the Horsehead Nebula, which protrudes distinctively from the dark molecular cloud to the left. The photograph was taken by amateur astronomer Rick Hull with a 12.5-inch (31-cm) telescope at f/4 on hypered Konica 400 film. The resulting print was recopied onto slide film to enhance the contrast.

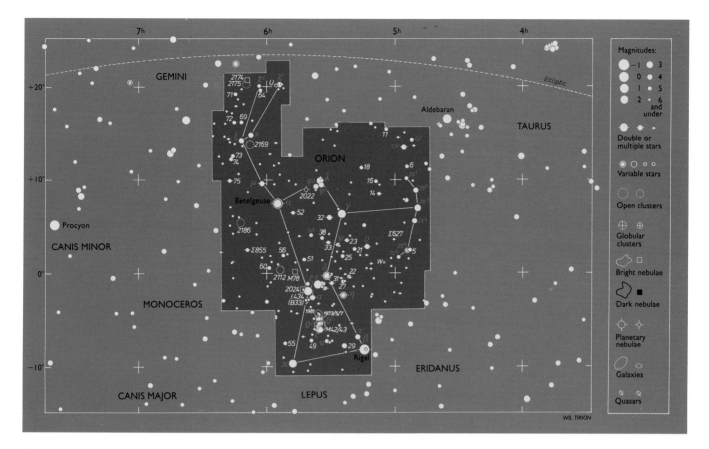

the naked-eye view, we will progress to the more exotic astrophysical specimens, which are in the realm of the professional astronomer. Orion contains dozens of naked-eye stars, including the bright orange Alpha (α), Betelgeuse, of magnitude 0.5 (slightly variable), and Beta (β) Rigel, a blue giant star, slightly brighter, at 0.12 magnitude. Betelgeuse is a red giant, which pulstates irregularly and varies in apparent magnitude from 0.4 at brightest, to about 1.2. Betelgeuse is about 1,400 light years distant and yet it is such an immense globe that its diameter has been established by direct interferometric measures as approximately 4 astronomical units (AU), or 4 times the Earth–Sun distance. So the diameter of Betelgeuse would include the orbit of Mars were it in our Sun's place.

Rigel is a hot blue supergiant star and may be about the same distance as Betelgeuse. It is burning its hydrogen fuel at a prodigious rate, having an absolute magnitude of − 7.1 (i.e. its brightness at a standard distance of 10 parsecs or 32.6 light years). This implies that Rigel is 57,000 times more luminous than the Sun. It contains as much matter as about 50 solar masses and is about 50 times as large as the Sun. It is this type of star that may collapse and create a supernova explosion when its hydrogen fuel is expended and possibly result in a black hole. Rigel has a small companion of the 7th magnitude at 9.5 arcseconds which appears bluish. Its gravitational connection with Rigel is unconfirmed by observation of orbital movement.

There are many exceptional doubles and multiples in Orion, many of which are listed below. Especially recommended are Sigma (σ), Zeta (ζ), Eta (η), 33, Delta (δ), Iota (ι), 52, and, of course, the multiple star Theta (θ) Orionis, the famous Trapezium at the heart of the Orion Nebula.

The Horsehead Nebula

The area around Zeta (ζ), the bottom, or easternmost, star in the belt is particularly remarkable. Zeta illuminates and/or excites the nebula NGC 2024, which is nearby. This nebula is easy to see with a 6-inch (15-cm) or larger aperture telescope, and has a dark lane splitting it. The unusual color of this nebula has been noted; in color photographs it usually appears yellow or at least a sort of orange color almost unique to this object. South of Zeta is the famous Horsehead Nebula or Barnard 33. It was discovered by Pickering at Harvard on some of the earliest astrophotographs of the region taken in 1889. This protrusion of dark matter in front of the dimly glowing emission nebula IC 434 looks more like a sea-horse head than a real horse, but the horsey connection is appropriate either way. However, trying to locate the nebula is very difficult at best. It has been seen in 6-inch (15-cm) and even smaller telescopes of the rich-field variety which have fast focal ratios of f/5 and below. My best view came in an 8-inch (20-cm) f/4.5 instrument on a calm, perfectly clear, and moonless night. A magnification of ×50 allowed the star Zeta to be placed outside the field. There is a little, elongated-kite-shaped asterism of faint stars around 12th magnitude which can be used as a guide. The intrusion of the Horsehead is just east of southern part of the kite shape. With large amateur telescopes (12-inch (30-cm) aperture and over) a nebular filter will help darken the sky and allow the light of IC 434 through so the dust shape stands out more definitely.

The Great Nebula

The centerpoint of Orion must be the Great Nebular M42 (NGC 1976), one of the few emission nebulae that can be seen with the naked eye. It is a slightly fuzzy gleam in the "sword" of Orion. Any optical aid will show a greenish or gray glow around a central star, the famous Trapezium. About half of a degree south is the brilliant star Iota (ι) Orionis (magnitude 2.76). About the same distance to the north is 42 Orionis, which is itself surrounded by a faint blue haze. The nebula stands as one of the most wonderful telescopic objects in the sky. As optical power (aperture and magnification) increases, the amount of detail brought forth becomes astounding. The great observers of the 19th century, such as the American William Cranch Bond, produced lovely drawings of the nebula as a result of many hours at the eyepiece. However, their work was surpassed by the first good astronomical photographs made of the area in the early 1880s. Most long-exposure photographs are "burned in" over the bright areas and some don't show the Trapezium at all, because of overexposure. The best photos have not only the exquisite outer detail but manage to show the Trapezium and small stars around it as well. The central area is the so-called Huygenian Region and is a bright zone sharply bounded on the south side, into which protrudes a dark mass, not unlike the Horsehead but more diffuse than it. The whole area is sprinkled with small stars, many of which are known to be "dust variables" which flicker as dust swirls in and out of their newly born atmospheres. Infrared photographs "see through" the nebula to a very young star cluster nearly behind the Trapezium, an apparently coincidental occurrence. The Trapezium is a remark-able multiple star with four easy components, two more that are much more difficult to observe and several faint stars discovered with large telescopes by such eagle-eyed observers as E.E. Barnard and A.G. Clark in the 19th century. Steady air conditions are needed to resolve the six major components. One simple test for steadiness of seeing is the "match test". If one can light a match out of doors, hold it up, and it doesn't blow appreciably, then chances are the steadiness will be superior when the telescope is employed. Simple, but it seems to work.

Cluster and Nebulae

There are many other interesting features in Orion. The reflection nebula M78 (NGC 2068), for example, would stand out as an interesting object on its own if it were placed in another constellation. There are two stars involved in a fairly bright nebulosity which is round. In photographs this nebula is very blue, as a result of starlight reflected off dust in the area. NGC 2022 is a small planetary nebula located between Betelgeuse and Lambda (λ). It is fairly bright, at 12th magnitude, and a darker center was visible to the author in an 8-inch (20-cm) Schmidt-Cassegrain telescope. NGC 2169 is a fine example of an open cluster, in the northeastern part of the constellation where the winter Milky Way flows by. It's easily found by making an isoceles triangle southwestwards between Xi (ξ) and Nu (ν). The cluster and nebula NGC 2174-5 are attractive subjects, appearing very red in photograph as many hydrogen emission nebulae do.

TELESCOPIC OBJECTS IN ORION
Double and Multiple Stars

Name	RA	Dec.		Separation (arcseconds)	Mags.		Year
Σ 627	05h 00.6m	+03° 37'		21.3	6.6	7.0	1932
β (Beta)	05h 14.5m	−08° 12'		9.5	0.1	6.8	1954
23	05h 22.8m	+03° 33'		32.1	5.0	7.1	1934
33	05h 31.2m	+03° 18'		1.8	5.8	7.1	1923
η (Eta)	05h 24.5m	−02° 24'		1.5	3.8	4.8	1959
δ (Delta)	05h 32.0m	−00° 18'	AB	32.8	2.2	13.7	1922
			AC	52.6	2.2	6.3	1932
λ (Lamba)	05h 35.1m	+09° 56'		4.4	3.6	5.5	1957
θ₁ (Theta 1)	05h 35.5m	−05° 23'	AB	8.8	6.7	7.9	1975
Trapezium			AC	12.8	6.7	5.1	1975
major components			AD	21.5	6.7	6.7	1975
			AE	4.1	6.7	11.1	1934
			CF	4.0	6.7	11.5	1957
ι (Iota)	05h 35.4m	−05° 55'		11.3	2.8	6.9	1932
σ (Sigma)	05h 38.7m	−02° 36'	AB	0.2	4.0	6.0	1960
			AB x C 11.4		4.0	10.3	1973
			AB x D 12.9		4.0	7.5	1969
			AB x E 42.6		4.0	6.5	1970
ζ (Zeta)	05h 40.8m	−01° 57'	AB	2.4	1.9	4.0	1970
			AC	57.6	1.9	9.9	1930
52	05h 48.0m	+06° 27'		1.6	6.1	6.1	1959
Σ 855	06h 09.0m	+02° 30'		29.3	6.0	7.0	1929

Deep Sky Objects

Name	RA	Dec.	Type	Size	Mag.
M42 Great Nebula also M43	05h 35.4m	−05° 27'	Diff. Neb.	66' × 60'	5
NGC 1977	05h 35.5m	−04° 52'	Refl. Neb.	20' × 10'	~7
B 33 (Horsehead)	05h 40.9m	−02° 28'	Dark Neb.	6' × 4'	...
NGC 2024	05h 40.7m	−02° 27'	Diff. Neb.	30' × 30'	~8
IC 434	05h 41.1m	−05° 16'	Diff. Neb.	60' × 10'	—
NGC 2022	05h 42.0m	+09° 04'	Pl. Neb.	28" × 27"	12.3pg
M78 (NGC 2068)	05h 46.7m	+00° 03'	Refl. Neb.	8' × 6'	~7
NGC 2169	06h 08.4m	+13° 57'	Open Cl.	7'	5.9
NGC 2174/5	06h 09.7m	+20° 30'	Open Cl./Diff. Neb.	25'	8

Starbirth

The bright white stars of Orion – including the belt and Rigel – are all part of the Orion Association. These hot B-type stars are all quite young (only a few million years old) and seem to have been born in the star-forming areas of dense clouds of dust and gas in the area – especially the Great Nebula itself. Astrophysicists are very interested in this area, probably the closest location to us (approximately 1,500 light years) in which extensive stellar birth is taking place.

The whole figure of Orion is alight with faint nebulous light coming from gas excited by the hot young stars within the association. There is no doubt that there are some reflection nebulae as well, near to the stars. The Infrared Astronomical Satellite (IRAS) showed huge concentrations of gas and dust all over the Orion/Monoceros region. Astronomers believe the dust and gas is a mixture of "raw" materials out of which stars form and matter blown off the "surfaces" of hot stars by so-called solar winds. This is particularly noted in the huge bubble or loop of gas around Lamba (λ) Orionis, one of the stars marking the hunter's beard.

The Great Nebula in Orion (M42) is perhaps the most photographed object in astronomy. This picture was made by the Reverend Ronald Royer using an 18-inch (46-cm) f/7 Newtonian telescope. It shows clearly the delicate white and pink traceries of the fan-shaped nebula. The small, almost round nebula directly above M42 is M43.

PEGASUS

Pegasus is a very well-known major constellation, centerpiece of the autumn sky for northern-hemisphere observers. The "Great Square of Pegasus" is one of the first things a beginner learns when observing the constellations. Several of the other fall groups are easily found once the square is located (Andromeda, Aquarius, Pisces, Cassiopeia). These other groups lie around the periphery of the large winged horse. The great square culminates at 10 pm on October 15. Pegasus contains many beautiful doubles, one of the best globular clusters (M15), and several fine galaxies for the telescopic observer.

The square is the body of the horse, and when it is rising in the east is often likened to a diamond. This is because of its orientation with one point up in the sky as it rises and the star on the northwest point, Scheat, Beta (β), appearing first before the rest of the diamond shape follows. The horse is orientated upside down for north temperate observers, upright for those south of the equator, with Enif, Epsilon (ε), the nose, the forelegs Mu (μ) and Eta (η). The star in the northeastern corner of the square, Alpheratz, is actually Alpha (α) Andromedae. There are many fine doubles in Pegasus, a few of which are detailed in the table below.

Deep Sky Objects

M15 (NGC 7078), a globular cluster of the strongly condensed type, is a showpiece for small telescopes. It is a large ball of stars rising in brightness rapidly to a luminous core. Since this object strongly emits X-rays, astronomers believe there may be a black hole at the center which sucks in any star coming too close. The destroyed star material joins the accretion disk of the black hole and as the material is finally stripped of electrons and accelerated into the hole, X-rays are produced which we detect. M15 is also the only globular cluster known to contain a planetary nebula, Pease 15, which is beyond the range of most backyard telescopes (3 arcseconds diameter, 15th magnitude). M15 is located west and a little north of Enif (ε). NGC 7331 is a large spiral galaxy of 9th-magnitude seen at 15° displacement from the edge-on position. It has a lot of dusty and closely wound arms, and there are several small galaxies to the east nearby. About half a degree to the southwest is the curious grouping of galaxies called Stephan's Quintet (NGC 7317, NGC 7318 A/B, NGC 7319, NGC 7320). Here are five galaxies, at least four of them interacting, with tidally disturbed matter streaming between them. The fifth galaxy is a little to one side, but close enough to be involved gravitationally. Curiously, one of the group, NGC 7320, has a much smaller redshift than the others. If they are all at the same distance, they should all have about the same redshift, assuming redshifts are proportional to the expansion rate of the Universe. Visually speaking, plenty of telescopic aperture is needed to identify the members. I usually see four fairly easily in a 10-inch (25-cm) f/6, with the two center galaxies (NGC 7318A and B) fused into one "faint fuzzy". These galaxies are 13th and 14th magnitudes, so don't expect to see what a long exposure on the 120-inch (3-meter) Shane Telescope produces!

Another galaxy in Pegasus worth pursuing is NGC 7479, a fine barred spiral located 3° south of Alpha Pegasi (α). Its arms are relatively bright, as is the cross-bar, and we are seeing this galaxy, almost flat-on. There is a field star at the western end of the galaxy, which shouldn't be mistaken for a supernova, which would have a similar brightness if it exploded in this object.

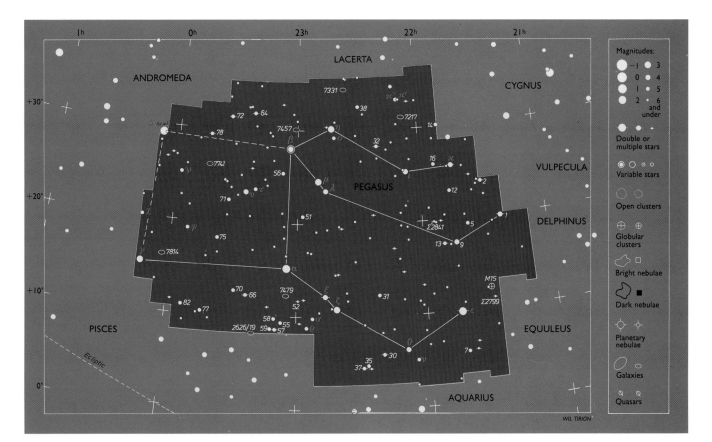

NGC 7331, a spiral galaxy in northwestern Pegasus, is one similar in form and size to our own Galaxy. It is about 50 million light years distant and has a luminosity of 50,000,000 Suns. The four small galaxies to the east of 7331 may be part of a complex system of galaxies including several more small faint companions. This is a 50-minute exposure with a 20-inch (50-cm) f/8 Ritchey-Chrétien on hypered Konica 400 by Kim Gordon.

TELESCOPIC OBJECTS IN PEGASUS

Double and Multiple Stars

Name	RA	Dec.	Separation (arcseconds)		Mags.		Year
Σ 2799	21h 28.9m	+11° 05'	AB	1.6	7.5	7.5	1959
			AC	136.2	7.5	9.3	1912
13	21h 50.1m	+17° 17'		0.4	5.5	7.5	1960
Σ 2841	21h 54.3m	+19° 43'	AB	22.3	6.4	7.9	1958
			BC	0.2	8.6	8.8	1969
37	22h 30.0m	+04° 26'		1.0	5.8	7.1	1969
52	22h 59.2m	+11° 44'		0.7	6.1	7.4	1969
72	23h 34.0m	+31° 20'		0.5	5.7	5.8	1960
78	23h 44.0m	+29° 22'		1.0	5.0	8.1	1959

Deep Sky Objects

Name	RA	Dec.	Type	Size	Mag.
M15 (NGC 7078)	21h 30.0m	+12° 10'	Glob. Cl.	12.3'	6.35
NGC 7217	22h 07.9m	+31° 22'	Gal. Sb	3.7' × 3.2'	10.2
NGC 7331	22h 37.1m	+34° 25'	Gal. Sb	10.7' × 4.0'	9.1
NGC 7479	23h 04.9m	+12° 19'	Gal. SBb	4.1' × 3.2'	11.0
NGC 7619	23h 20.2m	+08° 12'	Gal. E1	2.9' × 2.6'	11.1
NGC 7626	23h 20.7m	+08° 13'	Gal. E2p	2.5' × 2.0'	11.24
NGC 7814	00h 03.3m	+16° 09'	Gal. Sb	6.3' × 2.6'	10.9

PERSEUS

Perseus is one of the
more enduring of the
ancient legendary heroes,
whose most famous
deed was to kill Medusa,
a Gorgon whose
appearance was enough
to turn anyone
unfortunate enough to
look at her into stone.
Perseus was able to kill
her by using a shiny shield
to aim his sickle at her.
She was decapitated in
one blow, and the more
ornate constellation
drawings depict Perseus
holding Medusa's head.
As he returned, Perseus
rescued the hapless
Andromeda from the
clutches of the sea
monster Cetus. After
marrying Andromeda,
Perseus presented the
Gorgon's head to Athene.

Perseus is another Greek hero, immortalized in the form of an important and large fall–winter northern constellation. Perseus follows Cassiopeia and Andromeda, with whom he is mythologically associated. This grouping has many fairly bright stars but none of the first magnitude. If you locate the Pleiades, or Seven Sisters, look directly north of them toward Polaris. At about half the distance from the Pleiades to the pole, you will see a line of three fairly bright stars with many smaller, fainter ones around the brightest one. That star is Alpha Persei (α) or Mirfak, which marks the hero's elbow. To the southwest is another bright star, Algol, Beta Persei (β) which represents part of the head of Medusa whom the hero has just slain. The constellation is on the meridian at 10 pm about October 15.

Deep Sky Objects

Perseus has the Milky Way running through it from northwest to southeast, so it is a treasure-trove of telescopic objects. In addition, owing to the association of bright O/B stars centered on Alpha (α), Perseus has some of the best binocular objects in the sky. There are several open clusters crowned by the beautiful Double Cluster in Perseus. As the name suggests, this is composed of two clusters which are at slightly different distances, about half a degree apart. These were cataloged as h and Chi (χ) Persei, and appear to the eye as a fuzzy spot or condensation in the Milky Way between Cassiopeia and Mirfak. Either cluster would stand alone as a beautiful object, but in one field they are superb. You will need a low-power eyepiece and the more sky you can see around them, the better they are set off against the background. My best views have come in a pair of 20 × 80 binoculars and a 6-inch (15-cm) f/4 rich-field telescope.

The clusters are also designated NGC 869 (the western one) and NGC 884. NGC 884 contains several red stars with one near the center, while 869 numbers more bright stars and is a little richer, but has no red stars. About one degree east there is another smaller open cluster, NGC 957, with about 40 stars including two doubles.

M34 (NGC 1039) is a fine open cluster which can just be glimpsed with the naked eye. It lies on a line almost halfway between Algol and Gamma (γ) Andromedae, the easternmost bright star in that group. It contains about 80 stars in the half-degree diameter, including several pairs. Three degrees southwest of Mirfak is NGC 1245, a fairly rich cluster which constrasts nicely with two bright stars on either side. NGC 1528 is another charming open cluster with many fairly bright stars. M76 (NGC 650-1) is a small planetary nebula which is so small and faint it's a wonder that Messier saw it with his 3-inch (75-mm) telescope! It is a small planetary of about the 12th magnitude, which shows little detail. It takes a medium-sized telescope 8-inch (20-cm) or larger to see its dumbbell shape.

For owners of larger amateur telescopes (a growing fraternity), the Perseus Cluster of Galaxies is a fair target. Centered on NGC 1275 – which is an eruptive radio galaxy (Perseus A) – there is a string of galaxies about a degree long spreading west of NGC 1275 and around it which are visible in 10-inch (25-cm) and larger instruments. Photographs of NGC 1275 taken with a red filter show an amazing system of filaments erupting outwards from the galaxy, similar to those of Messier 82 or the Crab Nebula. NGC 1499 is known as the California Nebula because of its resemblance to the shape of the West Coast state. It is primarily a photographic subject, quite easy to capture in a 5-

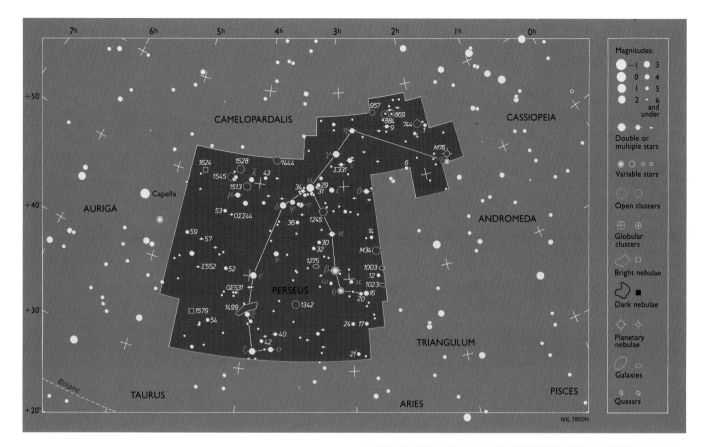

minute exposure with a piggybacked camera and 50-mm lens with ISO 1600 or ISO 3200 film (shoot at f/2.8). It is 2.5° long, and north of the star X₁ (ξ) which also illuminates it, with predominantly hydrogen emission, giving it a characteristic reddish or orange color. Astronomical binoculars or a small telescope – preferably equipped with nebular filters – seem to provide the best chance of seeing this low surface brightness object.

TELESCOPIC OBJECTS IN PERSEUS
Double and Multiple Stars

Name	RA	Dec.	Separation (arcseconds)		Mags.		Year
θ (Theta)	02h 44.2m	+49° 14'		18.3 (1953)	4.1	9.9	1953
η (Eta)	02h 50.7m	+55° 54'	AB	28.3	3.8	8.5	1932
			AC	66.6	3.8	9.8	1925
τ (Tau)	02h 54.3m	+52° 46'		51.7	4.0	10.6	1923
Σ 331	03h 00.9m	+52° 21'		12.1	5.3	6.7	1954
o (Omicron)	03h 44.3m	+32° 17'		1.0	3.8	8.3	1958
ζ (Zeta)	03h 54.1m	+32° 53'	AB	12.9	2.9	9.5	1968
			AC	32.8	2.9	11.3	1923
			AD	94.2	2.9	9.5	1957
			AE	120.3	2.9	10.2	1925
ε (Epsilon)	03h 57.9m	+40° 01'		8.8	2.9	8.1	1938
OΣ 531	04h 07.6m	+38° 04'		1.5	7.4	8.9	1969
OΣΣ 44	04h 17.3m	+46° 13'		58.4	7.2	8.6	1924
Σ 552	04h 31.4m	+40° 01'		9.0	7.0	7.2	1949
57	04h 33.4m	+43° 04'		116.2	6.1	6.8	1913

Variable Star

Name	RA	Dec.	Type	Range	Period
β (Beta) Algol	03h 08.2m	+40° 57'	Ecl. Bin.	2.12–3.40	2.8673d

Deep Sky Objects

Name	RA	Dec.	Type	Size	Mag.
M76 (NGC 650-1)	01h 42.4m	+51° 34'	Plan. Neb.	65"	12.2
NGC 869	02h 19.0m	+57° 09'	Open Cl.	30'	4.3pg
NGC 884	02h 22.4m	+57° 07'	Open Cl.	30'	4.4pg
NGC 957	02h 33.6m	+57° 32'	Open Cl.	11'	7.6
M34 (NGC 1039)	02h 42.0m	+42° 47'	Open Cl.	35'	5.2
NGC 1245	03h 14.7m	+47° 15'	Open Cl.	20'	6.9
NGC 1528	04h 15.4m	+51° 14'	Open Cl.	24'	6.4
NGC 1275	03h 19.8m	+41° 31'	Gal. P	0.7' × 0.6'	13
NGC 1499	04h 00.7m	+36° 37'	Diff. Neb. (E)	145' × 40'	14
NGC 1579	04h 30.2m	+35° 16'	Diff. Neb. (R)	12' × 8'	–

The Winking Demon

Beta Persei (β) or Algol, the Demon Star, is the best-known eclipsing binary star in the sky. Burnham's description is succinct: "The star is normally of magnitude 2.1 but at intervals of 2.86739 days it fades away to magnitude 3.4 and then slowly brightens again. The entire eclipse lasts some 10 hours; the exact period between minima is 2d 20h 48m 56s." John Goodricke had found the period accurately by 1782 and suggested that a brighter star was being eclipsed at least partially by a fainter companion. There is a smaller secondary dip in the light curve when in turn the brighter star eclipses the dimmer. The stars are about 100 light years away from the Earth, and the components are far too close to be resolved with Earth-based instruments (their centers are only 6.5 million miles apart).

PICTOR

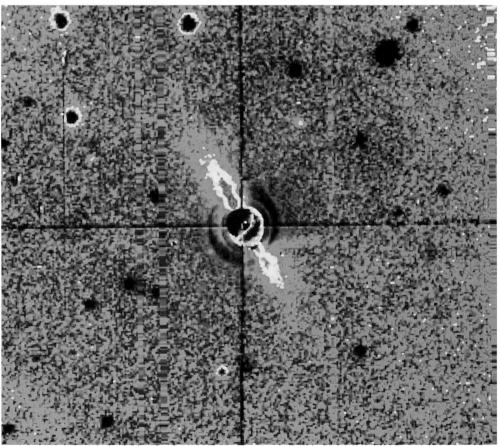

Pictor, the Painter's Easel, *is one of the constellations that Nicolas Louis de Lacaille created in 1752, in which he raised the most important implements of art and science to the heavens. There is no ancient mythology known for most of these groups, which were created out of amorphae or "left over" stars.*

Beta Pictoris. *What may be another solar system 50 light years away is seen in this CCD image of a circumstellar disk of material (red and yellow) seen edge-on around the star Beta Pictoris. The disk is thought to consist of ices, carbonaceous organic substances and silicates; it exends 60 billion kilometers from the star, which is hidden behind a circular occulting mask at the center of the picture. The fine dark lines that intersect in the middle of the picture and the black arcs around Beta Pictoris itself are artefacts of the imaging technique. The picture was recorded on the 100-inch (2.5-m) telescope at Las Campanas Observatory, Chile.*

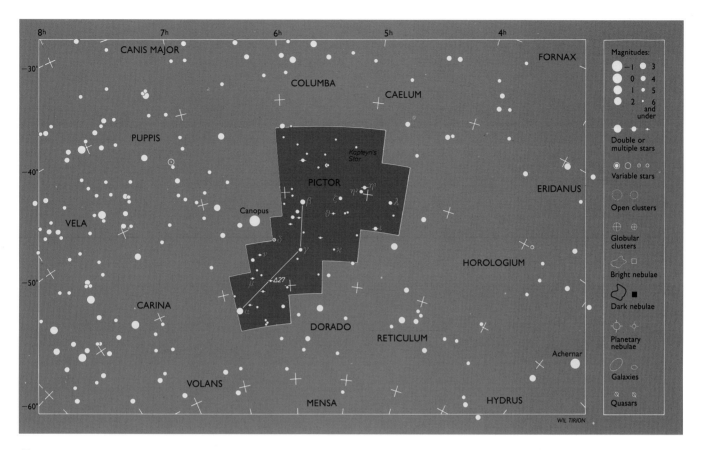

*P*ictor is a small southern constellation preceeding Canopus, with which its Beta (β) and Gamma (γ) stars make an almost equilateral triangle. It is largely circumpolar for those in temperate southern latitudes, and culminates at 10 pm on January 15 – the middle of summer in those climes. The constellation lies quite far from the Milky Way and contains little of telescopic interest.

The distance from the Galaxy and relative paucity of stars suggest that novae would be rare events, but a nova was seen in Pictor in 1925. A star which had been at 12th magnitude rose somewhat slowly and irregularly to almost 1st magnitude and then dropped (again, irregularly) until it rose again to 2nd magnitude 50 days later. Once again, after a drop it brightened only 5 days later, and then began a slow, somewhat irregular drop back to its pre-nova brightness. This is known as a recurring nova, and other examples have been studied. Apparently, considerable gas was blown off the star during the episode, as nebulosity was seen shortly after the nova dropped back in brightness. This kind of explosion/expulsion can happen when a star burns so much of its hydrogen core that the radiation pressure cannot hold up the outer layers of the star, and a sudden "settling" occurs. Then, as the collapse happens, a layer rebounds and blows off the surface of the contracted star. Current theory calls for material to transfer to the nova star from a close binary companion, leading to the collapse as the outer layers become "too heavy" to remain supported by radiation from the core. This star is probably about 1,000 light years distant, although too far for direct trigonometric measurement.

Kapteyn's Star

Kayteyn's Star is a red dwarf of about 9th magnitude, which has the second most rapid proper motion in the sky, 8.70 arcseconds per year. It is travelling southeastwards and covers a degree of sky in only 414 years. The distance to this fast-moving star is 12.7 light years, making it one of the nearest stars (actually ranking 24th on a recent list). It is a small red star about 250 times fainter in luminosity than our Sun. The observer should find it easy to detect motion in a year or two's observations, as it has just made a close pass (as seen from the Earth) by a more distant star and will be pulling away from it during the 1990s.

Multiple Stars

A few of the doubles located in Pictor are listed below. Iota (ι) is one of the most striking pairs with two bright components at an easy 12.3 arcseconds separation. Theta (θ) is a triple but the close stars are very difficult to resolve at about 0.2 arcseconds. Hartung reports they are opening, so this star is worth trying to observe. Dunlop (Δ) 27 is an optical double which is slowly diminishing in separation, and the components have a nice color contrast, blue and gold. There are a number of faint galaxies but none brighter than about magnitude 12.

TELESCOPIC OBJECTS IN PICTOR
Double Stars

Name	RA	Dec.	Separation (arcseconds)	Mags.		Year
ι (Iota)	04h 50.9m	−53° 28′	12.3	5.6	6.4	1952
θ (Theta)	05h 24.8m	−52° 19′	AB 0.2	6.9	7.2	1960
			AC 38.2	6.9	6.8	1938
Δ 27	06h 16.3m	−59° 13′	40.1	6.4	8.0	1950
μ (Mu)	06h 32.0m	−58° 45′	2.4	5.8	9.0	1937

PISCES

Pisces, the Fishes, is without doubt a very old constellation, and appears as a fish or two fishes in several ancient cultures. In more familiar Greco–Roman mythology, the fishes represented Venus and her son Cupid, who plunged into the Euphrates when the monster Typhon attacked, and became the fishes whose images were raised into the sky. Pisces has a connection with the seasons, as the celestial equator and ecliptic (Sun's apparent path) cross at the First Point of Aries, now moved into Pisces by precession of the equinoxes. When the Sun crosses this point on its way north, it is called the Vernal Equinox.

TELESCOPIC OBJECTS IN PISCES
Double and Multiple Stars

Name	RA	Dec.	Separation (arcseconds)	Mags.		Year
27	23h 58.7m	−03° 33'	1.3	4.9	10.2	1958
34 (UU)	00h 10.0m	+11° 09'	7.7	5.5	9.4	1958
35	00h 15.0m	+08° 49'	11.6	6.0	7.6	1958
51	00h 32.4m	+06° 57'	27.5	5.7	9.5	1933
65	00h 49.9m	+27° 43'	4.4	6.3	6.3	1959
ψ₁ (Psi 1)	01h 05.6m	+21° 28'	30.0	5.6	5.8	1959
φ (Phi)	01h 13.7m	+24° 35'	7.8	4.7	10.1	1936
ζ (Zeta)	01h 13.7m	+07° 35'	23.0	5.6	6.5	1974
Σ 145	01h 41.3m	+25° 45'	AB 10.5	6.2	10.8	1974
			AB 82.4	6.2	11.0	1959
α (Alpha)	02h 02.0m	+02° 46'	1.9	4.2	5.1	1966
Wolf 28 (Van Maanen's Star)	00h 49.1m	+05° 25'	distance = 14.1 light years	proper motion = 2.99"/year		
				Mag. 12.4		

Deep Sky Objects

Name	RA	Dec.	Type	Size	Mag.
NGC 128	00h 29.25m	+02° 52'	Gal. S0p	3.4' × 1.0'	11.6
NGC 488	01h 21.8m	+05° 15'	Gal. Sb−	5.2' × 4.1'	10.3
NGC 520	01h 24.6m	+03° 48'	Gal. P	4.8' × 2.1'	11.2
M74 (NGC 628)	01h 36.7m	+15° 47'	Gal. Sc	10.2' × 9.5'	9.2

Pisces is the twelfth zodiacal constellation, and is best seen during the fall for northern-hemisphere observers. Pisces contains no very bright stars, but there are asterisms in the group that can be put together to make the complete figure. It is a large constellation whose center is on the meridian at 10 pm on November 1. Just south of the Great Square of Pegasus is the "Circlet" of Pisces, an elliptical figure of stars of fourth magnitude and fainter. It is easy to pick out because of the absence of many stars in the region. This represents the western fish, the other appearing upright and about 30° eastwards. There is a "chord" or line of stars which leads from the circlet to the other fish, which then is shown by a line almost north–south, of the stars Omicron (o), Eta (η), Theta (θ), Chi (χ), Phi (φ), Psi (ψ) and Pi (π). The upper fish's head is near Alpha (α) Andromedae, Mirach.

Pisces contains several double star systems of interest, a star of high proper motion (Van Maanen's Star) and several nice galaxies for the amateur telescope. The very red variable star TX Piscium is an easily found example of the N spectral type – cool giant stars presumably near the end of their heat-producing lives. The star brightens only a third of a magnitude sporadically, presumably as the layers settle down, producing a short period of increased radiation. It is the easternmost star of the circlet marking the western fish, and at about 5.5 magnitude is an easy binocular object. It is easily recognized by its brick-red color.

The very bright object in the photograph just above and between Nu and Mu is the planet Jupiter.

Van Maanen's Star

Van Maanen's Star is a fast-moving star also known as Wolf 28. It is a white dwarf and has an apparent visual magnitude of 12.4. Its

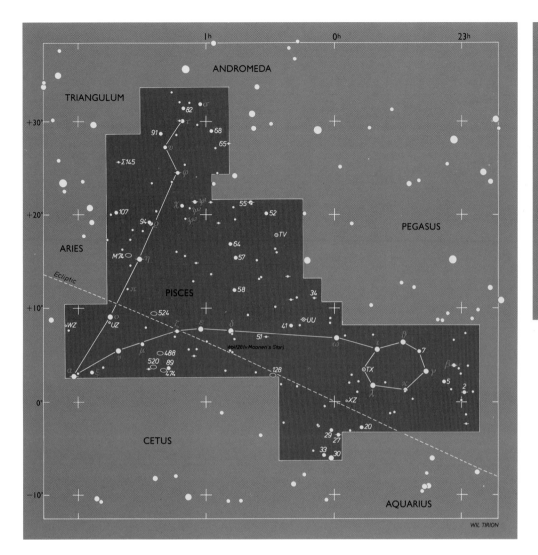

relatively faint absolute magnitude of 14.2 means the star is about 1/5800 the brightness of the Sun. It is made of "degenerate" matter, that is, mostly neutrons with no electrons, and must be only about the size of the Earth! It has, however, the mass of our Sun, so the density must be about one million times that of water. Burnham remarks that this star may have ceased energy production eons ago and is still hot from its active period. It is most probably slowly cooling down and retaining heat owing to its dense mass. This star has the large proper motion of almost 3 arcseconds per year.

Multiple Stars

Some of the doubles to enjoy are Alpha (α), a double with 4th-magnitude and 5th-magnitude stars which are closing and under one arcsecond apart. Here they will remain until about 2085, when they will start to open again. The colors of stars of Alpha have been remarked upon, so when you look at it examine closely the B star for color. A is A2 and B is A3, a small difference in color, but it has been proven in color photographic studies that the eye can perceive differences as small as 50°. In double star observation, it is often the contrast between the two stars which is important. Zeta (ζ) is an easy double for the small telescope with components separated by 23 arcseconds. 65 is a

fine pair of equally bright pale-yellow stars resolvable in almost any telescope. Psi I (ψ_1) is another easy pair, consisting of two 5th-magnitude stars 30 arcseconds apart.

Deep Sky Objects

The deep sky objects in Pisces are all galaxies. There are several unusually shaped ones seen in long-exposure photographs with large telescopes. NGC 128 has what appears to be a rectangular nuclear area and requires at least a 10-inch (25-cm) aperture telescope to see this well. NGC 488 is a lovely face-on spiral with faint, closely-wound arms. An 8-inch (20-cm) 'scope shows a softly glowing disk, rising in brightness towards the center. NGC 520 is an eruptive galaxy or possibly two galaxies in collision, and needs at least a 10-inch (25-cm) telescope to appreciate.

M74 (NGC 628) is the best galaxy in Pisces and is easily found a degree east, and slightly north, of Eta (η). It was discovered by Messier's associate P. Méchain from Paris in 1780, and later incorporated into Messier's catalog of non-stellar objects. It is, however, not a bright object, and in an 8-inch (20-cm) instrument appears as a featureless disk with a bright core. The Orange County Astronomers Kuhn Telescope (22-inch (54-cm)) at Anza shows the brighter arms quite well, however, demonstrating the power of aperture in observing galaxies.

PUPPIS

Puppis is the Poop (raised stern portion) of the sailing ship Argo Navis, which was a huge, ancient constellation broken up in the 1750s by Lacaille to form Vela (the Sails), Puppis, Carina (the Keel) and Pyxis (the Compass). In Greek myth, the Argo carried her crew of 50, captained by Jason, on an epic voyage from Thessaly to the Black Sea (Euxine Sea), to bring back the fleece of a winged golden ram and with it the soul of Phrixus, who the ram had rescued from sacrifice many years earlier. The image of the Argo was placed in the sky after the voyage by Athene.

M46 is an open star cluster located east of Sirius and adjacent to M47, which is just out of the picture. M46 is a fairly condensed cloud of stars of 10th magnitude and fainter. The small, red, ring-shaped planetary nebula is NGC 2438; it is about twice as far as M46. The photograph was taken by California amateur Rick Hull with his 12-inch (30-cm) f/4 Newtonian telescope. The exposure was 40 minutes on hypered Konica 400 negative film.

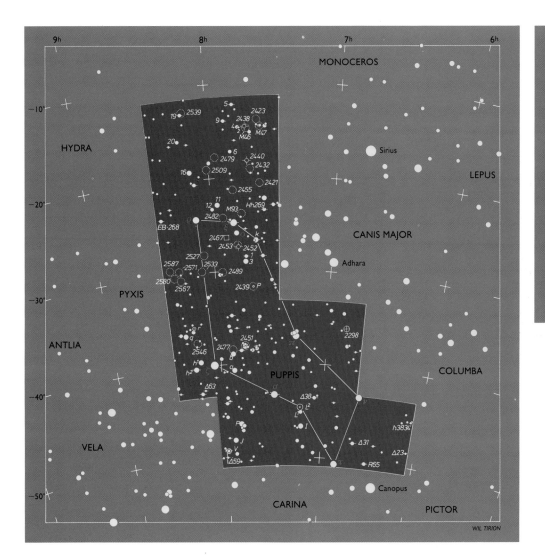

Puppis is a southern constellation which begins east of Sirius, so can be seen south of +40° latitude. It has many bright stars, and the Milky Way runs right down the middle providing a large number of telescopic objects, especially galactic open clusters. It has no strongly recognizable figure, but there are many bright stars, and, once found, Puppis is unmistakable. It is a winter group for northern-hemisphere observers, culminating at 10 pm on January 15. Its main stars are found in two groups; the first just east (following) of the hind feet of Canis Major, with another group 15° further south.

Puppis has 73 open clusters listed in Hirshfield and Sinnott's *Sky Catalogue 2000.0*, but many of these are simply condensations in the Milky Way. Hartung says 40, while Burnham lists 25, a more realistic number in terms of actually observing them all with amateur-sized instruments. There are also several good planetary nebulae and a diffuse nebula, NGC 2467. One small globular cluster (NGC 2298) is found in the western, less-obscured part of the group. Naturally, in this rich galactic region there are many impressive double and multiple stars. This is a particularly good constellation for binocular observers, with the bright Milky Way and its groupings of star clusters. Although rather low for many northern observers, Puppis is worth exploring when weather conditions allow.

Multiple Stars

A few of the many fine doubles in Puppis include R65, a triple, with a close (half-arcsecond) pair and a third star of magnitude 8.5, 12.4 arcseconds distant. The close stars have a 50-year period. Dunlop (Δ) 38 is an easy pair of yellow suns at some 20 arcseconds distance. k Puppis is a bright couple of white stars, separated by 9.9 arcseconds, which can be resolved in virtually any telescope. V is a delicate triple, whose primary is an eclipsing binary with a brightness range of from 4.74 to 5.25. The other three companions are of 10th and 11th magnitude. Dunlop (Δ) 59 is another almost equal double of 6th-magnitude stars separated by 16.4 arcseconds. Sigma Puppis (σ) presents a nice color contrast, with stars of orange and white (K5 and G5 stars).

Deep Sky Objects

A telescope or binoculars will open up many new sights in Puppis. NGC 2298 is a small globular cluster on the western side of the constellation where galactic absorption isn't heavy. It has irregular edges and resolves in an 8-inch (20-cm) instrument. It is a distant 75,000 light years away. M47 (NGC 2422) leads the parade of open clusters in Puppis, being 20 arcminutes in diameter and a bright cluster of stars from 6th magnitude downwards. There is a bright-orange star just preceeding it, along with two fairly easy double stars, Σ1120 and Σ1121. M46 (NGC 2437) lies just following M47 and is a cloud of small stars. The two clusters make a nice contrast, with M47 a coarse, sparser grouping and M46 a richer, but fainter, cluster. If you look closely at M46 you'll see a 50-arcsecond-diameter planetary nebula among the stars in its northeast quadrant. With 8-inch (20-cm) telescopic apertures and above you can see that it is a round nebula, with the three stars projected upon it. In fact, the nebula is about twice as far away as the cluster, and they just happen to be in our line of sight together. M93 (NGC 2447) is another bright cluster in the rich Milky Way which runs through Puppis. It's a compact group of about 50 bright stars lying 9° south of M46-7. NGC 2477 is a wonderful group of about 300 stars which appears like a cloud with a small telescope or binoculars. It is similar in concentration to M11 in Aquila, in that it looks like a very loose globular cluster, or a very compact galactic cluster. Spectral analysis tells us the difference in the ages and composition of the stars, since most of the galactic clusters are fairly young, and most of the globulars very ancient (2477 is a galactic cluster). NGC 2539 is another fine galactic or open cluster, with 100 stars of 11th magnitude and fainter in a 20-arcminute diameter region of the sky.

The planetaries in Puppis are good examples of the type. NGC 2440 is an 11th-magnitude ellipse, about 15 × 30 arcseconds in size and bluish in color. NGC 2452 is small and of 13th magnitude, but easy to pick out with an 8-inch (20-cm) or larger telescope. NGC 2467 is not a planetary but is a strange nebulous object, about 4 arcminutes in diameter and round. Burnham mentions faint streamers out to a radius of 15 arcminutes, sometimes seen on photographs. This nebula is gaseous, apparently excited to luminosity by the stars imbedded in the gas, several of which can be seen in the telescope. Deep photographs of this area show NGC 2467 and several other objects in the field. One appears to be a protostar (Herbig–Haro object) which has a peculiar jet of gas coming out of it, looking like the famous jet in M 87 (beaded) which is glowing near 2467. This jet is near two faint stars. If you have access to a 12-inch (30-cm) or larger telescope and can see this far south, see if you can see this peculiar feature.

Variable Stars

If you are far enough south, there is an interesting field south of Pi (π). This is the area of L2 and V Puppis, both variable stars. L2 is a semi-regular, or long period variable star, which has a period of 140 days on average, and a range from 2.6 to 6.2. V Puppis, located just southwest of brilliant Gamma γ Velorum, is an eclipsing binary. It has the short period of 1.454 days and a range from 4.7 to 5.2.

TELESCOPIC OBJECTS IN PUPPIS
Double and Multiple Stars

Name	RA	Dec.		Separation (arcseconds)	Mags.		Year
h3834	06h 04.7m	−45° 05′	AB	4.8	5.9	9.4	1951
			AC	196.7	5.9	6.2	1854
R 65	06h 29.8m	−50° 14′	AB	0.5 (1926)	6.0	6.1	1926
			AC	12.4	6.0	9.0	1938
Δ 31	06h 38.6m	−48° 13′		13.0	5.0	8.3	1937
Δ 38	07h 04.0m	−43° 36′	AB	20.5	5.6	7.2	1932
			AC	184.8	5.6	8.1	1900
σ (Sigma)	07h 29.2m	−43° 18′		22.3	3.3	8.5	1952
Hh 269	07h 34.3m	−23° 28′		9.6	5.8	5.9	1952
k	07h 38.8m	−26° 48′		9.9	4.5	4.7	1951
2	07h 45.5m	−14° 41′	AB	16.8	6.1	6.8	1933
			AC	100.5	6.1	10.4	1932
5	07h 47.9m	−12° 12′		2.2	5.6	7.7	1960
V	07h 58.2m	−49° 15′	AB	7.0	4.5	10	1933
			AC	19.0	4.5	11.5	1933
			AD	39.2	4.5	10	1933
Δ 59	07h 59.2m	−49° 59′		16.4	6.5	6.5	1954
EB-268	08h 25.1m	−24° 03′		41.0	5.3	8.8	1917

Deep Sky Objects

Name	RA	Dec.	Type	Size	Mag.
NGC 2298	06h 49.0m	−36° 00′	Glob. Cl.	6.8′	9.4
M47 (NGC 2422)	07h 36.6m	−14° 30′	Open Cl.	30′	4.4
M46 (NGC 2437)	07h 41.8m	−14° 49′	Open Cl.	27′	6.1
NGC 2440	07h 41.9m	−18° 13′	Plan. Neb.	14″ × 32″	10.8pg
M93 (NGC 2447)	07h 44.6m	−23° 52′	Open Cl.	22′	6.2
NGC 2452	07h 47.4m	−27° 29′	Plan. Neb.	15″ × 20″	12.6pg
NGC 2477	07h 52.3m	−38° 33′	Open Cl.	20′	5.8
NGC 2467	07h 52.5m	−26° 24′	Diff. Neb.	8′ × 7′	10?
NGC 2539	08h 10.7m	−12° 50′	Open Cl.	22′	6.5

The Puppis A supernova remnant is an expanding cloud of gas and dust resulting from the explosion of a massive star some 4000 years ago. This false-color image shows Puppis A at X-ray wavelengths. The bright blue, yellow and red regions are where the gas thrown out by the supernova is being heated to temperatures of millions of degrees as it sweeps up the tenuous interstellar gas and dust. The picture was obtained by the European Space Agency, Exosat X-ray astronomy satellite.

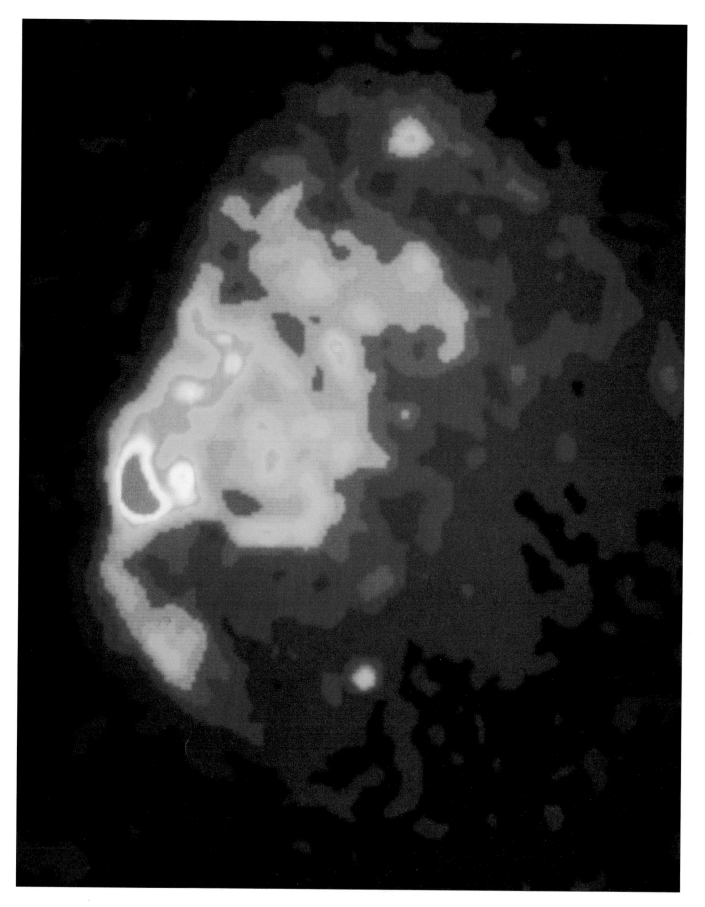

SAGITTA/VULPECULA

These two small northern constellations are grouped here for convenience. Sagitta is easy to find, located directly between Albireo, in Cygnus, and Altair, the brightest star in Aquila. There is a little line of several stars with the back end of the arrow a naked-eye double, Alpha (α) and Beta (β). The constellation is in the midst of the summer Milky Way with its crowded star fields and delightful multiple star array. Sagitta culminates at 10 pm on August 15. If you have found Sagitta, then Vulpecula is the amorphous group of stars between it and the southern boundary of Cygnus. Vulpecula's brighter stars are scattered across the Milky Way, which comes down through the center of this wide constellation. Vulpecula is 2.5 hours of Right Ascension wide, with two streams of the Galaxy passing through it.

Sagitta

This area has a number of good telescopic objects, an amusing asterism, and beautiful star fields for the binocular. In Sagitta, outstanding double and multiple stars are: Epsilon (ε), a wide optical double; HN 84, which has contrasting colors; and Theta (θ), a triple star of which the primary and tertiary stars are optically aligned.

The main attraction in Sagitta is the loose globular cluster M71 (NGC 6838). It is easy to locate about halfway between Gamma (γ) and Delta (δ) Sagittae. This was once classed as an open cluster, but now that interstellar absorption has been recognized, we realize there must be many faint stars which "fill in" the group. A small telescope will in fact show it as a scattering of stars with only a nebulous suspicion of richness. A 10-inch (25-cm) or larger aperture with medium to high powers will show the cluster as a richly resolved ball with many scattered brighter

points around the field. The distance is about 18,000 light-years. IC 4997 is a tiny planetary nebula, fairly bright, and making a 1 arcminute double object with a yellowish star nearby. High powers are needed to see the small disk of the nebula.

The eclipsing binary U Sagittae is an outstanding example of its type. The star is just west of the bottom star of the "Coathanger" asterism (see below). It has a magnitude range of from 6.4 to 9.0 with steep light curves. The eclipses come every 3 days, 9 hours and 8 minutes, and the minima occur for 1 hour and 40 minutes. The drop and brightening at the end of the eclipse is dramatic and can be seen over a period of a few minutes.

Vulpecula

Vulpecula contains the charming "Coathanger" asterism, officially known as Brocchi's Cluster. This group of 10 stars is visible to the naked eye as a small fuzzy spot and has no NGC designation. The slightest optical aid will show an almost perfectly straight line of six stars with four more making a hook protruding from the center of the line. It looks exactly like a small upside-down coathanger. This form was distorted in 1976 by the presence of a nova just north of the easternmost bright star, which reached magnitude 6.5. It is beyond visibility in small telescopes.

NGC 6802 is a small open cluster immediately following 7 Vulpeculae, the easternmost bright star in the Coathanger. It needs at least an 8-inch (20-cm) aperture and medium powers to appreciate the concentrated, but rather faint, grouping of 13th magnitude and fainter stars.

The Dumbbell Nebula

M27 (NGC 6853), the Dumbbell Nebula, is a superb object for

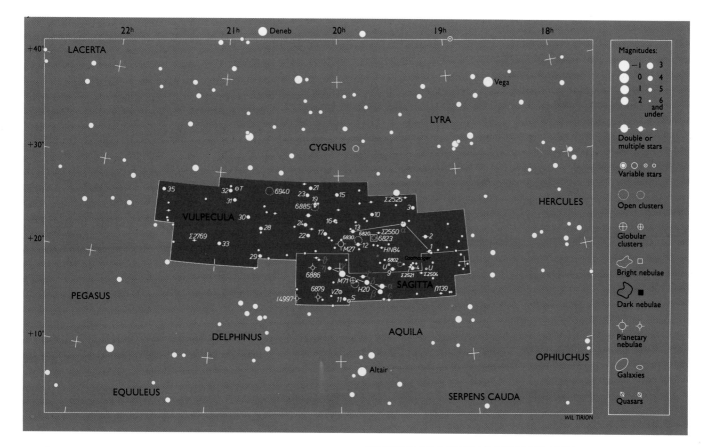

small telescopes, and exceptional in larger ones. It can be glimpsed with 7 × 50 binoculars as a fuzzy star. A foolproof way of finding it in this rich Milky Way region is to fix your telescope on the point of the arrow, Gamma (γ) Sagittae, lock the RA axis, and move the telescope 3° north in declination. The nebula should now appear in a low power eyepiece. In an 8-inch (20-cm) telescope, it has a dumbbell shape, not quite fully round, with a couple of faint stars involved. It takes a larger telescope to see the magnitude 13.5 central star, one of several stars conspicuous with a 22-inch (54-cm) telescope as a completely round object, with the dumbbell area very bright. A nebular filter helps define the edges in the 22-inch telescope. This is the largest bright planetary nebula, and is a showpiece for small telescopes, although rather featureless. NGC 6940 is a lovely, large open cluster in the northeast part of the constellation. It is rich in small stars and reminds one of M46 in Puppis. In the rich Milky Way, it is a distinctive group. Lying close to the Cygnus Loop supernova remnant in Cygnus, it appears on wide field photographs of that wonderful nebula. Vulpecula has several doubles which tend to be of unequal brightness, which are detailed in the table below.

TELESCOPIC OBJECTS IN SAGITTA
Double and Multiple Stars

Name	RA	Dec.	Separation (arcseconds)	Mags.		Year
Burnham 139	19h 12.6m	+16° 51'	AB 0.7	6.7	8.0	1958
			AC 113.4		7.9	1919
			AD 28.6		12.7	1958
Σ 2504	19h 21.0m	+19° 09'	8.9	7.0	8.7	1968
ε (Epsilon)	19h 37.3m	+16° 28'	89.2	5.7	8.0	1949

TELESCOPIC OBJECTS IN SAGITTA continued
Double and Multiple Stars

Name	RA	Dec.	Separation (arcseconds)	Mags.		Year
HN 84	19h 39.4m	+22° 15'	28.2	6.5	8.9	1931
θ (Theta)	20h 09.9m	+20° 55'	AB 11.9	6.5	9.0	1951
			83.9		7.4	1949

Deep Sky Objects

Name	RA	Dec.	Type	Size	Mag.
M71 (NGC 6838)	19h 53.8m	+18° 47'	Glob. Cl.	7.2'	8.3v
IC 4997	20h 20.2m	+16° 45'	Plan. Neb.	5"	11.6pg

TELESCOPIC OBJECTS IN VULPECULA
Double and Multiple Stars

Name	RA	Dec.	Separation (arcseconds)	Mags.		Year
2 Vul	19h 17.7m	+23° 02'	AB 1.8	5.4	9.2	1953
			AC 50.8		11.0	1881
4 Vul	19h 25.5m	+19° 48'	18.9	5.2	9.9	1957
Σ 2521	19h 26.5m	+19° 53'	AB 26.7	5.9	10.7	1958
			AC 70.4		9.9	1918
			ADI 49.6		9.9	1918
Σ 2525	19h 26.6m	+27° 19'	1.6	8.1	8.4	1959
Σ 2560	19h 40.7m	+23° 43'	15.3	6.6	8.9	1958
13 Vul	19h 53.5m	+24° 05'	0.8	4.6	7.8	1960
Σ 2769	21h 10.5m	+22° 27'	17.9	6.9	7.7	1954

Deep Sky Objects

Name	RA	Dec.	Type	Size	Mag.
Coathanger (Brocchi's Cluster)	19h 25.4m	+20° 11'	Asterism	60'	3.6
NGC 6802	19h 30.6m	+20° 16'	Open Cl.	3.2'	8.8
NGC 6820	19h 43.1m	+23° 17'	Diff. Neb.	40' × 30'	...
M27 (NGC 6853) The Dumbbell Nebula	19h 59.6m	+22° 43'	Plan. Neb.	350"	7.6pg
NGC 6940	20h 34.6m	+28° 18'	Open Cl.	31'	6.3

SAGITTARIUS

Sagittarius, the Archer, is one of the more prominent constellations. Probably it originated in ancient Babylon or Assyria, and was well known by the time of the Greeks. The figure appears with a lion's head on the Zodiac of Dendera, an Egyptian depiction of the sky. The centaur was a favorite creature of the Assyrians, seen as warlike and uncivilized, unlike his cousin to the west (Centaurus). He is depicted as holding a bow and arrow which is pointed at Antares, the heart of the Scorpion. Today's stargazers often describe a ladle or teapot.

The Sagittarius Star Cloud is the densest star cloud of the entire Milky Way. Although it lies in the direction of the center of the galaxy, it is in fact located in the nearby spiral arm and not in the galactic hub. The photograph was made by the author with a 5.5-inch (13.75-cm) f/1.65 Schmidt camera. The exposure was 10 minutes on Fujichrome 100 film.

Sagittarius is a large constellation which is seen towards the southern horizon in later summer. It has many fairly bright stars, but its chief glory is the central Milky Way, which runs through the western part of the constellation with many condensations and bright spots visible to the naked eye. Indeed, the center of our Galaxy is located on the west shoulder of the Large Sagittarius Star Cloud. Sagittarius is the ninth constellation of the ancient zodiac, and covers an area of sky of 867 square degrees. It has been depicted as an archer, a bow and arrow, and today's centaur archer, pointing his arrow at the heart of the Scorpion to the west.

It is with the telescope or binoculars that the real richness of Sagittarius becomes apparent. The Large Sagittarius Star Cloud is bright to the naked eye, and increases in brightness the farther south you are because it is higher in the sky. For southern-hemisphere observers, the constellation is overhead in July, August and September in the evening hours, and even with the naked eye, several clusters, dark dust nebulae, and glowing nebulae are seen from a dark sky site. 7 × 50 or larger binoculars will show many of the Deep Sky objects which are tabulated below. Particularly well seen in binoculars are the star clouds of the Galaxy. On the east side of the constellation the star density smoothly falls off away from the disk of the Galaxy (in which we are located), while the western side is limited and obscured by dust clouds, interesting dark places in the Milky Way we now know are obscurations rather than sparsely populated voids. There is perhaps ten times more dark matter in the Milky Way than is contained in stars or glowing nebular material. The center of the galaxy is obscured by as much as 30 magnitudes of absorbing material!

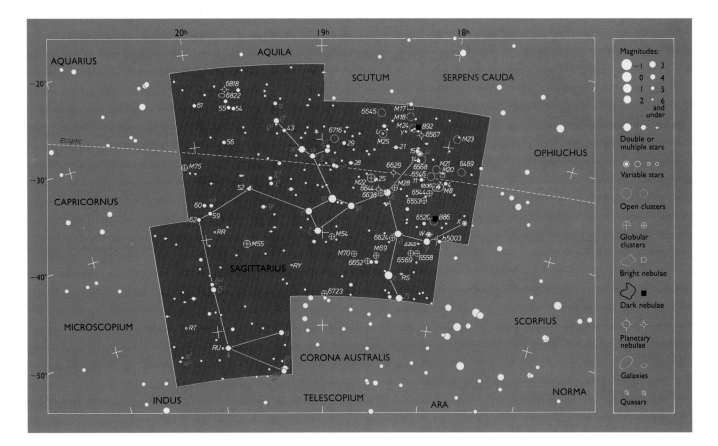

Deep Sky Objects

With astronomical binoculars, the many globular star clusters in Sagittarius are easily found. Over 20 are known, and in fact almost 10 per cent of all those cataloged are found here. The several galactic, or "open", clusters in Sagittarius are also well seen in smaller telescopes or large binoculars. The Small Sagittarius Star Cloud appears, with a little imagination, like a pilot with flying helmet, seen as the darker dusty areas surrounding the cloud of stars and passing behind it. The whole star cloud bears the description of M24 (NGC 6603). In photographs – and even with the naked eye on a very clear night – this Small Sagittarius Star Cloud is distinctively more blue-colored than the Large Sagittarius Cloud to the south. This shows up in color photographs too, and is probably because the small cloud is less obscured by reddening interstellar dust, and also perhaps by a larger population of bluer, younger stars.

M23 (NGC 6494) is a large open cluster lying to the west of the Small Cloud. It is made up of about 100 stars clustered in a 25 arcminute diameter with attractive curves of stars of similar brightness. M20 (NGC 6514) is the "Trifid" Nebula, so named because of the prominent dark lanes which break the round glowing cloud into three major parts. This nebula is sometimes a bit disappointing to the beginner familiar with the spectacular photographs of it made with long exposures. But it does have its rewards, especially if seen in a good dark sky with a fast telescope. If there is enough light, a nebular filter will help show the object against the sky background. The nebulosity which is just north of the round part is apparently a reflection nebula, since it is blue in color. It is much fainter than the main body, but shows up well in photographs. One of the attractive features of

M20 is the multiple star near the center. This is named HN 40 and has three major components of 7th, 8th and 10th magnitude lined up in a row, and separated by 10.6 and 5.4 arcseconds. With enough power, this is a spectacular object, and other faint components have been found by the great visual observers at the turn of the century (Burnham and Barnard). M21 (NGC 6531) is a cluster of bright stars northeast of the Trifid, with several dozen covering a diameter of 12 arcminutes.

Barnard 86 is a black spot in the Large Sagittarius Star Cloud, towards its northern extremities. It is charmingly placed next to the little open cluster NGC 6520, and together they make a nice contrast. B86 is just a little smaller than the cluster and is essentially a dust cloud absorbing the starlight from behind it. M8 (NGC 6523) is one of the major features of Sagittarius, and is a large cloud of glowing hydrogen with a star cluster associated with the nebula. This large object can be seen with the naked eye just west of the Large Sagittarius Star Cloud against a dimmer part of the Milky Way. Any optical aid will show an elongated patch of nebulous haze with a dark lane across the middle. Against the eastern section is an open cluster of a hundred or so stars of similar brightness (10th–12th magnitude). The Lagoon Nebula, as M8 is called (from the shape of the dark lane), has many small dark globules, which may eventually condense into stars. These "Bok Globules" are difficult to see visually but show up well to the camera. This object responds well to use of a nebular filter, which darkens the sky background and lets the nebular light through. With a 22-inch (54-cm) aperture telescope the Lagoon shows bright edges, the Bok globules, and a bright hourglass-shaped nucleus.

Another bright emission nebula is the Swan, Omega, or

Horseshoe Nebula, M17 (NGC 6618). This nebula is smaller and more concentrated than M8 and therefore a little easier to see. It lies north of the Small Cloud and the sky behind it is dark, although scattered with stars. There is no prominent star cluster associated with M17. This luminous cloud is elongated and has a patch protruding at a right angle on the eastern side, which resembles the swan's neck and head. There are dust protrusions into the side of the nebula, and the whole object is mottled and not uniform. In a larger telescope with a nebular filter, there is a background cloud glowing around the bright parts.

A major object in Sagittarius is M22 (NGC 6656), one of the top five globulars in the sky. It is a fat ball of stars, slightly flattened, which resolves well in almost any telescope. This cluster and the small group of stars nearby are visible with the naked eye when the air is very clear. The innumerable stars seen in this cluster make a beautiful sight in an 8-inch (20-cm) or larger instrument. In photographs there is an interesting dark spot visible in the cluster where there appear to be no stars. This may be an interstellar dust cloud superimposed on the cluster stars or a place where just by chance there aren't as many stars as in the rest of the cluster. This must be one of the nearer globulars, estimated to be 9,600 light years distant. The absorption of M22 is nearly 2 magnitudes, so it would be even more spectacular if we could see it unveiled by interstellar dust.

Of the many other globular clusters in Sagittarius, M55 (NGC 6809) stands out. It is a loose aggregation of thousands of faint stars spread over a 10 arcminute area. The cluster was discovered by Nicolas de Lacaille, whose 2-inch (5-cm) aperture telescope couldn't resolve it from Cape Town in the 1750s. There is a strange object in eastern Sagittarius called Barnard's Dwarf Galaxy, or NGC 6822. This irregular miniature of the Small Magellanic Cloud is fun to hunt up. It's visible in 7 × 50 binoculars, but due to its size (9 × 10 arcminutes) the galaxy is difficult to see with more than about × 50 magnification. It's quite easy in 20 × 80 astronomical binoculars, but a bigger instrument requires movement of the telescope to help identify the edges of the object. In a 10-inch (25-cm) or above it appears lumpy and two HII regions are easily observed at the north end. This is a member of the Local Group of galaxies and is located about 1,700,000 light years distant. It's small compared with the Small Magellanic Cloud, despite a luminosity of 50 million Suns.

The center of our Galaxy is in Sagittarius, buried 30,000 light years beyond visual penetration at about RA 17h 42m, Dec. −29°. This is located on the "shoulder" of the Large Sagittarius Star Cloud just north of M6 in Scorpius. Infrared and microwave radio studies show a massive cluster of stars and swirling gas there, perhaps the home of a black hole.

TELESCOPIC OBJECTS IN SAGITTARIUS
Double and Multiple Stars

Name	RA	Dec.	Separation (arcseconds)	Mags.		Year
h 5003	17h 59.1m	−30° 15′	5.5	5.2	6.9	1952
Burnham 245	18h 10.1m	−30° 44′	4.0	5.6	8.6	1951
μ (Mu)	18h 13.8m	−21° 04′	16.9	3.9	11.4	1932
η (Eta)	18h 17.6m	−36° 46′	AB 3.6	3.2	7.8	1959
			AC 33.3	3.2	13.0	1896
			AD 93.2	3.2	10.0	1896
ζ (Zeta)	19h 02.6m	−29° 53′	AB 0.4	3.2	3.4	1959
			AC 75	3.2	9.9	1905
β₁ (Beta 1)	19h 22.6m	−44° 28′	28.3	4.0	7.1	1953
52	19h 36.7m	−24° 53′	2.5	4.7	9.2	1959
κ₂ (Kappa 2)	20h 23.9m	−42° 25′	0.8	6.0	6.9	1952

Deep Sky Objects

Name	RA	Dec.	Type	Size	Mag.
M23 (NGC 6494)	17h 56.8m	−19° 01′	Open Cl.	27′	5.5
M20 (NGC 6514)	18h 02.6m	−23° 02′	Diff. Neb.	29′ × 27′	7
B 86	18h 02.7m	−27° 50′	Dark. Neb.	4′ × 3′	....
M8 (NGC 6523)	18h 03.8m	−24° 23′	Diff. Neb. + Cl.	90′ × 40′	5
M21 (NGC 6531)	18h 04.6m	−22° 30′	Open Cl.	13′	5.9
B92	18h 15.5m	−18° 11′	Dark Neb.	15′	....
M24 (NGC 6603)	18h 18.4m	−18° 25′	Open Cl.	5′	6.5
M17 (NGC 6618)	18h 20.8m	−16° 11′	Diff. Neb. + Cl.	46′ × 37′	5
M28 (NGC 6626)	18h 24.5m	−24° 52′	Glob. Cl.	11.2′	6.9
M69 (NGC 6637)	18h 31.4m	−32° 21′	Glob. Cl.	7.1′	7.7
M25 (IC4725)	18h 31.6m	−19° 15′	Open Cl.	32′	4.6
M22 (NGC 6656)	18h 36.4m	−23° 54′	Glob. Cl.	24.0′	5.10
M70 (NGC 6681)	18h 43.2m	−32° 18′	Glob. Cl.	7.8′	8.08
M54 (NGC 6715)	18h 55.1m	−30° 29′	Glob. Cl.	9.1′	7.7
M55 (NGC 6809)	19h 40.0m	−30° 58′	Glob. Cl.	19.0′	7
NGC 6818	19h 44.9m	−14° 09′	Plan. Neb.	15″ × 22″	9.9pg
NGC 6822	19h 44.9m	−14° 48′	Gal. Irr.	10.2′ × 9.5′	12?
M75 (NGC 6864)	20h 06.1m	−21° 55′	Glob. Cl.	6.0′	8.55

Trifid Nebula (M20) and Lagoon Nebula (M8). The Trifid (top) is a rare combination of an emission and a reflection nebula. Hot young stars in the southern part of the Trifid have excited the hydrogen atoms in the surrounding gas, causing them to emit red light. In the northern part of the Trifid, in contrast, the stars are not hot enough to excite the gas; the blue glow is the result of starlight being reflected by a myriad dust particles. The Lagoon Nebula, on the other hand, is a straightforward emission nebula. The photograph was made with the 48-inch (1.2-m) UK Schmidt telescope in New South Wales, Australia.

Scorpius

Scorpius was a double constellation in pre-Roman times, when it was combined with Libra, the Scales, as the insect's claws. This double group was called Scorpio cum Chelae, or Scorpius with Claws. The scorpion was the creature sent by Apollo to kill Orion, so the gods placed them on opposite sides of the sky. The scorpion is, however, itself being threatened by Sagittarius' arrow, aimed straight at Antares (Orion's arrows having bounced off its shell). The figure has recently been shown as a kite, with its long tail, which also fits the shape of the stars well.

*S*corpius is an ancient and important zodiacal constellation which is best seen in summer for northern hemisphere observers. It has many bright stars and they outline a figure remarkably like the animal they represent. Scorpius lies in the western part of the rich summer Milky Way, providing many objects worthy of visual and photographic appreciation. The Galaxy glows behind the stars of Scorpius, and even a naked-eye view reveals dusty dark lanes here and there on a dark clear night. 7 × 50 or larger binoculars confirm the dustiness of the area east of Antares and also west of the "sting in the tail" where a little cluster of nebulae glow softly against the dusty background. Scorpius is on the meridian at 10pm on June 22.

The heart of the Scorpion is its red giant Alpha (α) star, Antares. This star is one which has had its diameter measured using an interferometer and was found to have a diameter of about 0.04 arcsecond, which translates into a diameter which is 700 times that of the Sun at the star's distance of about 520 light years. This huge star's luminosity must be about 9,000 times that of our star. Antares is surrounded by a huge red nebula which may be shining as a reflection of its bright glow. This nebula is probably the same material which shines with a blue color around nearby Rho (ρ) Ophiuchi, a hotter, younger star (see Ophiuchus). This is mostly a photographic subject, since the eye sees little color at these low light intensities.

It is noticeable that the claws of the Scorpion as well as the Gamma (γ) star are missing. These were originally part of the creature, but were transferred to Libra in Roman times. Gamma is now Beta (β) Librae, marking the northern claw. The southern claw starts at Pi (π) and curves up at least as far as Sigma (σ) Librae. Many of the stars in this area are members of a group with common proper motions, and most appear to be about the same age. This is the Scorpius Association, discovered by the Dutch astronomer Jacobus Kapteyn early in this century. Many O and B spectral-type young stars in Scorpius, Lupus, Centaurus, and Crux are members. The center is about 550 light years away, near to Alpha Lupi. Viewed from several thousand light years away, this grouping might appear like an open star cluster such as M7 (NGC 6745) in Scorpius.

Multiple Stars

Beta (β) Scorpii is an exceptionally bright double star for small telescopes, with a third star near the primary at less than an arcsecond's distance. Beta is occulted by the Moon occasionally (i.e. the Moon passes in front of it) and the fainter companion can be studied by the way in which the light curve changes as observed with a high speed photometer. Zeta 1 (ζ_1) and Zeta 2 (ζ_2) are a naked-eye double star in what is known as the "Table of Scorpius", a curious designation for the region around Zeta, approximately from −40° to −43° in declination. It includes several wonderful clusters and nebulae. Zeta 1 is an orange star and Zeta 2 an extremely luminous blue giant at the great distance of 5,700 light years. This star exceeds Rigel in output according to Burnham, with an absolute magnitude of −8. Nu (ν) Scorpii is an interesting object, a quadruple star. The brighter pair is close, at just over 1 arcsecond separation, and requires very steady seeing to resolve. The other double is some 43.7 arcseconds away, and its components are a relatively easy 2.3 arcseconds apart. The whole picture is striking with an 11-inch (27.5-cm) Schmidt-Cassegrain with a 9mm Nagler eyepiece. Xi (ξ) is also a multiple system, the primary stars closing between

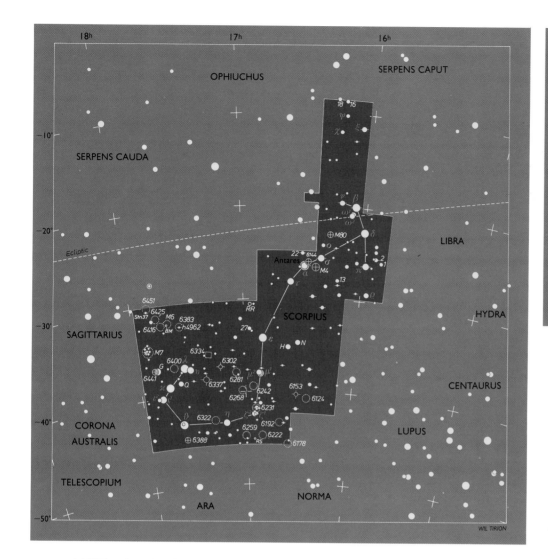

now and 1997 to less than 0.5 arcsecond. In the 1970s this pair was quite easy to resolve, being over 1.25 arcseconds apart. Some 7.4 arcseconds away to the northeast is a third star which can easily be resolved, of 7.2 magnitude. Adding interest to the field, there is a lovely double only 283 arcseconds south, named Σ1999. These stars are travelling with the Xi triple system, so there are at least five stars in the Xi family.

Deep Sky Objects

Scorpius is the home of many globular clusters, but there is room here to list only the best examples. M80 (NGC 6093) is a compact-type globular located almost exactly halfway between Antares and Beta (β). It is somewhat difficult to resolve even in an 8-inch (20-cm) telescope, as the stars are magnitude 14 and fainter, but the cluster as a whole is relatively bright. This globular was host to an unusual nova in 1860 which reached 7th magnitude. Only one other nova in a globular cluster is known, so the event is rare indeed. There is a suggestion that perhaps two stars merged or collided to create the outburst, since stars are crowded together closely in the cores of such a cluster.

M4 (NGC 6121) is a nearby globular of a less concentrated type and is quite conspicuous as it is only 1.2° west of Antares. Here the stars resolve easily, and the nucleus is not strongly

brighter. There is a "bar" of 11th magnitude and fainter stars across the center running almost vertically. M4 is a showpiece for any telescope, and one of the better globulars for smaller instruments. M62 (NGC 6266) is another fine globular which resides southeast of Antares, and is obscured by interstellar dust by as much as 2.4 magnitudes. This may be the reason for the appearance of the nucleus being off center, with the southern edge of the cluster fading away. The stars are faint here, needing a good 12-inch (30-cm) to observe them. NGC 6441 is perhaps one of the easiest globulars to find. The cluster is immediately east of the 3.5 magnitude star G Scorpii, 4.5 minutes distant and making an interesting contrast with it. G Scorpii and NGC 6441 are straight east of Shaula (λ), the sting in the tail of the Scorpion. NGC 6441 is highly obscured and is difficult to resolve even with a 22-inch (54-cm) telescope.

The open clusters of the Scorpius Table and those near to the sting are fine examples of their genre. NGC 6231 in the Table near the Zeta stars is visible to the naked eye and is a tight grouping of brilliant white stars of early spectral type (O and B). This exceptionally bright grouping is one condensation of the Galaxy which includes members of the scattered cluster H12 just to the north. Together these stars are known as the I Scorpii Association, located in the next spiral arm of the Galaxy toward its center. North of H12 is another fine open cluster, NGC 6242. This group has a bright orange star just on the edge and is beautiful with an 8-inch (20-cm) or larger instrument.

M6 (NGC 6405) and M7 (NGC 6475) are large, bright open clusters which are naked eye objects. They can be appreciated in any instrument from field glasses to a large amateur telescope such as a 16-inch (40-cm). M7 is much the larger, appearing as a fuzzy spot to the eye, against the background of the bright Milky Way. The diameter is nearly double that of the full Moon, or about a degree, and contains about 80 members brighter than 10th magnitude, with the center being 818 light years distant.

The Butterfly Cluster

M6, known as the "Butterfly Cluster" is 3.5 degrees northwest of M7. M6 shines against a darker background than M7, and can be seen with the unaided eye as a fuzzy star almost directly north of Shaula (λ Sco). This group appears to be a little richer than M7 owing to its concentration. The Butterfly description comes from the arrangement of the principle stars into a butterfly-like figure with a body and two wings formed by four rough lines of stars extending approximately east–west. Apparently this lovely cluster is about twice the distance of M7, at 1,300 light years.

Nebulae

Several nebulae of note shine in Scorpius, of both the diffuse and the planetary varieties, as well as the dark dusty shapes best shown by long-exposure photography. The red nebula around Antares and blue section around Rho Ophiuchi have been discussed above. The so-called planetary nebulae of Scorpius are numerous and worth finding. NGC 6072 is found about a degree northeast of the star Theta (θ) in neighboring Lupus. It's a 40 arcsecond diameter disk with little apparent detail, and easily seen with 8 inches (20cm) of aperture.

The Bug Nebula

NGC 6302, known as the "Bug Nebula", is a peculiar object. It is classed as a bipolar nebula – a two-lobed nebula – apparently the product of gas and dust being thrown off a central star. In the telescope, we see a nebula with a dark lane running through it unsymmetrically, looking like a galaxy with an off-center nucleus. Long-exposure photographs show a typical "footprint"-type nebula with many faint streamers emanating from the pinched center. Nearby is NGC 6337, a beautiful ring nebula about 40 arcseconds in diameter with several small stars involved. It is rather faint, however, and requires telescopes of about 10-inch and larger aperture. Lastly, there is a lovely little "nest" of nebulae, NGC 6334, which are really photographic objects, but which I have seen well with a 16-inch (40-cm) f/5 telescope with a nebular filter. They are apparently really one luminous cloud which is split up by intervening dust, something like the Trifid Nebula. These are very red objects, and show up well on only a few minutes' exposure, providing the film is sensitive to Hα light towards the red end of the visible spectrum. NGC 6334 is northwest of the Bug, between Shaula (λ) and Epsilon (ε).

TELESCOPIC OBJECTS IN SCORPIUS
Double and Multiple Stars

Name	RA	Dec.	Separation (arcseconds)		Mags.		Year
2	15h 53.6m	−25° 30′		2.5	4.7	7.4	1946
ξ (Xi)	16h 04.4m	−11° 22′	AB	0.9	4.8	5.1	1960
			AC	7.6	4.8	7.3	1975
β (Beta)	16h 05.4m	−19° 48′	AB	0.5	2.6	10.3	1959
			AC	13.6	2.6	4.9	1976
ν (Nu)	16h 12.0m	−19° 28′		0.9	4.3	6.8	1955
σ (Sigma)	16h 21.2m	−25° 36′		20.0	2.9	8.5	1959
α (Alpha)	16h 29.4m	−26° 26′		2.9	1.2	5.4	1959
ζ₁ + ζ₂ (Zeta 1 & 2)	16h 54.3m	−42° 20.2′		6.8	4.8	6.2	1989
h 4962	17h 34.7m	−32° 35′	AB	5.4	5.7	10.5	1933
			AC	13.3	5.7	10.5	1907
Stn 37	17h 51.2m	−30° 33′		10.1	6.8	8.2	1952

Deep Sky Objects

Name	RA	Dec.	Type	Size	Mag.
M80 (NGC 6093)	16h 17.0m	−22° 59′	Glob. Cl.	8.0′	7.2
M4 (NGC 6121)	16h 23.6m	−26° 32′	Glob. Cl.	26.3′	5.9
NGC 6144	16h 27.3m	−26° 02′	Glob. Cl.	9.3′	9.1
NGC 6231	16h 54.0m	−41° 48′	Open Cl.	15′	2.6
H 12 (cluster)	16h 57.0m	−40° 40′	Open Cl.	60′	8.6pg
NGC 6242	16h 55.6m	−39° 30′	Open Cl.	9′	6.4
NGC 6072	16h 13.0m	−36° 14′	Plan. Neb.	40″ × 70″	14.1
NGC 6153	16h 31.5m	−40° 15′	Plan. Neb.	25″	11.5
NGC 6337	17h 22.3m	−38° 29′	Plan. Neb.	48″	12.5
NGC 6302	17h 13.7m	−37° 06′	Plan. Neb. bipl.	50″	12.8pg
NGC 6334	17h 20.5m	−35° 43′	Diff. Neb.	40′ × 30′	9
M6 (NGC 6405)	17h 40.1m	−32° 13′	Open Cl.	15′	4.2
NGC 6441	17h 50.2m	−37° 03′	Glob. Cl.	3.0′	8.0
M7 (NGC 6475)	17h 53.9m	−34° 49′	Open Cl.	80′	3.3

Table of Scorpius. This area about half way down the tail of Scorpius bears the curious nickname of "the Table of Scorpius". It was apparently first used by English astronomer John Herschel during his expedition in the 1830s to observe at Feldhausen, near Table Mountain, in South Africa. The red arc of nebulosity is IC 4628, and the loose association of stars in and below it is called H12. The rich galactic star cluster near the bottom of the picture is NGC 6231. Zeta 1 (ζ₁) and Zeta 2 (ζ₂) Scorpii are the yellow stars below it. The photograph was made with a 180-mm f/2.8 lens on Fujichrome 100 film pushed two stops.

SCUTUM/SERPENS CAUDA

Scutum is a small constellation through which the summer Milky Way runs in all its glory, paired here with neighboring Serpens Cauda for photographic convenience. Scutum is a shield but its stars do not form a recognizable figure. However, if some stars in Aquila are included, the northernmost stars of Scutum form an oval which is quite recognizable. Scutum is most easily picked out by the presence of a star cloud within it, a bright patch of Milky Way (roughly circular in form) with three relatively bright stars at the top. These are Lambda (λ) Aquilae, 12 Aquilae, and Beta (β) Scuti, from east to west respectively. This area is on the meridian at 10pm on August 1. Serpens Cauda, the body or tail of the snake being held by Ophiuchus, is the eastern portion of this two-part group. The head, Serpens Caput, is on the west side of Ophiuchus, below Corona Borealis, with which it is paired in this book for convenience.

Scutum

Scutum is worth exploring, as it contains several very interesting telescopic objects. The star cloud itself is best seen with 7×50 binoculars (or similar). It has quite definite boundaries to the north and west, and blends in with the Milky Way to the south and east. The beautiful open cluster M11 (NGC 6705) is imbedded in the northeast shoulder of the cloud. It is one of the most concentrated open clusters, and appears like a globular in long exposure photographs. The stars are of similar brightness except for the orange lead star, which is about a magnitude brighter, at about magnitude 8. A wide field eyepiece will help appreciate the form of this popular cluster. With higher powers, you can look straight "in" to the center of the starry wonderland.

Another field in Scutum is of interest, that of the globular cluster NGC 6712 and planetary nebula IC 1295. This pair of disparate objects can just be seen together in a half-degree field as they are 24 arcminutes apart. The cluster is fairly large and is easily resolved in an 11-inch (24-cm) aperture telescope. It appears suppressed in brightness, which indeed it is, with the absorption estimated at 2.7 magnitudes here. Just east is the fairly large planetary nebula IC 1295. This planetary is a gray, round disk with little detail in the 11-inch. The open cluster M26 (NGC 6694) is nearby to the west, but is not a strong object in an 8-inch (20-cm). It contains about 40 stars gathered into a 15 arcminute field.

Scutum is noted for the variable star class named after Delta (δ) Scuti. This is a class of pulsating variable stars of low amplitude (i.e. range of brightnesses), with periods of several days. They are subgiants of A or B spectral class, and are identified with the disk of the Galaxy (Population I) rather than its halo.

Serpens Cauda

The only recognizable shape in Serpens Cauda is a triangle of 4th-magnitude stars between Eta (η) and Nu (ν) Ophiuchi, and the 3rd-magnitude star Eta Serpentis (η) 4 degrees northwest of the star cloud. Doubles in this section of Serpens include the triple β 131, which is just west of M17 in Sagittarius, 59 Serpentis and Theta (θ), a bright double, easily seen in any telescope. It has three bright field stars as well, making it an attractive object. To the naked eye, there is an interesting "wing" or extension to the Galaxy which terminates in Ophiuchus near the north end of the snake. A large open cluster, IC 4756, is on the south side of this extension, and is in Serpens. This constellation's chief claim to

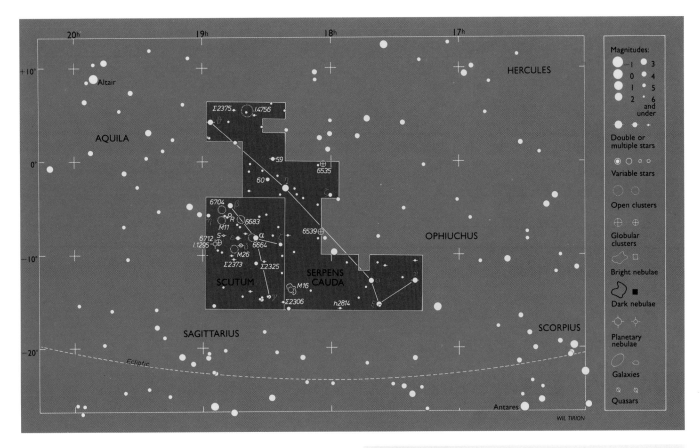

fame is the cluster and nebula M16, known as the Eagle Nebula. The outlines of this nebula are actually something like a three-leafed clover, but the name stems from dust features shown in long exposure photographs. Virtually in the center of the nebulous glow is a bird outlined by dark absorption. This is only the most prominent of several dust features brought out by photography. At the eastern side there is a dark protrusion reminiscent of the Fishes Mouth in the Orion Nebula. This is evidently part of a huge dark cloud which in fact surrounds the entire glowing area of the nebula. There is also a strange dark column of stellar smoke below the wedge-shaped intrusion. In photographs this has a luminous rim in spots. There are also several "Bok globules", small dark blobs of dust which may eventually contract into stars. These might be visible with a nebular filter, but in normal light the bright stars of the cluster make details in the nebula difficult to see. A 10-inch (25-cm) aperture will bring all these features out, although fairly faintly. The cluster is a young grouping, and the whole area is reminiscent of the S Monocerotis region with its Cone Nebula and hot cluster of stars.

IC 4756 is a scattered open cluster at the north end of Serpens Cauda, most effectively seen in binoculars as there is little central condensation and the group is about a degree in diameter. NGC 6539 is a globular cluster which if unobscured by the Milky Way would be spectacular, for the absorption here is reckoned to reduce its brightness by 7 magnitudes. We see a rather faint haze, with little resolution with even an 11-inch (27.5-cm) f/10 Schmidt-Cassegrain telescope.

TELESCOPIC OBJECTS IN SCUTUM
Double and Multiple Stars

Name	RA	Dec.	Separation (arcseconds)		Mags.		Year
Σ 2306	18h 22.2m	−15° 05′	AB	10.2	7.9	8.6	1959
			AC	10.1	7.9	9.0	1936
Σ 2325	18h 31.4m	−10° 48′		12.3	5.8	9.1	1925
δ (Delta)	18h 42.3m	−09° 03′	AB	15.2	4.7	12.2	1943
			AC	52.6	4.7	9.2	1976
Σ 2373	18h 45.9m	−10° 30′		4.2	7.2	8.2	1953

Deep Sky Objects

Name	RA	Dec.	Type	Size	Mag.
M26 (NGC 6694)	18h 45.2m	−09° 24′	Open Cl.	15′	8.0
M11 (NGC 6705)	18h 51.1m	−06° 16′	Open Cl.	14′	5.8
NGC 6712	18h 53.1m	−08° 42′	Glob. Cl.	7.2′	8.2
IC 1295	18h 54.6m	−08° 50′	Plan. Neb.	>86″	15pg

TELESCOPIC OBJECTS IN SERPENS CAUDA
Double and Multiple Stars

Name	RA	Dec.	Separation (arcseconds)		Mags.		Year
ν (Nu)	17h 20.8m	−12° 51′		46.3	4.3	8.3	1959
h2814	17h 56.3m	−15° 49′	AB	20.8	6.1	8.6	1904
			AC	33.7	6.1	11.5	1904
59	18h 27.2m	+00° 12′		3.8	5.3	7.6	1958
Σ 2375	18h 45.5m	+05° 30′		2.5	6.9	7.9	1960
θ (Theta)	18h 56.2m	+04° 12′		22.3	4.5	5.4	1973

Deep Sky Objects

Name	RA	Dec.	Type	Size	Mag.
NGC 6539	18h 04.8m	−07° 35′	Glob. Cl.	6.9′	9.6
M16 (NGC 6611)	18h 18.8m	−13° 47′	Diff. Neb. + Cl.	35′ × 28′	6?
IC 4756	18h 39.0m	+05° 27′	Open Cl.	52′	5.4

TAURUS

Taurus, the second sign of the old zodiac, is very ancient: the bull was worshipped in several Mediterranean civilizations, and is associated with many stories involving the gods. The bull is seen simply threatening Orion, who holds up his shield to ward it off. In Greek mythology, Taurus was the snow-white bull which carried Europa off, only to be revealed as Zeus in disguise. The Pleiades have their own myths, the seven sisters being associated with spring and agriculture due to their heliacal rising just before dawn at the beginning of the planting season. They were apparently worshipped by many ancient peoples.

*T*he myth of the Bull predates written history. By the time of the Egyptians and Tigris–Euphrates cultures (about 2500 BC) the association of a bull or bull's head with the stars of the Hyades cluster was well established. Taurus is a fall star figure in the northern hemisphere, announced by the rising of the bright open cluster, the Pleiades. The bull's head with the Hyades follows about an hour later. The group is virtually overhead and dominates the sky with Orion until late winter. The Pleiades are on the meridian at 10pm about December 15. Taurus is recognized by the "V"-shaped bull's head with the Alpha (α) star, 1st-magnitude Aldebaran, as its eye. The long horns are tipped by Zeta (ζ) and Beta (β).

The winter Milky Way passes through eastern Taurus, but is not particularly bright. Edward Emerson Barnard's extremely long (4–8 h) exposures early this century show wonderful dark lanes and extensive faint nebulosity here, but these are completely photographic subjects. There are several small and one large open cluster (NGC 1647). The nebulae available for observation by amateurs are associated with the stars of the Pleiades and a couple of dusty stars. There is also the interesting and easy to see Crab Nebula, M1, the first object in Messier's catalogue, which is classed as a planetary nebula by some and supernova remnant by others. As might be expected, there are many double stars here in this large and populous constellation.

The Pleiades

The Pleiades, or Seven Sisters (M45), is a nearby young galactic cluster, the stars of which are imbedded in nebulosity shining by light reflected from microscopic solid particles. In color photos this light is blue, the color deriving from the very hot stars providing the light. Seeing the members of the Pleiades individually is a test for acuity in eyesight, as they are close together and vary in magnitude from Alcyone's 2.86 to Pleione's 5.09. William Rutter Dawes, keen-eyed double star observer of the mid-1800s, saw 13 stars here without optical aid. Burnham remarks that there are at least 20 stars in the vicinity which could be glimpsed, although the brighter ones tend to obscure the smaller members. Binoculars or a small telescope allow full appreciation of the lovely group. In a larger instrument with a wide field ocular, the view is stunning, with dozens of blue-white gems, the brighter ones surrounded with delicate stains of nebulosity. Many of the stars are double and there are several wide bright pairs. Pleione is a young variable star with extremely fast rotation (about 6 hours), which may have been brighter in antiquity, when there were apparently 7 relatively easy-to-see members (Alcyone, Atlas, Electra, Maia, Merope, Taygeta and Pleione – all in the magnitude range 4.77–5.50). The remarkable nebulosity surrounding these stars contains striations which may be orientated at right angles to the rotational axis of the stars. Perhaps the material has been thrown off by the rapidly spinning stars.

The Hyades

The Hyades is one of the nearest open clusters to the Solar System. By observing the proper motions of the Hyades stars astronomers have found the cluster is receding towards a point east of Betelgeuse. The center of the cluster is about 130 light years away near the center of the "V". Aldebaran is less than half the distance to the center, at 68 light years distant, and is not associated with the cluster.

The Hyades contains many stars which have evolved for a

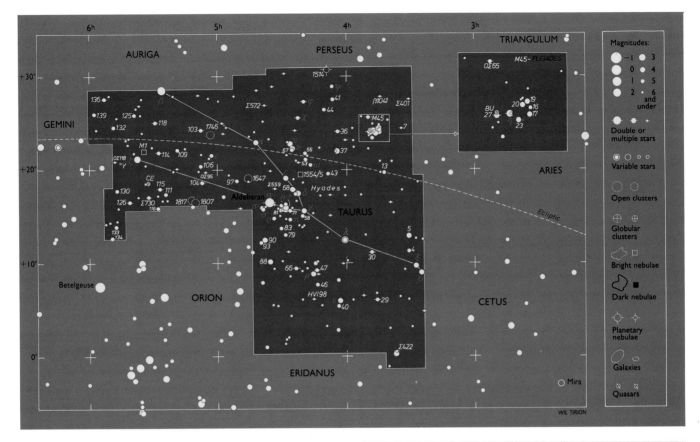

longer time than the Pleiades. The age has been estimated at 400 million years, whereas the Pleiades may be as young as 10 to 20 million years. Some fine doubles are found here. Chi (χ) is north of the "V"-shape in Taurus. Kappa (κ) + 67 are two yellow stars, 339 arcseconds apart with a delicate double between them, Σ541 with 9th and 10th magnitude stars at 5.6 arcseconds.

The Crab Nebula

The Crab Nebula, M1 (NGC 1952), is an object which is important astrophysically, as a supernova remnant whose age is precisely known. The Chinese court astronomers reported a "guest star" near Zeta (ζ) Tauri on July 4, 1054. The "guest" blazed so brightly that it could be seen in daylight for 23 days. The nebula is seen to be expanding rapidly, movement which can be measured on large telescope photographs over only a year's interval. Today, we see a 9th-magnitude oval, which reveals progressively more detail as optical power is increased. The central double star – one component of which is the pulsar remnant of the exploded star – is of 16th magnitude and is marginally observed with a 16-inch aperture. The filaments which are so prominent in red light photographs are dim but detectable with a large telescope such as one with a 22-inch (54-cm) aperture. In smaller amateur telescopes, an oval glow with a few faint stars scattered around it is all that may be seen. The other nebulae in Taurus are the interesting T-Tauri nebula, NGC 1555, known as Hind's Variable Nebula" and IC 359, another faint dust nebula illuminated by a 12th-magnitude star. NGC 1555 is similar to Hubble's Variable Nebula in Monoceros in that its light and form vary with the star's episodes of variability.

TELESCOPIC OBJECTS IN TAURUS
Double and Multiple Stars

Name	RA	Dec.	Separation (arcseconds)		Mags.		Year
Σ 401	03h 31.3m	+27° 34'		11.3	6.4	6.9	1949
7	03h 34.4m	+24° 28'	AB	0.6	6.6	6.7	1959
			AB × C	22.4	6.6	10.0	1958
Σ 422	3h 36.8m	+00° 35'		6.6	5.9	8.8	1975
Burnham 1041	03h 44.6m	+27° 54'		126.7	6.7	7.0	1920
30	03h 48.3m	+11° 09'		9.0	5.1	10.2	1933
OΣ 65	03h 50.3m	+25° 35'		0.6	5.8	6.2	1960
HVI 98	04h 15.5m	+06° 11'	AB	65.5	6.3	7.0	1937
			AC	214.5	6.3	10.0	1907
χ (Chi)	04h 22.6m	+25° 38'		19.4	5.5	7.6	1931
Σ 541	05h 25.4m	+22° 18'		5.6	9.5	10	1956
κ + 67	04h 25.4m	+22° 18'		339.5	4.4	5.4	1900
Σ 559	04h 33.5m	+18° 01'		3.1	6.9	7.0	1968
Σ 572	04h 38.5m	+26° 56'		4.0	7.3	7.3	1959
OΣ 95	05h 05.5m	+19° 48'		1.1	6.9	7.5	1960
118	05h 29.3m	+25° 09'	AB	4.8	5.8	6.6	1957
			AC	141.3	5.8	11.6	1912
Σ 730	05h 32.2m	+17° 03'		9.6	6.0	6.5	1972
OΣ 118	05h 48.4m	+20° 52'	AB	0.4 ('53)	6.1	7.6	1953
			AB × C	75.5	6.1	8.6	1933

Deep Sky Objects

Name	RA	Dec.	Type	Size	Mag.
M45 Pleiades	03h 47.0m	+24° 07'	Open Cl.	110'	1.2
NGC 1554-5 (Hind's Var. Neb.)	04h 21.8m	+19° 32'	Diff. Neb.	var.	9.4 var.
NGC 1647	04h 46.0m	+19° 04'	Open Cl.	45'	6.4
M1 (NGC 1952) (Crab Nebula)	05h 34.5m	+22° 01'	SNR	6' × 4'	9

TRIANGULUM

M33. This beautiful computer-processed image of the M33 spiral galaxy shows it in enhanced true color. The ragged spiral arms are dominated by young, hot blue stars. Giant pink clouds of hydrogen gas, notably NGC 604 towards the bottom right edge of the galaxy, are the sites of current star formation. The image was derived by Dr John Lorre from photographs taken through blue, green, and red filters on the 48-inch (1.2-m) Schmidt Telescope at Mount Palomar.

Triangulum occupies an area north of Aries and south of Andromeda. It consists of a long right-angled triangle of 3rd- and 4th-magnitude stars. The constellation predates Ptolemy of the 2nd century AD, who gave it 4 stars in his *Almagest*, the book which survived the Dark Ages of Europe, remaining known and used in the Moslem world. It is on the meridian at 10 pm about November 20.

M33

The only interesting object in Triangulum is the nearby face-on spiral galaxy M33. Although very large, stretching for over a degree from north to south, the galaxy is not very bright. I have seen it unmistakably with the unaided eye on dark nights, lying between Alpha (α) Triangulum and Beta (β) Andromedae. On that kind of beautiful night, a small pair of binoculars will show a fairly large glow. 20 × 80 binoculars begin to show the ellipticity of the object and its brighter center. This member of the Local Group of galaxies is only 2.4 million light years away, slightly farther than the great galaxy M31 in Andromeda.

This is an Sc spiral, meaning that it is highly evolved and has well-defined spiral arms with stars, dust, gas, and active nebulous areas in the arms. There is also a small, brighter nucleus from which the arms appear to be rotating. The visible extent of this huge collection of stars, gas and dust is about 62 arcminutes in large telescope photographs, which is about 46,000 light years. This compares with an extent of some 100,000 light years for our galaxy, and is about one-third the size of M31 in Andromeda.

Large amateur telescopes will show the spiral arms in M33 as well as several of the brighter HII regions, or diffuse nebulae.

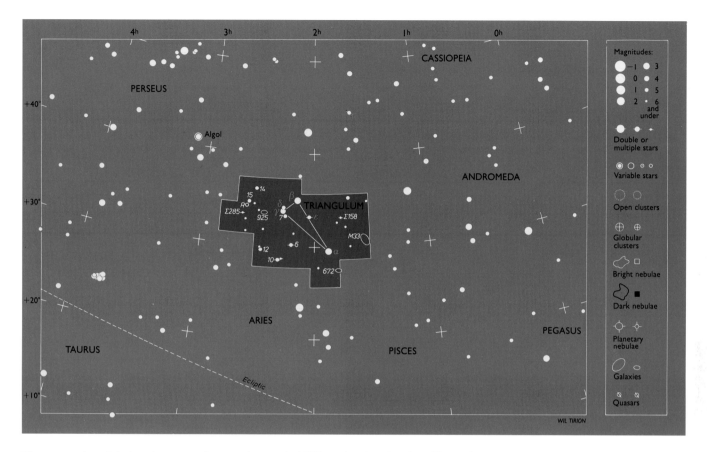

There are also globular clusters and open clusters in M33, and one of the most prominent features, the association of bright blue giant stars. These groupings in the arms are similar to our Perseus or Orion Associations, for example. With its many associations, and the presence of dust and gas, it appears that there is still star formation going on in M33. No supernovae have been observed here, probably because none of its stars has evolved to the point where the core burns out and the structure of the star is overloaded by material transferring from a binary companion, two conditions which current theory requires to produce the catastrophic collapse of a massive star we see as a supernova. If there was one, and we saw it unobstructed by dust, it would be about 6th magnitude, outshining the whole galaxy.

NGC 604

The most prominent nebula in M33 is NGC 604, which is a huge cloud of gas, larger than the nebula in Orion, and more like the Tarantula Nebula in the Large Magellanic Cloud in size. It appears in the telescope as a one arcminute diameter fuzz ball, about 10 arcminutes from the nucleus. It photographs red, and the spectrum is similar to our galaxy's Hydrogen II regions, like the Lagoon Nebula (M8). With a large amateur telescope, arms may be traced from the nucleus, and there is a short line of 4 foreground stars. The arms are diffuse and wide in the telescope, and a wide field is needed to see the whole object. The dusty mottling is quite obvious in a 12-inch (30-cm) or larger telescope on a clear dark night. The OB star clouds and individual stars begin to resolve in a 16-inch (40-cm) with higher powers.

Other galaxies in Triangulum are faint, but NGC 672 and NGC 925 are good sized and worth finding. Double stars are

few, but Iota (ι) stands out as a nice color contrast pair, with G5 and F6 combination providing blue and yellow by contrast. These stars are about 200 light years distant. Σ 285 at 1.7 arcseconds is a good test for a 3-inch lens. At high power the components should stand just apart.

TELESCOPIC OBJECTS IN TRIANGULUM

Double and Multiple Stars

Name	RA	Dec.	Separation (arcseconds)	Mags.		Year
Σ 158	01h 46.8m	+33° 10′	AB 2.1	8.5	9	1962
			AC 55	8.5	12.5	1912
			AD 100	8.5	11.5	1912
6	02h 12.4m	+30° 18′	3.9	5.3	6.9	1973
Σ 285	02h 38.8m	+33° 25′	1.7	7.5	8.2	1959

Deep Sky Objects

Name	RA	Dec.	Type	Size	Mag.
M33 (NGC 598)	01h 33.9m	+30° 39′	Gal. Sc (s)	62′ × 39′	5.7
NGC 672	01h 47.9m	+27° 26′	Gal. SBc	6.6′ × 2.7′	10.8
NGC 925	02h 27.3m	+33° 35′	Gal. Sb/c	9.8′ × 6.0′	10.0

URSA MAJOR

*U*rsa Major is third in size among all the star groups. It is circumpolar and thus never sets for most of the north temperate zone population. Ursa Major is marked by the Big Dipper (or Plough), but its area is much larger than that taken up by those seven bright stars. The figure is of a bear, with the dipper making up the hind quarters and tail. The rest of the bear is made up of fairly bright stars, with Omicron (o) as the nose, Theta (θ), Kappa (κ) and Iota (ι) as the front foot, and Chi (χ), Psi (ψ) and Lambda (λ) and Mu (μ) the rear foot. Circumpolar constellations can be said to have two culminations, an upper one when the constellation is on the meridian south of the pole and a second or lower one when it passes due north under the pole. Ursa Major passes virtually overhead for North American and European viewers, and its upper culmination is at about 10 pm on May 1, making this a spring group.

Stars in the Big Dipper

The Big Dipper or Plough part of the constellation contains the famous "Pointer" stars, Alpha (α) and Beta (β). If a line is extended northwards through them, it will come very near Polaris, about 28° away. This was not always the case, as Dubhe, Alpha (α), is moving westwards, and is "opening" the bowl of the Dipper relative to the other stars making up this sub-group. For the telescopic observer, Ursa Major contains many galaxies, members of two major groups or clusters of galaxies. These are the Messier 81–82 group and the Ursa Major section of the great stream of the Ursa Major–Coma–Virgo cluster. There is also a fine planetary nebula, M97, the Owl. As might be expected in so large a group, there are dozens of fine doubles, and some of the best are listed below. There are no nebulae,

and the known globular clusters are very faint extragalactic objects only recently discovered by photography.

The bright stars of the Dipper are all named; Alpha (α) at the front of the figure is Dubhe, "The Back of the Great Bear"; Beta (β), Mirak, "The Loin of the Bear"; Gamma (γ), Phecda, "The Thigh"; Delta (δ), Megrez, "The Root of the Tail"; Epsilon (ε), Alioth, of unsure meaning, perhaps "Fat Tail"; Zeta (ζ), Mizar, a girdle, or waistband; and Eta (η), Alkaid, "The Governor of the Daughters of the Bier" (the Arabs sometimes had the dipper as a casket or hearse with mourners strung out behind).

Ursa Major also includes two fast moving stars, Groombridge 1830, and Lalande 21185. These stars have proper motions of 7.04 arcseconds and 4.78 arcseconds per year. This places them in third and eighth place in a list of high proper motion stars. Groombridge 1830 is a yellow star of magnitude 6.5, and is moving at an unusually high velocity through space, 216 miles per second (348 km/sec). It is also approaching us at 61 miles per second (98 km/sec). The star is located almost halfway between Beta (β) Canum Venaticorum and Nu (ν) Ursae Majoris. The proper motion should be detectable over a year or two.

The variable star W Ursae Majoris is a prototypical star for a class of eclipsing dwarf binaries. These are intrinsically faint stars approximately as luminous as our Sun. They are almost in contact, and the periods are short. W is two dwarf suns whose period is just a little over 8 hours. The drop in magnitude is from 8.3 to 9.6, and there is a secondary eclipse almost as deep. These stars are distorted by gravity since their surfaces almost touch and they are engulfed in the same atmosphere. There are almost 400 of these pairs known, more than 20 times as many as any other kind of binary star.

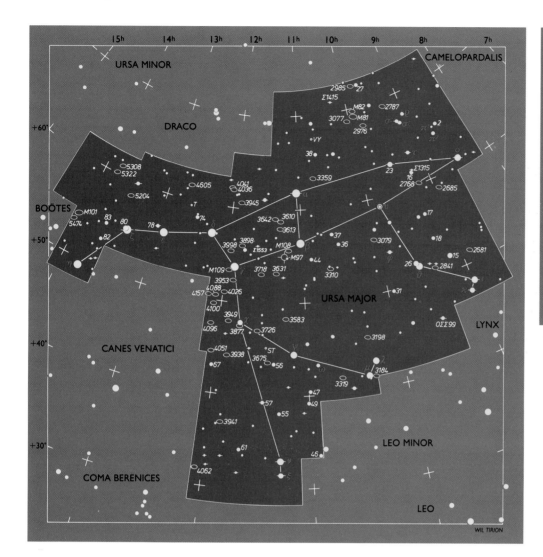

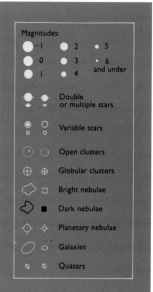

The Moving Cluster

Many of the bright stars of Ursa Major are travelling together through space. The group's center is about 75 light years away, and its destination is eastern Sagittarius. The Ursa Major Moving Cluster is the closest grouping of stars to the Solar System. This group of about 17 stars includes the stars of the Dipper, excluding the first star in the bowl, Alpha (α), and the last star in the tail, Eta (η). Also included in this group are: Alcor (wide companion of Mizar), Zeta (ζ), 21 Leonis Minoris, 78, 37, GC 17919 and GC 17404 Ursae Majoris, Σ 1878 in Draco, and possibly Alpha (α) Coronae Borealis.

Mizar

One of the most notable double stars in the sky is the double star Mizar in the bend of the dipper's handle. It forms a visual double star with 4th-magnitude Alcor. This combination has traditionally been an eyesight test for various armies, although it does not seem very difficult today, perhaps because Alcor may have brightened somewhat in the past millenium or so. Mizar itself is perhaps the most prominent double star in the sky, having been discovered by Riccioli in 1650. It consists of two bright stars 2.4 and 4.0, which are at an easy 14.4 arcseconds separation. I see them both as white, but there have been colors

described such as Allen's "brilliant white and pale emerald". Each of these brilliant points is itself a spectroscopic binary, and there is a fifth star indicated by changes in the radial velocities of the others. This fascinating system is about 88 light years away and is a member of the moving Ursa Major group.

The Owl Nebula

Before diving into the sea of galaxies, M97, the Owl Nebula, should be noted. This ghostly disk is not a bright example, but one that is interesting and easily found near Beta (β). It is one of the larger planetaries at about 150 arcseconds in diameter. In a good-sized amateur 'scope (12-inch (30-cm) or larger) a faint central star and two dark patches inside the disk are visible (hence the Owl's eyes). If you start at Beta to find the Owl, perhaps you will notice a cigar-shaped galaxy roughly between the star and the Owl. This is M108, or NGC 3556. It is a dusty edge-on system, probably similar to our own Galaxy, but at the huge distance of about 35 million light years.

Galaxies

M81 and M82 are at the center of a small grouping of galaxies which, in intergalactic terms, places them right in the neighborhood. There are about 12 members in this cluster and the center is about 7 million light years away. M81 is one of the brightest spiral galaxies to be seen in a telescope, and I have also seen it (and M82) in 7 × 50 binoculars. In astronomical binoculars, which are increasing in popularity, with 15 or 20 magnification and 80mm objective lenses, the pair is obvious. M81 has faint thin arms, which a 16-inch (40-cm) aperture will show under good conditions. The disk of the galaxy is bright and large, with a stellar nucleus. The dust lanes on the nucleus only appear in photographs. M82, 38 arcminutes northward, is one of the enigmas of modern astronomy. Conflicting studies have appeared, first contending that the galaxy is exploding, and more recently that its prominent dusty features are falling inwards. These features are photographic, especially in the red light of glowing hydrogen. In a telescope, we see a fairly bright cigar-shaped object with several dark lanes running through it, especially across the middle. These are part of the enormous ejection/contraction features revealed by photography. The filaments are oddly similar to those in the Crab Nebula, the supernova remnant in Taurus. Evidently something awesome is going on in M82!

Many other galaxies in Ursa Major compete for our attention. NGC 2841 is a favorite of mine, probably because of the ease of finding it. It is also one of the brightest galaxies in the sky after those in the Local Group. NGC 2841 is just between the stars Theta (θ) and 15 in the front foot of the Bear. Medium-sized telescopes will show a fairly bright oval with a star near one end. In 12-inch (30-cm) telescopes, or over, a delicate haze outside the nuclear bulge betrays the presence of multiple tightly wound spiral arms. NGC 3184 is another galaxy which is easily found, within a low power field containing Mu (μ).

M101 above the handle of the dipper is a very large spiral galaxy seen face-on with several major arms. It is one of the galaxies whose arms can most easily be seen in fairly small telescopes. My 10-inch (25-cm) f/6 shows their existence on a dark night with low power. There are many condensations and emission nebulae in the arms which are cataloged separately in the *New General Catalog* (NGC), originated by J. L. E. Dreyer (1852–1926), and subsequently extended. There is a small, virtually stellar nucleus which can be seen in small telescopes. Astronomical binoculars show M101 as a large, dim disk with several faint stars involved. These should be learned because M101 has produced at least three supernovae in this century which reached 11th or 12th magnitude. This galaxy and M74 in Pisces look almost identical, except that M74 is much smaller.

TELESCOPIC OBJECTS IN URSA MAJOR
Double Stars

Name	RA	Dec.	Separation (arcseconds)		Mags.		Year
Σ 1315	09h 12.8m	+61° 41'		24.9	7.7	7.7	1925
ΟΣΣ 99	09h 28.7m	+45° 36'	AB	77.3	5.5	8.0	1924
			AC	83.5	5.5	9.7	1923
23	09h 31.5m	+63° 04'	AB	22.7	3.7	8.9	1975
				99.6	3.7	10.4	1957
φ (Phi)	09h 52.1m	+54° 04'		0.4 (1966)	5.3	5.4	1960
Σ 1415	10h 17.9m	+71° 03'	AB	16.7	6.7	7.3	1968
			AC	150.1	6.7	10.6	1956
α (Alpha)	11h 03.7m	+61° 45'		0.6 (1944)	1.9	4.8	1945
ξ (Xi)	11h 18.2m	+31° 32'		2.9 (1968)	4.3	4.8	1977
57	11h 29.1m	+39° 20'		5.4	5.3	8.3	1958
Σ 1553	11h 36.6m	+56° 08'		6.0	7.9	8.4	1968
78	13h 00.7m	+56° 22'		1.0 (1967)	5.0	7.4	1959
ζ (Zeta)	13h 23.9m	+54° 56'		14.4	2.3	4.0	1977

Deep Sky Objects

Name	RA	Dec.	Type	Size	Mag.
NGC 2841	09h 22.0m	+50° 58'	Gal. Sb–	8.1' × 3.8'	9.3
NGC 2976	09h 47.3m	+67° 55'	Gal. Scp	4.9' × 2.5'	10.2
M81 (NGC 3031)	09h 55.6m	+69° 04'	Gal. Sb	25.7' × 14.1'	6.9
M82 (NGC 3034)	09h 55.8m	+69° 41'	Gal. P	11.2' × 4.6'	8.4
NGC 3079	10h 02.0m	+55° 41'	Gal. Sb	7.6' × 1.7'	10.6
NGC 3184	10h 18.3m	+41° 25'	Gal. Sc	6.9' × 6.8'	9.8
NGC 3198	10h 19.9m	+45° 33'	Gal. Sc	8.3' × 3.7'	10.4
NGC 3319	10h 39.2m	+41° 41'	Gal. SBc	6.8' × 3.9'	11.3
M108 (NGC 3556)	11h 11.5m	+55° 40'	Gal. Sc	8.3' × 2.5'	10.1
M97 (NGC 3507)	11h 14.8m	+55° 02'	Plan. Neb.	194"	12.0pg
NGC 3726	11h 33.3m	+47° 02'	Gal. Sc	6.0' × 4.5'	10.4
NGC 3938	11h 52.8m	+44° 07'	Gal. Sc	5.4' × 4.9'	10.4
NGC 3953	11h 53.8m	+52° 20'	Gal. Sb+	6.6' × 3.6'	10.1
M109 (NGC 3992)	11h 57.6m	+53° 23'	Gal. SBb+	7.6' × 4.9'	9.8
NGC 4605	12h 40.0m	+61° 37'	Gal. Sbcp	5.5' × 2.3'	11.0
M101 (NGC 5457)	14h 03.2m	+54° 21'	Gal.Sc	26.9' × 26.9'	7.7

Spiral galaxy M81 (NGC 3031). This beautiful galaxy is located 10.5 million light years away and is not unlike our own galaxy. It has a similar large increase in the concentration of stars towards its center, as is clearly seen in this computer enhancement of a photograph taken with the 200-inch (5-m) Hale Telescope at Mount Palomar. The dense central area is portrayed in orange. The thin spiral arms are dominated by knots of hot young stars, colored blue.

VELA

Vela, the Sails of the ship Argo, is one of the divisions made by Nicolas Louis de Lacaille in the 1750s from the old constellation Argo Navis, based on the mythical Greek ship in which Jason and the Argonauts sailed from Thessaly to the Black Sea on an epic voyage to recover the Golden Fleece.

The Gum Nebula is the largest nebula in the sky, with a diameter of 30°. It is named after its discoverer, Australian astronomer Colin Gum who found it when he made a mosaic of photographs of Vela and Puppis. The stars Gamma (γ) Velorum and Zeta (ζ) Puppis lie within the nebula, but appear not to be powerful enough to light it. One explanation is that the nebula's hydrogen is still glowing as a result of the nearby Vela supernova explosion some 12,000 years ago. This picture was taken by the European Southern Observatory.

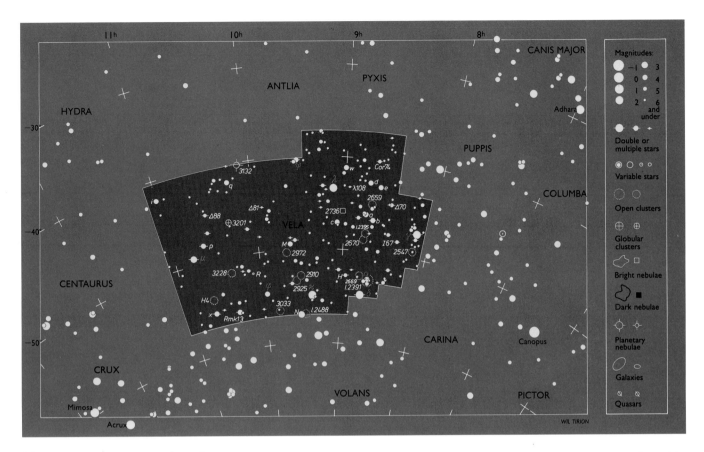

Vela is part of the old ship Argo Navis, which Lacaille dismembered to get Vela, Puppis, and Carina. The four bright stars of Vela carry designations used for Argo, so its brightest stars are Gamma (γ), Delta (δ), Kappa (κ), and Lambda (λ). This is a southern constellation lying between Puppis and Centaurus east–west, and south of Pyxis and Antlia. In the south, it is at culmination around 10pm on March 15. Its four bright stars make a skewed rhomboid across the Milky Way, but it may be found more easily by identifying the "false cross", a figure somewhat like Crux but larger and not as symmetrical. It is made up of Delta (δ) and Kappa (κ) Velorum, and Epsilon (ε) and Iota (ι) in Carina to the south.

The Galaxy runs through Vela from northwest to southeast, and there is a great band of absorbing dust cutting all the way across the Milky Way right in the middle of Vela. This is not very obvious since the Galaxy is not particularly bright here, but does show up on long exposure photographs. There are many rather small star clusters here, but only two nebulous areas, one globular cluster, and two planetaries, one of which is one of the best in the sky for any telescope (NGC 3132). Also, as one might expect in a large constellation housing the Galaxy, there are many beautiful double and multiple stars.

Double Stars

First among the doubles must stand Gamma (γ) Velorum. A bright double of easy separation, Gamma has two stars of magnitude 1.9 and 4.2 at 41 arcseconds. There is also another double star nearby, the components of which may be associated gravitationally with Gamma. Gamma's brighter star is the prime example of an unusual spectral type, the Wolf-Rayet star. These

stars have spectra that show a continuum crossed by bright emission lines (mainly of helium). These lines or bands are up to 100 angstroms wide (1 angstrom = 10^{-10} meters), betraying great velocity and turbulence in the source gasses, which are ionized helium, nitrogen, oxygen, carbon and silicon. These stars have a very strong solar wind which is blowing gasses off the star into space. As they leave the star's vicinity, the gases ionize and glow, providing the emission lines seen in the spectroscope. Although Gamma is low in the sky for northern observers (at −47°), if you can reach it it's well worthwhile.

Many other fine multiple stars are found in Vela. Among the best are: Dunlop 70, called deep and pale yellow by Hartung, at 4.5 arcseconds separation; Delta (δ) in which the components are magnitude 2.1 and 5.1 at about 2.6 arcseconds; Lambda (λ) 108, a quadruple star with 7th-, 9th- and 10th-magnitude components; Psi (ψ), a 34-year binary which was widest at 1981 at 0.9 arcseconds and will close to 0.6 arcseconds by 1993; Dunlop 81, a color contrast pair of yellow and blue at 5.4 arcseconds (6th and 8th magnitudes); Dunlop 88, a bright almost equal 6th-magnitude double which makes a great small telescope object; and Mu (μ), two solar type stars which are widening (2.3 arcseconds in 1990, 2.5 arcseconds in 2000).

Clusters

Many good open clusters dot the sails of Vela. NGC 2547 is a 20 arcminute diameter group requiring a wide field, low power ocular lens. IC 2391 is a sparse but bright group including Omicron (ο), a 4th-magnitude star, great in binoculars; H3 (NGC 2669) has 35 stars in 7 arcminutes, including the double Hu 1590 (8.3 and 8.8 at 0.3 arcseconds). IC 2488 is a fairly large cluster of

11th-magnitude stars and fainter, 15 arcminutes in diameter. NGC 3201 is a globular cluster which is quite obscured by galactic smog, by about 2.2 magnitudes according to Hartung. A photograph shows a less condensed type of globular with several interesting sub-groupings of small stars.

Nebulae

Two different nebulae are found in Vela. Herschel found a long narrow nebula, NGC 2736, which is some 20 arcminutes long and only 30 arcseconds wide. This is part of the Gum 12 Nebula, a supernova remnant. The famous Vela Pulsar is found about 45 arcminutes west of this streak. NGC 3132 is a bright planetary nebula, elliptical, with a bright central star (9th magnitude) and complex structure to be seen in large telescopes.

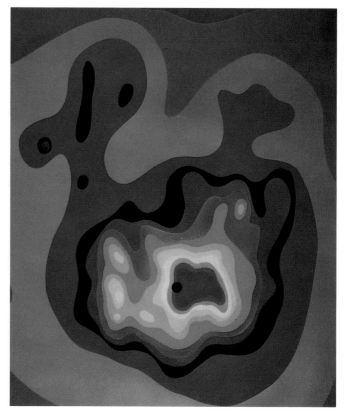

Vela supernova remnant. The uncanny resemblance of this 11-cm radio image of the Vela supernova remnant to Donald Duck is entirely accidental! The image, recorded by the Parkes radio telescope in Australia, is color-coded according to the intensity of the radio emission. The radio remnant is 4° (about 100 light years) across. The position of the Vela pulsar is marked by the black dot. An optical picture of part of the remnant is shown opposite.

TELESCOPIC OBJECTS IN VELA

Double and Multiple Stars

Name	RA	Dec.	Separation (arcseconds)		Mags.		Year
γ (Gamma)	08h 09.5m	−47° 20′	AB	41.2	1.9	4.2	1951
			AC	62.3	1.9	8.2	1907
			AD	93.5	1.9	9.1	1902
I 67	08h 22.5m	−48° 29′		0.8	5.2	6.2	1946
Δ 70	08h 29.5m	−44° 44′		4.5	5.2	6.8	1951
Cor 74	08h 40.3m	−40° 16′		4.0	5.2	8.5	1935
δ (Delta)	08h 44.7m	−54° 43′	AB	2.6	2.1	5.1	1952
				69.2	2.1	11.0	1913
H	08h 56.3m	−52° 43′		2.7	4.8	7.4	1938
λ 108	08h 57.1m	−43° 15′	AB	3.1	7.6	9.6	1935
			AC	43.1	7.6	10.1	1935
			AD	48.1	7.6	9.2	1935
ψ (Psi)	09h 30.7m	−40° 28′		0.5 (1961)	4.1	4.6	1956
Δ 81	09h 54.3m	−45° 17′		5.4	5.8	7.9	1952
Rmk 13	10h 20.9m	−56° 03′	AB	7.2	4.7	8.4	1952
			AC	36.8	4.7	9.5	1931
Δ 88	10h 31.9m	−45° 04′		13.5	6.2	6.5	1951
μ (Mu)	10h 46.8m	−49° 25′		0.7	2.7	6.4	1942

Deep Sky Objects

Name	RA	Dec.	Type	Size	Mag.
IC 2391	08h 40.2m	−53° 04′	Open Cl.	50′	2.5
NGC 2669 (H3)	08h 44.9m	−52° 58′	Open Cl.	12′	6.1
NGC 2547	08h 10.7m	−49° 16′	Open Cl.	20′	4.7
NGC 2736	09h 00.4m	−45° 54′	SNR	>20′	12.0
IC 2488	09h 27.6m	−56° 59′	Open Cl.	15′	7.4pg
NGC 3132	10h 07.7m	−40° 26′	Plan. Neb.	>47″	8.2pg
NGC 3201	10h 17.6m	−46° 25′	Glob. Cl.	18.2′	6.8

The Vela supernova remnant is the result of a stellar explosion that is estimated to have taken place around 9000 BC. It consists of many wispy filaments of gas and dust spread across several degrees of sky, almost ten Moon widths in total. This picture, which shows only about a quarter of the whole remnant, was produced by combining three photographs taken through different filters at the 48-inch (1.2-m) UK Schmidt Telescope in Australia.

VIRGO

Virgo is a very large equatorial and zodiacal constellation which covers 1,294 square degrees of sky. It has few bright stars, but is led by Spica, its Alpha (α) star, the 16th brightest star in the sky. This is a spring group for northern observers and a fall one for southern-hemisphere astronomers. The center culminates at 10pm, about May 10. There is no Milky Way in this area, although it is liberally sprinkled with galactic stars. She is generally shown standing or lying on her side, feet to the east and holding a sheaf of wheat in her left hand at Spica. Outside astrology, Virgo is known chiefly as the location of the "Realm of the Nebulae", a term coined by Edwin Hubble in the 1920s to describe the region of sky north of Gamma (γ), west of Eta (η), and approximately bounded by Beta (β) Leonis, Denebola, to the west. In this pocket of sky are hundreds of relatively bright galaxies which are members of the Coma–Virgo Cluster.

The Coma–Virgo Cluster

These galaxies are in one of the nearest clusters of galaxies to the Milky Way. It is also one of the most massive known, with about 3,000 members discovered so far.

The distance to the Virgo Cluster has been controversial since Hubble's announcement that many of the "nebulae" known at the time (mid-1920s) were in fact island universes millions of light years away and isolated in space. Modern estimates have the center of the cluster approximately 40 million light years distant, with those on the nearer side about 20, and those on the far side about 70, million light years away.

The Virgo Cluster of galaxies is but the nearest major grouping of galaxies in the sky. There are many other clusters of galaxies, all the way out to the photographic limit of about 25th magnitude. The Virgo grouping appears to be the core of an even larger aggregation called the Virgo Supercluster. Many owners of small telescopes are, however, keen deep sky observers, who list and perhaps draw such "faint fuzzies" as well as monitor them for unexpected supernova appearances. Around the world there are several such groups and individuals who are finding novae, supernovae, and comets which professional astronomers then study. At the typical distances of the Virgo galaxies, supernovae appear about 12–14th magnitude, easily seen in a 10-inch (25-cm) telescope.

Beginning at the western border of Virgo, I have listed most of the galaxies which are brighter than 12th magnitude, and will describe the best examples of those. NGC 4030 is a face-on spiral halfway between Eta (η) and Upsilon (υ) Leonis. NGC 4216 is a nearly edge-on spiral similar to NGC 253 in Sculptor but smaller. It is a pair with NGC 4123, found by making a flattened isoceles triangle north between Eta (η) and Beta (β). There is a 13th-magnitude star on the eastern (following) edge; don't mistake it for a supernova. M61 is one of the brightest Virgo galaxies at magnitude 10.2. This is a galaxy with prominent arms which can be glimpsed with a 12-inch aperture. This, like many face-on spirals, is a supernova producer, the latest in 1964. M61 is just a bit over 1° north of the first bright finder star straight north of Eta (η). M84 and M86 are almost twin elliptical galaxies located at the heart or nucleus of the Virgo Cluster. M84 is the westernmost of the two, and is a round, bright diffuse object, rising strongly to the center. It produced a supernova in 1957, unusually for elliptical type galaxies. Just 17 arcminutes eastward is M86, which is slightly elliptical, but also has the smooth brightening towards the center typical of ellipticals. M86

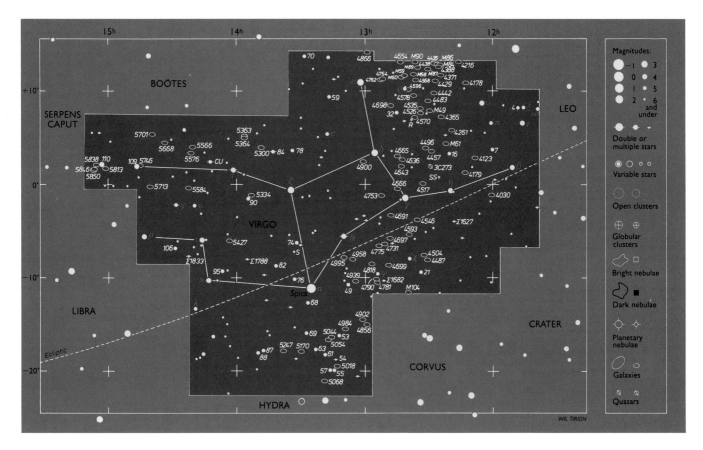

has another elliptical companion within its halo, which I estimate to be about 15th magnitude, on the northeast side. NGC 4438/5 are the next two galaxies in this peculiar chain at the heart of the Virgo Cluster. NGC 4438 is a peculiar edge-on spiral with an extension to the south. It has faint filaments north–south which are seen in long exposure, large instrument pictures. These may come from an encounter with NGC 4435, a fainter elliptical just to the north.

M87

The huge ball of stars M87 possesses many more stars than the Andromeda Galaxy, or the Milky Way. It also has two other interesting features. The galaxy is surrounded by a halo of globular clusters, numbering perhaps 4,000! (Our Galaxy has 110 known.) Something very strange is going on in the nucleus of M87. It emits strong radio signals (Virgo A). There is a very blue jet of unusual matter emerging from the center. This jet has been intensely studied by astronomers in many wavelengths from ultraviolet to infrared and radio. It has several small condensations or beads, and the whole jet is moving outwards from the nucleus at high speed. Calculations suggest that there may be a source of radiation powering the jet, which could mean a massive black hole exists in the core of M87. Owners of 16-inch (40-cm) and larger telescopes might want to look for the jet, which is on the northwest side and is 20 arcseconds long and 2 arcseconds wide. A nebular filter might help you see it by suppressing the continuum from the galaxy's stars. There are two small ellipticals in the field with M87 to the southwest.

M90 is a beautiful spiral located east of the core group. It is a threequarter-view spiral which has soft outlines in photographs,

but are not seen visually. It appears as an ellipse which has a brighter, almost stellar, nucleus.

The Sombrero Galaxy

M104, the Sombrero Galaxy, lies southwards on the border with Corvus. It was discovered after Messier finished his catalog with 102 objects, by his colleague Méchain, and added to Messier's list in 1784. In the telescope it is a fairly bright oval rising to the center. In an 8-inch (20-cm) or larger, a dark line is seen crossing the southern half. This is the famous dark lane, well seen in photographs. Long exposure photographs show not only a lane but that the galaxy has a great number of globular clusters around it, and spiral structure in a disk of dust, gas and stars. Studies show the galaxy at about 40 million light years, and that it is one of the largest galaxies known, with a mass of 1.3 trillion (1.3 million million, or 1.3×10^{12}) Suns! Its diameter is at least 130,000 light years, surpassing our Galaxy by about 30%.

M60 is directly north of Sigma (σ) and is among another group of galaxies. It is a round diffuse ball rising in brightness toward the center. Another galaxy is close northwest, NGC 4647, and much fainter. This is a face-on spiral but most amateur telescopes see it as a featureless faint round haze.

NGC 4699 is one of the brighter Virgo spirals, and has tightly wound multiple spiral arms. The arms are much fainter than the nuclear region which is probably all we see in smaller telescopes. This galaxy is 2° east and about 0.5° south of Chi (χ). NGC 4939 is a 12th-magnitude spiral 1° northwest of 49, west of Spica. NGC 5247, a faint face-on spiral, has reversed S arms which should be visible in a 16-inch (40-cm) or larger aperture. This southern galaxy is about 8° south and a little east of Spica. 4°

north of Tau (τ) there are two galaxies together in the same field; the northern one is NGC 5363, a fairly bright round elliptical, and 14.5 arcminutes south is NGC 5364, a low surface brightness spiral 5′ × 4′ in size. Another elliptical/spiral pair is NGC 5846 and NGC 5850.

Quasar Challenge

Owners of larger amateur telescopes might want to try the unimaginably remote quasar 3C 273, one of the most luminous objects in the Universe, thought to be the nucleus of a young galaxy. This 13th-magnitude, somewhat variable, object appears stellar and makes a right-angled triangle with two stars of similar brightness. 3C 273 is estimated to be more than 3 billion (3,000 million or 3.0×10^9) light years away! The brightest known galaxies would appear 19th magnitude at this distance. Thousands of quasars have now been found, and very deep photographs reaching 25th magnitude and fainter show large numbers of them at vast distances, 3–12 billion light years away. This is of course equivalent to looking back in time 3-12 billion years, to a period of galaxy formation. The most recent, deepest CCD (charge coupled device – a highly sensitive light detector used to image very faint objects) images penetrate beyond this period of galaxy formation, from 12 billion years back towards the beginning of the Universe some 18 billion years ago.

TELESCOPIC OBJECTS IN VIRGO
Double Stars

Name	RA	Dec.	Separation (arcseconds)	Mags.		Year
Σ 1627	12h 18.2m	−03° 57′	20.1	6.6	6.9	1958
γ (Gamma)	12h 41.7m	−01° 27′	4.7 (1966)	3.6	3.6	1966
Σ 1682	12h 51.4m	−10° 20′	AB 30.2	6.5	9.3	1959
			AC 143.9	6.5	10.9	1911
48	13h 03.9m	−03° 40′	0.8	7.2	7.5	1960
θ (Theta)	13h 09.9m	−05° 32′	AB 7.1	4.4	9.4	1958
			AC 69.6	4.4	10.4	1934
54	13h 13.4m	−18° 50′	5.4	6.8	7.3	1958
84	13h 43.1m	+03° 32′	2.9	5.5	7.9	1958
Σ 1788	13h 55.0m	−08° 04′	3.4	6.5	7.7	1977
Σ 1833	14h 22.6m	−07° 46′	5.7	7.6	7.6	1954
φ (Phi)	14h 28.2m	−02° 14′	4.8	4.8	9.3	1958

Deep Sky Objects

Name	RA	Dec.	Type	Size	Mag.
NGC 4030	12h 00.4m	−01° 06′	Gal. Sc	4.3′ × 3.2′	11.9
NGC 4178	12h 12.8m	+10° 52′	Gal. SBc	5.0′ × 2.0′	11.4
NGC 4216	12h 15.9m	+13° 09′	Gal. Sb	8.3′ × 2.2′	10.0
M61 (NGC 4303)	12h 21.7m	+04° 28′	Gal. Sc	6.0′ × 5.5′	9.8
M84 (NGC 4374)	12h 25.1m	+12° 53′	Gal. E1	5.0′ × 4.4′	9.3
M86 (NGC 4406)	12h 26.2m	+12° 57′	Gal. E3	7.4′ × 5.5′	9.2
NGC 4429	12h 27.4m	+11° 07′	Gal. S0	5.5′ × 2.6′	10.2
NGC 4435 Siamese	12h 27.7m	+13° 05′	Gal. E4	3.0′ × 1.9′	10.9
NGC 4438 Twins	12h 28.7m	+13° 00′	Gal. Sap	4.0′ × 1.5′	11.0
3C 273	12h 29.1m	+02° 03′	QSO	5″?	13.8 var.
M49 (NGC 4472)	12h 29.8m	+08° 00′	Gal. E4	8.9′ × 7.4′	8.4
M87 (NGC 4486)	12h 30.8m	+12° 24′	Gal. E1	7.2′ × 6.8′	8.6
NGC 4517	12h 32.8m	+00° 07′	Gal. Sc	10.2′ × 1.9′	10.5
NGC 4535	12h 34.3m	+08° 12′	Gal. SBc	6.8′ × 5.0′	9.8
M90 (NGC 4569)	12h 36.8m	+13° 10′	Gal. Sb+	9.5′ × 4.7′	9.5
M58 (NGC 4579)	12h 37.7m	+11° 49′	Gal. Sb	5.4′ × 4.4′	9.8
M104 (NGC 4594)	12h 40.0m	−11° 37′	Gal. Sb−	8.9′ × 4.1′	8.3
NGC 4647	12h 43.5m	+11° 35′	Gal. Sc	3.0′ × 2.5′	11.9pg
M60 (NGC 4649)	12h 43.7m	+11° 33′	Gal. E1	7.2′ × 6.2′	8.8
NGC 4699	12h 49.0m	−08° 40′	Gal. Sa	3.5′ × 2.7′	9.6
NGC 4753	12h 52.4m	−01° 12′	Gal. P	5.4′ × 2.9′	9.9
NGC 4939	13h 04.2m	−10° 20′	Gal. Sb+	5.8′ × 3.2′	11.4
NGC 5247	13h 38.1m	−17° 53′	Gal. Sb	5.4′ × 4.7′	10.5
NGC 5363	13h 56.1m	+05° 15′	Gal. Ep	4.2′ × 2.7′	10.2
NGC 5364	13h 56.2m	+05° 01′	Gal. Sb+p	7.1′ × 5.0′	10.4
NGC 5566	14h 20.3m	+03° 56′	Gal. Sb+	6.5′ × 2.4′	10.5
NGC 5713	14h 40.2m	−00° 17′	Gal. Sc	2.8′ × 2.5′	11.4
NGC 5846	15h 06.48m	+01° 36.3′	Gal. E0	3.4′ × 3.2′	10.2
NGC 5850	15h 07.1m	+01° 33′	Gal. SBb−	4.3′ × 3.9′	11.0

Giant elliptical galaxy M87. The small spots that surround the brilliance of M87 in this photograph are some of its retinue of over 400 globular clusters, each consisting of up to a million stars. The two larger, diffuse objects at lower right are small galaxies which are also members of the Virgo Cluster. The photograph was taken by the 154-inch (3.9-m) Anglo-Australian Telescope.

GLOSSARY

Almagest The Arabic name for the book written by Ptolomy of Alexandria in about 115 AD which catalogued the constellations then known and assigned them their stars.

Angular Separation The apparent distance apart of any two points at infinity as measured in a circle of 360°. Each degree is broken up into minutes and seconds of arc.

Association Any grouping, particularly of stars of a type, common proper motion, age, or just in the same area of sky.

Asteroid Literally meaning small star. But this now means a small member of the solar system. About 3000 have known orbits, mostly between Mars and Jupiter. Largest is Ceres, about 480 miles diameter.

Astrometry The study of the positions of astronomical objects (by measurement).

Astronomical Unit (AU) The mean distance from Earth to the Sun's center. This is 92,955,630 miles or 149,597,870 kilometers.

Astrophysics Study of the physical matter and states of the heavenly bodies.

Barred Spiral A type of galaxy which has a "bar" or straight structure through its nucleus from which the arms usually start.

Binary Star Actually two stars which orbit a common center of gravity. These range from two in actual physical contact to two which are separated by thousands of AUs.

Black Hole A body so compact and dense that light cannot escape from it. There is often a rotating accretion disk around the black hole and stars and other matter may be "sucked into" the hole, releasing large amounts of energy, detectable from earth.

Blue Giant A very luminous star which is burning its hydrogen very rapidly; by definition young in age.

Bok Globules Named for the Dutch-American astronomer who studied them, these are nodules of dust several AUs in diameter usually seen as dark against a luminous nebula.

Celestial Equator The projection of the Earth's equator onto the sky. Divides the sky into northern and southern hemispheres.

Cepheid A type of variable star which pulsates regularly. Their absolute luminosity is directly related to the period, making them valuable distance indicators.

Classification of Galaxies Sa to Sd are spiral galaxies of simple spiral form with a to d indicating increasing pitch angle. SBa to SBd are barred spiral galaxies, with a to d again describing spiral tightness. E0 to E7 represent elliptical galaxies, the number indicating increasing ellipticity (flattening). Irr. are irregular galaxies. S0 galaxies are lenticular, having a central bulge like a spiral galaxy but no spiral arms.

Cluster of Galaxies Seen in many places in the sky, galaxies tend to clump into groups, from a few to hundreds.

Coccoon Nebula A recently catagorized type of nebula which has a young star in the center and heavy dust obscuration around it.

Coma Literally means "hair" in Latin. Used two ways; as the gaseous envelope around a comet when active (near the Sun), and as the optical effect which causes star images off axis to look like tiny comets, sharp at one end but fuzzy at the other.

Constellation A group of stars seen as connected to form a figure in the sky such as a hero, triangle, animal, etc.

Culmination The highest point an astronomical body can reach during the 24-hour diurnal cycle, as it crosses the meridian.

Dark Nebula Dust which obscures a star or nebulous light behind it, such as the Horsehead Nebula in Orion.

Declination The north-south measurement in the sky (the equivalent of earthly latitude), starting with 0° at the equator and rising to + or − 90° at the celestial poles.

Double Star Two stars which appear to be close together in the sky. May be physically connected by gravity (binary) or just appear together by being in line of sight (optical double).

Dwarf Star Small star which has collapsed to form a dense body or simply a small star (Sun size down to a few miles in diameter).

Ecliptic The projection of the Earth's orbit around the Sun onto the celestial sphere.

Elliptical (galaxy) Type of galaxy which has no visible structure except perhaps a nucleus. May be elongated or round.

Extragalactic Outside of our home galaxy (all other galaxies).

Footprint Nebula Nebula with a young star (protostar) at its center. Because of its rotation, the dust and gas it lights up appears like an hourglass or footprint.

Galactic Cluster Cluster of stars in a galaxy. Also known as open clusters.

Galaxy An association of stars, gas and dust, gravitationally bound together, presumably rotating. The three basic types are spiral, elliptical and irregular. Thousands are known.

Globular Cluster A roughly spherical association of stars apparently of similar age. Usually very old, and comprising tens of thousands to millions of stars.

Gravitational Attraction The force which is proportional to the inverse square of the distances between bodies. It is also directly proportional to the mass of a body.

Hubble Constant The ratio between the apparent velocity of recession of galaxies (red shift) and their distance. Currently accepted figure is 50-80 kilometers per second per Megaparsec.

Hydrogen The simplest element, and most predominate in the Universe. Consists of one proton and one electron. Lightest element.

Hydrogen Alpha A wavelength in the spectrum at which ionozed hydrogen atoms radiate, at 656.3 nanometers (10^{-9} meter). (Red end of visual area.)

Hydrogen II Region A region of doubly ionized hydrogen.

Index Catalog (IC) An addendum to the New General Catalog published as IC I and IC II in 1895 and 1908 respectively.

Infrared Longer wavelengths than those visible to the eye. Approximately 0.75 to 1000 μm (10^{-6} meter).

Interstellar Absorption The blocking of starlight by dust in space.

Ionization Excitation of atoms by energetic radiation such as ultraviolet photons from a nearby star. Causes fluorescence in some gases such as hydrogen, oxygen, nitrogen.

Light Pollution Filter A filter for visual or photographic use which selectively absorbs light from man-made sources.

Light year The distance travelled by light in space in one year, approximately 5.88×10^{12} miles (9.46×10^{12} kilometers).

Luminosity The intrinsic or absolute amount of energy radiated per second by a celestial object. The unit of measurement is magnitude.

Magnitude: Apparent A scale of brightness in which stars (or other astronomical bodies) are graded by intervals of the 5th root of 100 or 2.512 times. Naked eye limit is about +6. **Absolute** The brightness a star would be if seen at a distance of 10 parsecs or 32.6 light years.

Mass The quantity of matter in a body. (Weight is mass times acceleration due to gravity.)

Meridian The great circle passing through the poles of the celestial sphere which cuts the observer's horizon at the north and south points, and also passes through his zenith.

Milky Way The name for our Galaxy seen in our sky.

Multiple Star A system of more than two stars gravitationally bound. More than 5 would usually constitute a cluster, but the borderline is unclear.

Nebula A glowing cloud of gas or dust or a dark cloud seen against a lighter background. Types are emission, reflection, and dark, or absorbing. Planetary nebulae are a type of emission nebula.

Nebular Filter A filter used visually or photographically which allows various emission lines of nebulae to pass but which absorbs continuous light and artificial light (pollution).

Neutron Star A very dense body, made up of neutrons, the result of the collapse of a normal star. They are observed as pulsars.

New General Catalog (NGC) Catalog by Dreyer published in 1888, of non stellar objects, largely based on observations of the Herschels and other 19th century (prephotography) observers.

Nova A "new" star that suddenly becomes visible.

Ocular Another name for eyepiece.

OB Association A loose grouping of young hot stars of O and B spectral types. Seen in spiral arms of dusty spiral galaxies.

Open Cluster A name for a loose galactic cluster of stars, containing at most a few hundred stars.

Parallax The apparent change in position of a star relative to the distant, background stars as seen from the Earth at opposite points in its orbit of the Sun.

Parsec Parallax-second, a measurement of astronomical distance equivalent to 3.26 light years. Defined as the distance at which a star would subtend a parallax of one second of arc.

Photographic Magnitude A largely outmoded system of brightness measurement derived from star diameters on the photographic plate.

Photometry The study of brightnesses, using a photometer, which converts light into electrical current which is measured accurately by a meter.

Planetary Nebula A small gaseous nebula around a late evolutionary type star (which has blown off atmosphere to form the nebula).

Population I/II Walter Baade in the 1950s identified two types of stars in galaxies. Type I compose the galactic disk, and are rich in heavy elements. Population II are older stars, located in the nuclear bulge and in the halo of stars around the disk. Globular cluster stars are examples. Low abundances of heavy elements are typical.

Position Angle Relation of one star to another in the field of view of a telescope. Measured from north to east and around the circle 360 degrees.

Proper Motion Motion on the sky of a star (over a year).

Protostars Very young stars just beginning to shine, usually in the cloud of material they are forming from.

Pulsar Rapidly rotating neutron stars. Observed in radio and other wavelengths including visual. Bursts of radiation regularly detected.

Quasar Extremely remote starlike bluish astronomical object. Contraction of quasi-stellar object. Thought to be bright nuclei of active forming galaxies.

Radial Velocity Velocity directly away from or towards the observer.

Red Giant A star with low surface brightness and density with a diameter 10–100 times that of the Sun, and more luminous than the Sun.

Red Dwarf A cool small star.

Redshift The lengthening of wavelengths caused by the recession of the source from the observer. In an expanding Universe, the more distant the source the greater the redshift.

Reflection Nebula The reflection of starlight off dust in space. Usually near a luminous star.

Reflector Type of astronomical telescope using a mirror to form the main image.

Refractor Type of telescope which uses lenses to form an image.

Right Ascension (RA) The measurement of position in the sky "from right to left" laterally. Measured in hours, minutes and seconds from the Vernal Equinox, or First Point of Aries, 24 hours around the sky. The Earthly equivalent is longitude.

Schmidt Telescope A type of telescope originally built as a camera, which uses an aspheric corrector lens to eliminate aberration.

Seeing The steadiness of a telescopic image which is degraded by atmospheric motions.

Spectral Classification The color of a star is an indication of its temperature, and is classified by spectral type. O and B type are the hottest stars and are bluish. Then in order of decreasing temperature, A stars are blue-white, F are white, G are yellow-white, K are orange and M are red. Each spectral type is subdivided in steps from 0 to 9. The Sun is a G2 star, for example.

Spectrum, Visible Band of colored light produced when white light is dispersed by a prism or diffraction grating.

Spectroscopic Binary Binary star detected only by the periodic doubling of spectroscopic lines. The components are too close to resolve visually.

Spiral Galaxy Type of galaxy which has identifiable arms.

Supergiant Classification of enormous, highly luminous, late type stars which may have over 100,000 times the Sun's radiation.

Supernova Cataclysmic explosion of a massive star caused by collapse. Leaves a remnant of expanding gas and sometimes a pulsar.

Supernova Remnant Shell of gas blown out by a supernova explosion.

Variable Star Any star whose brightness changes with time. Variable stars have been found in all the constellations. They are designated as follows: The brightest is usually named R and the letters from R through Z are then used to designate the next 7 brightest variables. After that, RR, RS, etc. are used. After ZZ, the 55th star is named AA, AB . . . AZ, BB, BC, etc. omitting combinations with the letter J. This system ends with QZ, and 334 variables have been named. After this, the letter V and a number such as V278 is used.

White Dwarf Remains of a collapsed star, hot and small, radiating heat from the collapse, but not actually producing new heat internally.

Wolf-Rayet stars Massive luminous stars with gaseous envelopes around them, often members of binary systems.

Zenith The point on the celestial sphere vertically above the observer's head.

Index